GW00361224

JOHNNY MARR

THE SMITHS *&* THE ART OF GUN-SLINGING

RICHARD CARMAN

Independent Music Press

Published in 2006 by
INDEPENDENT MUSIC PRESS
Independent Music Press is an imprint of I.M. P. Publishing Limited
This Work is Copyright © I. M. P. Publishing Ltd 2006

Johnny Marr: The Smiths & The Art of Gun-slinging
by Richard Carman

All Rights Reserved

This book is sold subject to the condition that it shall not, by way of
trade or otherwise, be lent, re-sold, hired out or otherwise circulated
without the publisher's prior consent in any form of binding or cover
other than that which it is published and without a similar condition
being imposed on the subsequent purchaser.

No part of this publication may be reproduced, stored in a retrieval system,
or transmitted in any form or by any means, electronic, mechanical,
photocopying, recording or otherwise, without the prior
permission of the copyright owner.

British Library Cataloguing-in-Publication Data.
A catalogue for this book is available from The British Library.
ISBN: 0-9549704-8-9 and 978-0-9549704-8-2

Cover Design by Fresh Lemon.
Edited by Martin Roach.

Printed in the UK.

Independent Music Press
P.O. Box 69,
Church Stretton, Shropshire
SY6 6WZ

Visit us on the web at: www.impbooks.com

For a free catalogue, e-mail us at: info@impbooks.com
Fax: 01694 720049

JOHNNY
MARR

THE SMITHS & THE ART OF GUN-SLINGING

Contents

Acknowledgements

I wrote this book during a very difficult period for my wife, and dedicate it therefore to Linda, and to her mother Winifred Hopwood... there is, of course, a light that never goes out.

Immeasurable thanks again to my editor and friend Martin Roach, to Kaye Roach and the inestimable Alfie Blue. Thanks also, 'in anticipation', to Korda Ace.

Many people helped me along the way, and I am particularly grateful to the following for their support: Grant Showbiz; Billy Bragg; Jonathan Schofield; CP Lee; Shaun Lawlor; Paul Carrack; Steve Korta; David Byrne; Joanne Carroll; Chris Frantz; Jose Maldonado and Dave Collett from Sweet And Tender Hooligans, Martin from Stoke Underground, Sarah Hyde at Sincere Management. I'd also like to thank the handful of people who generously gave their time and memories but asked to remain outside of this acknowledgement. You know who you are! I also plagued a few people endlessly for their contributions, without success... but thanks to all of you for your patience.

While they did not contribute to this book directly, if I failed to thank Johnny Marr, Morrissey, Andy Rourke, Mike Joyce for the music of a lifetime, I would be remiss. Thanks guys. Let sleeping beauties lie.

Introduction

I grew up in the Sixties. I was bathed in The Beatles' music from the age of three. George was my favourite. I still get the shivers when I hear those fabulous intros on the first four Beatles albums. At the age of twelve I fell in love with Bolan, Bowie and Bryan Ferry, and life was never the same again. I was too old to be a punk, but Buzzcocks and The Sex Pistols were as exciting as it got in 1976 – or any other year. By the time I was twenty three and living in Manchester, I thought I'd heard it all.

Then came The Smiths.

Ever since I first heard them, they have been my favourite band. While I thought I had heard it all, it was evident that they *had* it all. And in Johnny Marr they had a new George Harrison, a man who could set the room alight within the first bar and a half. And of course, in Morrissey, The Smiths had perhaps the last great lyricist, the last great vocalist.

Over the years that followed, I heard many great records, from Billy Bragg, Kirsty MacColl, Talking Heads and Electronic. And I found in so many cases that Johnny played on these records too. What I liked, and still like, about Johnny Marr, was his refusal to play the role of guitar hero whilst being, evidently, the greatest guitar 'hero' of his age. While Carlos Santana pulled faces over his endless solos that made it look as though he was enduring an intrusive rectal examination while he played, and countless onanistic solos screamed egotistically from under the yard-long hair of a thousand so-called 'geniuses', Johnny remained solo-free, cool, distanced and locked into tighter grooves than were good for any of us. While he never took centre-stage until relatively recently with The Healers, he lit up virtually everything he played on. For Johnny Marr, it has always seemed that the *guitar* was the key thing, not Johnny himself. While other more visible guitarists over the years have used the instrument to tell us far more about themselves than we really need to know, Marr has resolutely continued to promote *guitar playing* as the end in itself.

The Smiths' catalogue of recordings is much like any individual Smiths single: brief, concise, gorgeous, irresistible. Nearly every song is close to perfection, and theirs is a catalogue as near perfection as any band will get. For me in 1983, they were the best British band since The Beatles, and with hindsight they remain so. While any decent record collection should contain all The Beatles' albums, so should it contain every record The Smiths ever released. A handful of albums that shook the world.

Since then, the boy Marr has 'done tremendous.' He is still working, still passionately involved in project after project, still exciting to hear, still the same guitar player who graced a hundred thousand bedsits in the Eighties, still supporting his beloved Manchester City. His most famous band, and his be-quiffed former song-writing partner, have been the subject – or the victims – of many biographies, amongst which there have been some good ones. Dave Haslam, writing for *NME* in 1989, pertinently noted that "the Johnny Marr story will run and run," but nobody has yet chosen to look at Johnny's career exclusively. Since the last major biography of The Smiths, a generation of guitar players and lovers of great pop have discovered the band. This book is for them.

I have tried to tell the story of Johnny's career in full. It's the tale of a guy who picked the guitar up in his pre-teen years and went on to change the lives of millions of listeners. And whatever the world around him thought of it, he 'kept on keeping on.'

CHAPTER ONE

Manchester

"My first memory of guitar playing was this uncle," recalls Johnny Marr. "With big sideburns and Chelsea boots. He was well cool. He had a guitar, and did a little bit of playing. I thought he was really hip... I remember this red Stratocaster. I can recall the smell of the case and everything."

Johnny Marr's love of the guitar isn't unique. Millions of us have fallen under its spell over the years. Millions of us have gone on to learn to play. While some went on to become professionals, a tiny percentage actually make it big. And some became the most important guitarists of their generation. Marr is simply that – one of the most important players of his generation. His passion for the instrument is written across almost every record he has made and in nearly every interview he has given. Throughout his career, whatever has been spinning around him, it has always been about the music and the guitar. "For better or worse," Johnny has said, "it *happened* for me. I wanted to be known for what I did, not for what I said."

Marr joined a tradition stretching back decades. Johnny himself has been keen to emphasise that tradition, and over the years has referenced many musicians and producers who have influenced his own playing. Just as Marr dug back through old records to find the best guitar players he could find, so subsequent generations will use Johnny as their own route to the past. To understand Johnny, it is worth tracking back through the history of the world's sexiest instrument, to establish where Johnny Marr came from.

From the Thirties onwards, the guitar was the natural successor to the piano as the leading instrument in popular music. Rock 'n' roll guitar as we know it is born out of the American country blues players of the early decades of the twentieth century. Faced with a choice between the piano or the more portable guitar, the itinerant players of the early years of the century chose the piano. While the guitar allowed a musician to carry his own instrument from dime bar to juke joint, the key thing about the piano was that – above a hot and sweaty Saturday night crowd – the latter could be *heard*. While playing one's own guitar every night was preferable to turning up at a gig only to find that the venue's piano was out of tune, missing strings, or half a block away from the bar, the very fact that the audience could actually hear you was more important.

However, throughout the Twenties and Thirties, various people experimented with amplification, and by the time the guitar could be wired up to a speaker and heard as loudly as a piano, the future of pop music was etched out. A guitar player could drift from venue to venue, from town to town, and carry his own instrument with him. Migration from the rural southern states to the cities of the industrial north meant that itinerant guitar players could play night after night to a different audience and refine their sound and their playing. The guitarist became the leader of the dance, the bringer of news, the bearer of joys and sorrows. Both the musician and his instrument became adaptable and personal. As the guitarist hugged his instrument close to his chest, he seemed to welcome the audience into his soul too.

Such was the genesis of the modern rock guitarist. The wandering bluesman trawling the bars of Chicago for work isn't far from the modern rock star, globe-trotting around the world with a heap of flight cases in tow. Maybe the money's better, but the culture and ethos is pretty much the same.

We *need* guitar bands.

Throughout the developing years up to and including the Second World War the guitar became established both as an orchestral instrument in the major jazz and dance bands of the era and as a solo instrument in itself. On both sides of the Atlantic, as Fifties pop became more sophisticated, guitarists such as Bert Weedon and Chet Atkins became celebrity instrumentalists in their own right. While early rock 'n' rollers such as Little Richard and Jerry Lee Lewis were pianists, it was Buddy Holly who really cemented the image of the guitar band and established its format for ever more. His clipped, rough-strummed songs were irresistible, his band The Crickets the perfect foil for Holly's own delivery. In the UK, Buddy's influence was picked up by the young Hank Marvin, and his group The Shadows became England's premier guitar band, both in their own right and as backing for the young Cliff Richard. Guitar bands flourished throughout the country in their wake – influenced by Holly, The Shads, and the increasingly available imports of American country, blues, early R&B and soul records. Across the UK, the generation of players who would re-invigorate pop music as never before picked up the instrument and started to copy what they heard. Lonnie Donnegan and Hank Marvin learned from Buddy, and older blues players like Elmore James and Robert Johnson. Throughout the Fifties, Brian Jones, Eric Clapton, Jeff Beck, Paul McCartney, Jimmy Page, John Lennon, Keith Richards and George Harrison took these influences, copied their favourite American sounds on cheap guitars plugged into the family radiogram, and reinvented rock 'n' roll.

It was Dick Rowe at Decca Records who famously turned down The Beatles in 1962 on the grounds that "guitar groups are dead." By the time The Beatles, the Stones, The Who and the Yardbirds had proved him wrong, the guitar was established as *the* weapon of choice in pop and rock. Nearly all the bands and artists who established long-term careers in pop from the early Sixties onwards did so with the guitar as the leading sound in their band or backing. It was Jimi Hendrix who – when the major players were delving back into the rootsy blues past of the instrument – picked up the Fender Stratocaster and re-invented the guitar. No longer simply a tool with which great music was made, the guitar itself became as much the maker of the music as the players themselves. Hendrix gave the guitar a new language, offered musicians on every instrument a code by which they could investigate not only song-writing and music construction, but could explore the machine, the instrument itself. Hendrix took the guitar apart with both an actual and a metaphorical screwdriver, and gave the instrument its soul. From Jimi onwards, the guitar was a vehicle that would transport audiences to other worlds, a means by which future players would boldly go where no man had gone before.

Out of Hendrix came psychedelia, prog rock, heavy metal; likewise soul, blues and jazz were all enriched by his work. The guitar was re-established as the single most important musical instrument on the planet. Clapton, The Stones, Zappa, Free, The Grateful Dead all carried the guitar into the Seventies alive and well, prepared to excite us, enliven us, delight and move us. Through Ziggy and the glam rock phenomenon, Mick Ronson, Phil Manzanera and Dave Hill kept glitter-ball acts such as Bowie, Roxy and Slade deeply rooted in guitar-based rock. It was here that the schoolboy Johnny Marr would join the journey. Pop was exciting again; fun, silly, stylish, cool. Ronnie Wood's barrel-house chops made The Faces one of the best guitar boogie bands. Status Quo kept it simple, with twelve bars kicked firmly to the floor. More articulate acoustic pickers like John Martyn incorporated technologies into their playing that offered new sounds and new landscapes for guitarists that still inform the sounds of U2 and Coldplay. King Crimson guitarist Robert Fripp merged the heaviest of juggernaut guitar sounds with a shimmering tape-delay that is heard in chart bands well into the Twenty-First century too.

Just as all this potential and variety threatened to crawl up its own backside in self-regard, punk purified the art even further. Gone were the pixie hats and the mystical visions of other worlds. Out came the guitar, the bass and the drums, and up went the volume. If 'Anarchy In The UK' recalled nothing more than The Who at their mid-Sixties best, it did remind everyone that the most exciting thing in the world was the sound of a sneering front man spitting new music out over a crunching guitar – only a step or two away from Buddy Holly and the early Stones in its simplicity and ferocity. For two or three years punk was driven by three-chord wonders that refreshed the entire music scene, much as Hendrix had done a decade before. If old heads rallied against the sounds of Buzzcocks, X-Ray Spex and the Pistols, it was surely only because they subconsciously realised that they had themselves lost sight of what thirteen-year-old kids living on low income in a time of political paucity really wanted out of life.

By the early Eighties, style had overtaken content, and pop was in serious danger of collapsing as a medium. Bored by the simplicity of punk, some bands adopted a more edgy, creative role. Bands such as Talking Heads, XTC, Squeeze and Elvis Costello defined a new genre – 'new wave.'

For big-selling chart pop however, make-up and glamour took over from energy and content in a sub-Warhol celebrity-driven world. Eighties pop became musically bland – Culture Club, Spandau Ballet, Wham! and Duran Duran favoured new technologies and bad make-up, their songs superbly fashioned to appeal to the Lady Di-generation of Thatcherite wannabees. But music was so glossed with dazzling sheen that any decent content – if it was there – was invisible. Lyrically, pop could not have become more superficial. Synthesizers and sequencers took over from rocking electric guitars. At some point in the early Eighties someone was going to have to break this bubble of self-absorption and vapidity and get back to basics, or Dick Rowe's prediction would have come true – albeit twenty years late. We needed guitar bands again.

And so, on a white charger from the depths of Greater Manchester, came the saviours. Enter... The Smiths.

★

Johnny Marr was born John Martin Maher in Chorlton on Medlock, Manchester, on October 31, 1963, a Halloween baby in the bleakest winter that the north-west of England had seen in decades. John's birthplace was close to the centre of one of England's toughest, most engaging cities. Victorian Prime Minister David Lloyd George was born in the area almost exactly one hundred years before Maher, while novelist Elizabeth Gaskell and suffragette leader Emmeline Pankhurst both lived there. Buzzing around the nearby Manchester College of Art, LS Lowry and fashion designer Ossie Clarke would be regularly spotted in the area. Today the area still houses the BBC and Manchester University, St Mary's Hospital and Manchester Museum. As it was at the time of John Maher's birth, the area remains one of the main centres of activity on the fringes of the city centre.

Maher was born on Everton Road. Nicknamed 'Little Ireland', the area was awash with Irish immigrants recently settled in the area, and the Mahers was one such family. John's father was part of the mass emigration from Eire in the years following the Second World War, when country people from all over Ireland fled to Dublin in search of work. As jobs in the Irish capital became increasingly hard to find, they crossed the Irish Sea. Settling in Manchester, John Snr married Frances Doyle in 1962, and John – who would become known as Johnny – was born the following autumn. His mum and dad were young – his father only twenty years old, his mother a mere seventeen. The family, who originated in Kildare, lived in Ardwick, a little further from the city centre than Johnny's birthplace, a tough part of town with – like Harlem – its own nationally known theatre, The Apollo. Many of John Snr's relatives had made the journey to Manchester at the same time. "Four families lived next door to each other," says Johnny. "All Irish immigrants, all very young. There were parties every night." In the next street there were some seven related families. It seemed as though the entire extended family had moved to Manchester together – all of them young and spending much of their leisure time together, many of them working as labourers around the north-west.

The Maher family – like so many émigré Irish – carried the tradition of Irish music with them to England, and Johnny's father was an accomplished accordion player. While he described his father's occupation as "digging holes in roads", Johnny's parents were actually soon to be involved in promoting country music themselves. "Because it was a big family," recalls Johnny, "there were always christenings and weddings, and there was always what seemed like this same band playing at these functions." John Snr taught his son to play the harmonica and the accordion, and before he hit his teens, Johnny was experimenting with the guitar. "My parents had Beatles records, but they were more into the Irish stuff, country music, which spilled over into the Everly Brothers – who were really popular in my household." 'Walk Right Back', by The Everlys, is the first record that Johnny can remember being played around the house. Jim Reeves, and what Johnny came to refer to later as 'bad country' – the music of people like Hank Williams and Chet Atkins – was popular around the house too. Even the music Johnny didn't like influenced him. He still claims not to enjoy country music, saying that "no matter how much you believe otherwise, you upbringing indelibly affects your development." "It gives you your musical personality," says Johnny, "and in some cases your entire musical vocabulary." Even when he was ten or eleven years old and getting into glam rock, the influence was still there. Deliberately and unwittingly, Johnny's family shaped his early musical aspirations, and though he still retains an aversion for country, "the influence remains."

Johnny would spend long periods back in the home country, sometimes enjoying as much as four months of the year in Ireland. Alongside his immediate family in Manchester, Ireland itself influenced him strongly too – the atmosphere and the people. "The Irish connection is a big one," he has said during a webchat on jmarr.com. "There is a sensibility that affects your life… passion, humour, irreverence." Johnny was aware of the poetic nature of his Irish-ness, of its occasional surreality, and of the darkness in the Irish soul that is sometimes hard to ignore.

As a kid though, most of Johnny's earliest influences were most certainly poetic and occasionally surreal, but rarely dark. His first musical heroes were amongst the most incandescent of all. One of the first was Marc Bolan, and T. Rex one of his earliest and most abiding influences. Bolan epitomised all that was fine about post-Beatles pop, his guitar playing ballsy and rooted in the electric blues of Howlin' Wolf, his image glamorous and elusive. "If it hadn't been for Marc Bolan, Roxy Music and David Bowie," Marr recalled in *Designer* magazine in 2001, "kids of my generation would have been completely screwed." Glam gave access to pop that more sophisticated acts such as Little Feat denied the ten-year-old Maher. Sparks was another of the bands that turned Johnny on, at a time when the Bay City Rollers were perhaps the ghastly, inevitable alternative. At the same time, Keith Richards was one of Johnny's earliest icons. For the young Johnny Maher, pop music soon became a major preoccupation and took a complete hold on his imagination. It was the perfect time to be growing up in pop, and to be heavily influenced by the music of the early Seventies was to be introduced to a thousand different sounds, such was the diversity of the material around: The Beatles, Stones, Neil Young, Motown, blues, rock and soul – the wealth and the breadth of Sixties and early Seventies pop was astonishing. Throughout these years, Johnny soaked it all up, his appetite for the next cool band enormous. As it was for so many born in the early Sixties, it was a route outside of the formal education system via which we learned about the world. "I didn't really think the world made very much sense," Johnny has said, "until I discovered pop music. Music made me understand."

Like so many children whose imaginations were taken over by pop in the early Seventies, Maher would obsess over certain bands or albums for a while, and hungrily lap up every new influence as it came along. His music-crazy parents gave him a role model; "I learned the art of playing the same seven-inch twenty-seven times in succession from my mother," said Johnny. His love of music was intuitive and instinctive, and Johnny has always preferred that to any academic route into music. "It seems to me there are two ways you can go, and neither would include musical school," said Johnny when asked by author Martin Roach, in *The Right To Imagination And Madness*, whether a formal musical education would have helped his own development. "You can either come from the genetic thing, like I did, or you come from a completely non-musical situation... I don't know anyone who's had success from music school." Tuition in a formal sense, was the last thing the young Johnny Maher needed, preferring to rely on an understanding of music "on a spiritual level... a purely spiritual connection" for his impetus. "I would play records at really deafening volume at eight o'clock in the morning, just playing the same song over and over again," he admitted to one interviewer. Patti Smith, Television, The Stones, Rory Gallagher – they all came under his learning gaze and were gathered together one by one to appear by degrees in his playing as he matured.

From the age of ten, Johnny's future was almost pre-ordained. "I had always had guitars, for as long as I could remember," he recalls. "I thought once that maybe my parents were pushing me into it, but I soon realised that I was obsessed." One of the earliest influences on John were what he later called "crappy Elvis movies." The Beatles movies *Help* and *Hard Day's Night* were regularly on the television, and US Beatles cartoons were often repeated. Late night radio – John Peel in particular – had a huge influence. For Maher, pop music took him outside the ordinary life of school, family and friends, outside of the real world of rainy old Manchester.

★

Manchester is a tough town. It raises its musical children almost without kindness. In the early Sixties, the city's mills were indeed dark and satanic, its huge, brick-built warehouses foreboding and claustrophobic. Compared to its limestone cousin along the East Lancs Road, Manchester was sooty and dotted with Second World War bomb sites, while Liverpool was shiny and romantic: an Atlantic city, not a northern town. From the early Sixties and the rise of Beatlemania, it seemed that when something happened, it happened in Liverpool first. Liverpool was on TV every time you switched it on. The Beatles, Jimmy Tarbuck or Cilla, for example, as well as being professional entertainers were professional Liverpudlians and celebrity scousers.

But by the time Johnny Maher was entering his teenage years, Manchester's inherent delights had become obvious to all. For the kids of the north-west in the early Seventies, it was often in Manchester that they saw their first gigs, in Manchester where they bought their first records, posters and books. Manchester was the harder town, but it was cool: it might have lacked a famous and iconic bronze parrot on the town hall roof, but it worked hard, got its jobs done, then went down the pub and rocked. It had the best record shops, the best bookshops, the best venues for gigs.

In fact, the Manchester music scene had already shone brightly, both nationally and internationally. Though often eclipsed by the city some forty miles to the west, Manchester's innate competitive relationship with Liverpool meant that some of Britain's finest bands emerged from its environs over the years. In both Manchester and Liverpool, a huge influence came from the American airmen who flooded the region during the Forties, Fifties and Sixties. During the Second World War, nearly 75,000 aircraft that were used in the Allied campaign entered Europe through Liverpool's docks, and nearly a million-and-a-half US servicemen joined the war effort in the same way. Young people looking for the latest jazz, skiffle, R&B and rock 'n' roll music tuned into the American Forces Network, a radio station for the tens of thousands of Yanks away from home – at a time when the BBC's output catered for rather dainty minds in rather middle-class homes. In the north-west of England, the influence of the Americans was felt perhaps more keenly than anywhere else in the UK, and consequently the influence of the music the Yanks brought with them was fired there like nowhere else. Over the years, much of the correspondence between troops and civilians was centred around the huge US airbase at Burtonwood, halfway between Liverpool and Manchester. It was a phenomenal place, and until the Seventies its storage facilities – designed for aircraft and tanks – was the biggest single-span building space in the world. In the Eighties, it was rumoured that more nuclear armament was stored there than anywhere else in Britain, while gossip of un-named 'goods' being secretly removed in removal vans were rife.

The local love affair with imported American pop music started during the war years. It was jazz and swing for starters, rock 'n' roll and blues later on. After the war it was this romance with imported pop that led to the birth of great music in the region. While the short-trousered Harrison, Lennon, McCartney and Starr were picking up early Elvis and Buddy Holly records in Liverpool, at the other end of the Manchester Ship Canal the influence was equally keenly felt. Both cities had a burgeoning black market trade as sailors and airmen brought discs over from The States and sold them locally at mighty profits. With a vibrant immigrant community – Irish, Afro-Caribbean and Eastern Europeans in particular – and as a major inland port in its own right, Manchester was as likely as Liverpool or London to burst into cultural prominence.

With Elvis and movies such as *Rock Around The Clock* everywhere across the region, the first major post-war teenage cultural development was the appearance in Manchester of the coffee bar. A juke box and a coffee machine were all the teenagers of the city needed to develop their own cool hang-outs. The youth of Manchester started to drag the city out of its post-war austerity and into the modern world. The city centre boasted a plethora of such bars, and they were plentiful in the suburbs too. In the early Sixties, while clubs such as The Cavern flourished in Liverpool, in Manchester it was venues such as The Twisted Wheel, The Forty Thieves and The Oasis – labelled 'the north's top teenage rendezvous' – that attracted the kids of Ardwick, Chorlton, or Wythenshaw into the city centre. By 1965 there some 250 such clubs in central Manchester alone. They were largely alcohol-free affairs, open late into the night, as teenagers listened to the R&B and skiffle sounds that predated English pop proper. As Jonathan Schofield, guru of all things Mancunian, has pointed out on the website www.virtualmanchester.com/music/features, the Mersey river itself is actually born in Greater Manchester. If the Mersey bands claimed Liverpool as their spiritual home, then throughout the Sixties, Manchester answered back with a raft of Beat groups of its own. The Hollies – from whence Graham Nash went on to revolutionise Californian pop – Herman's Hermits, The Bee Gees, Wayne Fontana And The Mindbenders and Freddie Garretty all hailed from the Manchester suburbs, and all had enormous success both at home and abroad. The oft-derided Herman's Hermits clocked up sales of over sixty million records worldwide, while Freddie And The Dreamers and The Mindbenders both reached the number one singles slot in the USA. Manchester was exporting big-selling pop long before The Smiths or Oasis got in on the act.

By 1967, the number of Beat clubs in Manchester had been reduced – by legal intervention – from 250 to just three. The clubs were described in a police officer's report as "dirty and crudely decorated, with a minimum of furniture." The beatniks, mods and rockers came under the critical eye of the law too. Professor CP Lee of Salford University, and formerly vocalist with popular Manchester outfit Albertos Y Los Trios Paranoias, has researched this blitzkrieg of the Manchester scene extensively, and notes that in the wake of the demise of the smaller venues, larger clubs and discos flourished. The Ritz, run by DJ Jimmy Savile was one of the biggest, while audiences of up to 4,000 would attend similar nights at The Plaza and Belle Vue Ballroom. Yorkshire-born Savile was one of pop's first local impresarios to break nationally and a local myth claims that the enigmatic and later-to-be-knighted Sir Jim boosted his clubs' attendances by offering free polio jabs to punters. Other characters built popular and enduring venues around the city. When the BBC launched its premier pop TV show, *Top Of The Pops*, it did so from a converted chapel in the south Manchester suburbs, cementing Manchester at the heart of Britain's pop culture. For all the acts that appeared on the show, it was to Manchester that they travelled to make their reputations.

John Mayall was another Mancunian with a huge influence on British pop. One of the prime movers in the introduction of traditional American blues into Sixties Britain, his band The Bluesbreakers was a cradle for Eric Clapton, John McVie, Mick Taylor, Peter Green, and many other influential rock artists of the following decade. 10cc were one of the most popular Mancunian bands of the Seventies. Graham Gouldman, formerly of The Mockingbirds, had written hits for The Hollies, The Yardbirds and Herman's Hermits. Eric Stewart was an ex-Mindbender. With Kevin Godley and Lawrence Crème they developed into one of the most articulate, witty, accomplished songwriting and performing outfits of their time, described by one journalist as "the UK's Steely Dan." Rusholme's Roy Harper established his own musical voice internationally, helped along by his associations with Pink Floyd and Led Zeppelin, and his sensitive, romantic and woefully underrated work continues to influence to this day. Sad Café's album *Fanx Ta Ra* helped establish them as one of Manchester's most successful mid-Seventies bands, while Salford's Elaine Bookbinder, under the moniker Elkie Brooks, hit pay dirt in the late Seventies with 'Pearl's A Singer' and a run of other hit singles after a stint in Vinegar Joe, a band that also featured Robert Palmer. Thus while he was taking his first, rudimentary steps in guitar craft, the young John Maher had a healthy local culture on which to build his castle.

★

In the early Seventies the Maher family was to move to Baguley, Wythenshaw, a bus ride to the south from the city centre and one of Manchester's most significant urban sprawls. At the time, the area was the biggest council housing estate in Europe, a major part of the south Manchester conurbation. It was by no means a poor and down-and-out place however. Maher has said that the area was middle-class in comparison with the streets of his upbringing, "like Beverly Hills," compared to the tougher streets of his earliest years. Much of the area was 'village-ised' – the great urban sprawl divided up into smaller units with their own facilities and services, encouraging a village mentality among the residents. While it wasn't the haven of crime that many similar developments would become, the area was nevertheless a breeding ground for petty crime and thieving. Set as it was only a mile or so from the wealthy suburbs of Hale, Halebarns and Bowdon, the temptation to wander across the great divide was always there. It was said at the time that there were more millionaires per square mile in these areas than anywhere else in the UK.

Wythenshaw, says Johnny felt "like nirvana" in comparison to his former home. Initially placed at the Sacred Heart Primary School, Johnny earned a place at St Augustine's Grammar School, a traditional Catholic institution for boys where the staff wore traditional mortar boards and gowns. Children were expected to enter the school with an 11+ pass and to leave with nine or ten O-levels and the prospect of a university education. By the mid-Seventies, St Augustine's had, like the majority of grammar schools, joined the movement towards comprehensive education. It was renamed St John Pleasington, and, with a much broader net bringing in a greater variety of pupils, loosened up seriously. Johnny was happy at the school, excelling in English, Art and Music, but claims that by his fourth year there he was losing interest in academia and found himself increasingly poring over music rather than school books.

If the education system lost a potentially very able scholar in Johnny Marr, the youngster did get something out of school, even if it wasn't marked in percentages and grades. "I think the most useful thing about school for me," he told a webcast many years later,

26

"was that I learned to suss out different types of people, and they crop up later in life sometimes… especially loudmouths!" Johnny did go on to enrol at Wythenshaw College, but his real education was taking place elsewhere.

Johnny made friends easily, and one of the lads he teamed up with early in his secondary education was Andy Rourke, a kid from Ashton. Rourke was one of four brothers, whose parents had recently split up, and the two became firm friends, inspired by music, truancy and clothes. While they initially disliked one another – a keen sense of competition between long-haired rock fans – they got together because Johnny was wearing a Neil Young 'Tonight's The Night' badge. Within days they were friends for life, and Andy the better guitar player of the two. The boys led a mildly wild lifestyle – nothing too heavy, but there were soft drugs around the scene as there were in most teenage environments.

By the age of fourteen, Johnny had moved out of the family home and moved in with Andy and his dad *chez* Rourke. It was a short-term separation from parents whom Johnny would remain extremely close to and who had always supported his musical endeavours. While John and Frances Maher willingly helped Johnny out by buying him his first guitars and letting him practise around the house undisturbed, by the time their rebel son was hanging out with older kids and taking his music very seriously, they were naturally concerned that the lifestyle of the musician was too advanced for their young son. For Johnny though, his commitment was already absolute, and there was no going back. "They could see disaster looming," Johnny was to say towards the end of The Smiths' career, but by then, of course, it was too late.

Pop music – in the early-Seventies world before Playstations and video games – was the means to another world, a world of style and individuality, of achievement and of standing out from the crowd. Pop was the badge you wore, the currency you carried with you. Soul boys. Quo freaks. Metal heads. Prog rockers. Folk fans. The breadth of pop in the post-Beatles climate was exhilerating, and exciting, and every week on *Top Of The Pops* or John Peel's Radio One show there was something new to admire, dissect, reference in class or follow slavishly.

"The first record I ever bought," Johnny remembers, "was 'Jeepster.' But it wasn't until 'Metal Guru' got to number one that I really made the connection for the first time." Marr remembers riding his bike around the local streets and singing the song over and over. "It was a feeling that I'll never forget," says Johnny. "A new sensation. I got on my bike and rode and rode, singing this song... one of the best moments of my life." Johnny remembers stealing 'loads of glitter', putting it on his face, and emulating his favourite bands. "From then on my formative years were totally and utterly dedicated to music."

Maher, Rourke *et al* would get together at local youth clubs, meet in town or at one anothers' houses to compare notes, practice the guitar or simply hang out. "What I was doing was more interesting than what other kids were doing," he told one interviewer. "When I left school I had jobs and all that – but they were only a means to playing loads of records and tapes, and getting paid for it." A promising footballer – he tried out for Manchester City and was apparently pursued by Nottingham Forest – and potentially academically very capable, Johnny soon began to neglect both his sport and his homework for music and for the nights out with the boys.

★

Well before Margaret Thatcher entered Downing as Britain's first female Prime Minister in 1979, Britain's inner cities had become dirty, dishevelled and run-down centres of disaffection and unrest. From the summer of 1976, punk was a response to the culture in which flippant DJs and pompous, high-earning bands had taken the fun from the music business just as successive governments had taken the job prospects away from millions of school-leavers. If we'd 'never had it so good' in the late Fifties and early Sixties, by the time The Sex Pistols were launched upon an unsuspecting London public via their now legendary early gigs and TV shock tactics, the youth of Britain was ready for a chance to shout and scream. Just as the mods, rockers and beatniks had done before them, they really caused a stir. In Manchester, this was reflected in the famed summer of 1976 gig at the Lesser Free Trade Hall, when local scenesters Peter McNeish and Howard Trafford organised the first appearance of The Pistols in the city [the definitive account is David Nolan's *I Swear I Was There – The Gig That Changed The World*]. By the time the band returned in July, Peter and Howard's band Buzzcocks had the support slot, and Pete Shelley and Howard

28

Devoto (as they came to be known and loved by millions) were the leading lights of Manchester's nascent punk scene. Buzzcocks went on – even after Devoto's defection to form Magazine in 1977 – to be a long-standing favourite for many who remember that summer as one of the most exciting in pop music's history. Their singles 'Ever Fallen In Love (With Someone You Shouldn't Have)?', 'Orgasm Addict' and 'What Do I Get?' define all that was great about not just punk, but pop music in general. Tense, stylish and fun, witty and heartbreakingly sincere, with a wash of punk insouciance glazed over the top of lovelorn pop. Thirty years on, Buzzcocks are compared to The Ramones and The Velvet Underground, among the most influential bands of all. Buzzcocks remain one of Manchester's finest exports.

And then there was The Fall. There was Warsaw – soon to become Joy Division. Slaughter And The Dogs. The Nosebleeds. The Worst. The Blue Orchids. The Frantic Elevators. The Albertos. Manchester was responsible for some fine bands, and some pretty ropey ones. Alongside the first punk explosion sat John Cooper Clarke, the 'behind-the-shades' punk poet whose appearance owed more to hip Dylan as to Johnny Rotten. Joy Division and The Fall emerged as the two bands 'most likely to.' In Mark E Smith and Ian Curtis, they both had enigmatic, uncompromising front-men with clear agendas and a lot to say. The death of Curtis at once put an end to the potential of Joy Division and launched New Order upon the world. The influence of both bands is prime to this day.

The influence of Shelley and Devoto's early punk enthusiasm is not just felt in the sounds that Buzzcocks created however. In bringing The Sex Pistols into Manchester, they drew a crowd from which were born bands that would be amongst the most important in Manchester's musical heritage and would enliven immediate rock history. Mick Hucknall, Ian Curtis, Peter Hook, Bernard Sumner, Tony Wilson and Mike Pickering were all allegedly present to see the Sex Pistols at that feted Lesser Free Trade Hall show. New Order and Joy Division, Factory Records, Simply Red, The Hacienda club, M People – all were born in some sense out of these cathartic musical events. Pickering, one of the brains behind M People and Quando Quango, was the man to book The Smiths into their first public gig, and would later work with Johnny on at least two occasions.

But at the Sex Pistols gig was another kid looking for a reason to believe. A young man by the name of Steven.

★

Punk was an immediate call to arms for teenagers everywhere. Not since an army of Bowie clones had peopled a hundred high streets in the early Seventies was there such an immediate rush among across the nation's youth to join the movement. Punk was *the* excuse everyone had needed to dress up, get out and get into trouble. Have fun and cause offence. Of course, the movement was about much more than just music. The music attracted a crowd with a certain fashion sense, it didn't create it. A link between fashion and music features in the punk story and in Johnny Maher's. The Pistols were born of Malcolm McClaren's King's Road boutique Sex. In London in particular, punk was a fashion statement as much as a musical force, but by the time it had hit the provinces the two had become almost inextricably linked.

The most tangible evidence that punk had hit town was that kids went out and formed bands of their own. The Sex Pistols were at one and the same time both *so* good and *so* bad, that everyone recognised in them something that they could get off their backsides for and do themselves, at a time when nobody else in society seemed interested in them. Punk was the first truly DIY ethic in pop music since skiffle, when a guitar and a washboard were all a band needed to get started. In its earliest days, pop songs were written by professional song-writers, who would present finished songs to artists to perform under studio direction. Via Buddy and The Beatles, artists soon performed their own material. By the end of the Sixties, artists were not only writing and performing their own material, but the biggest owned their own labels too, like Apple and Beggars Banquet. But in order to be successful, even the most self-managing bands still had to be accomplished as musicians or singers. Punk demonstrated to everyone that if they had something to say they could simply go out and say it, and do all of the above, regardless of how well they could do so. And they could have it done by tomorrow. And in Manchester – as everywhere else – they said it loudly and proudly.

For Johnny Maher punk was a sword with two edges. The Smiths were never a punk group, but they had its influence scrawled all over their attitude to the record industry, their love of the three-minute single, their rhythm section, and their uncompromising belief in their own selves. At the time, Johnny watched the movement from a slight distance. He kicked against it largely because of his current interest in English folk music, derided by the hard-line punk movement. At the same time, he was too young to get in on punk's earliest flourish, those first, influential Manchester gigs. Only twelve years old when The Pistols first came to the city, the first gig that Johnny attended was The Faces. But punk was more than just suburban thrash from south London, if you had the ears to hear it. The American bands embraced by the movement appealed to Johnny much more. Early on, he managed to see Iggy Pop, and it was the related bands such as Television, Patti Smith and The Stooges who joined Bolan and Sparks in Johnny's pantheon of rock gods. Johnny also recalls seeing Rory Gallagher live at around the first time, and the Irish guitarist became an influence that Johnny still recognises today. "He scared the life out of me," Johnny said. "He was so intense – I couldn't believe it. I can remember staying off school for a few days... trying to play along with his records."

Johnny remembers that, after endless attempts, the day after seeing Rory live he finally cracked the Gallagher code and turned a corner in his own playing. "I sussed it out," said Johnny. "And the penny just dropped... 'I can play!'" Rod Stewart and his careering guitarist Ronnie Wood became major influences. The one thing that Johnny did that really expanded his knowledge of music and developed his own fluency and playing was to go out and source the people who had influenced these bands in the first place. The influence of Bo Diddley is heard throughout Johnny's career. He first heard it in the disco funk of Hamilton Bohannon, whose 'Disco Stomp' was a firm favourite, but traced the influence back to its original source. Television's Richard Hell had a clear effect on Johnny, but at the same time he was helplessly drawn to melodic old hats like Simon and Garfunkel.

Simultaneously, there was a huge cross-cultural process in progress. The Beatles had taken American pop music and sold it back to the States in a different guise. By the early Seventies, American bands were coming over to the UK to find their market. Most British kids had Americana about them at every turn. Bolan and Bowie were very 'English' in their original concepts, but washed with American input, so that while Ziggy stood heroically on the rain-washed streets off the back of London's Regent Street, by the time of *Aladdin Sane* Bowie was dissecting New York and Hollywood too. Bolan dipped into the American Riff Songbook on regular occasions to colour his psychedelic boogie. Gary Glitter could only have been born of a generation raised on holidays at Butlins or Pontins, but US bands like Sparks came over to the UK and found their most receptive markets.

In the mid-Seventies you could choose to take the ideological line, or accept that everything was there for you. While Marr didn't follow everything that appeared on *Top Of The Pops* he was not prepared to discard Motown, Phil Spector and The Ronettes – his next love – for the sake of The Clash. "I felt [punk] was definitely for the generation before me," Johnny was to say many years later in a published conversation with Matt Johnson on The The's website. "One of the things about punk in the UK was that, as I remember, it was very political… as if lines were drawn." If you were on the right side of the ideological line then you were in, but waver across that line at your peril. "To me that seemed to hang over our generation like an albatross," said Marr. If joining the club meant ignoring so many other great artists and bands, then Johnny was not interested.

★

Of all the kids whose interest turned to playing music rather than just listening to it, Maher was quickest among his peer group to learn the practical elements of guitar. Chord structures and progressions, picking techniques and fingering came easily to him, naturally, almost as though there was a predetermined route for him to follow. "By the time I was ten or eleven," he told *Guitar Player* in 1990, "I started to buy T. Rex records." 'Jeepster''s Howlin' Wolf riff was the first Johnny had learned, later back-tracking (as he put it) into Motown. "I'd try to cover the strings, piano and everything with my right hand, trying to play the whole record on six strings." This orchestral approach to the guitar mirrored that of impeccable Canadian guitarist Joni Mitchell, who herself has spoken at length of trying to cover an entire orchestra's sound across the six simple strings of the basic guitar. "That's one reason why I am so chordally oriented," Johnny went on to explain. "Why key changes and the strategy of arrangement are really important to me."

He picked up from everywhere and everybody. Johnny found he learned more, and enjoyed the life more, if he hung out with the older boys from around Wythenshaw. He stored every lick and chord that he could find. Johnny's wealth of musical knowledge gradually

32

became immense, a trait that he has continued to display over the years since. His enthusiasm for music, his ability to remember everything he hears and maybe one day use it somewhere in his own music, is legendary. Smiths soundman Grant Showbiz remembers visiting Johnny at home many, many times over the years, and testifies to the fact that music was *always* there. "Whenever I went to Johnny's house," recalls Grant, "which was an awful lot of the time in those days, Radio One was on absolutely permanently. And I can remember it being the same ten years later." Showbiz can only think of one other musician with the same kind of all-inclusive referencing, and the same enthusiasm to share the process of listening to music with anybody. "Peter Buck (of REM) has an absolutely encyclopaedic knowledge of music, and so has Johnny. And he'll just say, 'This B-side by The Dells – listen to the middle eight, listen to what the organ's doing' or whatever it is. And suddenly, it's eight hours later!" Such was the process of assimilating a myriad of musical influences for the young Johnny, as it remains today for the adult; hang out, listen to music, talk about music, play music.

Future Cult hero Billy Duffy was one of the older kids who showed Johnny new chords. Marr remembers how "I met guys who were only thirteen or fourteen, but took themselves so seriously as musicians, they were already legends in their own minds." As well as picking up guitar tips, Johnny was also open to the record collections of everyone he met. In addition to the bluesy rock of Rory Gallagher, Johnny breathed in the soulful West Coast folk of Neil Young, the articulate British picking of Martin Carthy, Davey Graham and Bert Jansch (to whom Johnny was introduced by Duffy). Along with Richard Thompson and Fairport Convention, Johnny also fell for Thin Lizzy, the pristine manufactured pop of Motown and the romantic, Byrds-influenced guitar jangling of Tom Petty. Like his friends, Johnny soon came to consider himself a musician, not just a music fan.

"When I got into Nils Lofgren," Johnny explained to Martin Roach in *The Right To Imagination And Madness*, "there was no turning back." Increasingly, and throughout his teenage years, Johnny was to be seen around the streets of Wythenshaw with a guitar case and a bagful of attitude and confidence. "It was just to let everybody know that my whole identity was as a guitar player," he continued. "I was very cocky..." Besotted by New York New Wave, intrigued by the old waves of acoustic British folk, Johnny's boundless enthusiasm made up for his inescapable youth. "I could pick like Bert Jansch, but I wanted to look like Ivan Kraal from the Patti Smith Group," he said.

At the same time, Johnny began to realise that there was only so far that he could get by playing other people's riffs. He needed people to play with and he needed to write. Marr was starting to write songs for himself, and he needed people around him off whom he could bounce ideas and share the playing more formally. "As soon as I could string a few chords together, I started putting them down on a cassette recorder," Johnny recalls. What was important to him was the guitar. The idea of being the next Jeff Beck or Eric Clapton was anathema to him: Johnny Marr never wanted to be a guitar hero. For Johnny it was always the guitar and the songs that were important. As it gradually dawned on him that he needed some kind of context in which to play and write, so he needed a band to play with.

The names of Johnny Marr's first bands have gone into the legend of pre-Smiths history. For one interviewer in the USA, Johnny claimed his first band was simply called 'Johnny Maher.' The Paris Valentinos was the first example of John Maher actually formalising an arrangement amongst his friends to form 'a group.' The Valentinos comprised Kevin Williams on vocals and bass guitar, Bobby Durkin on drums and Andy Rourke on second guitar. One half of The Smiths was almost in place at this very early stage in Maher's career, when the teenage lads would hang out and plan their route to fame and fortune. "We had more names than we did songs," Johnny was to say later. One day they were a Crosby, Stills, Nash and Young outfit, and the next they were Television. Those early gigs were heard in the echoing chambers of local church halls and at Sunday mass. Gradually it became apparent that Williams – older than Johnny by two years – had other fish to fry. While he handed the bass role in the band over to Andy, he pursued his other creative love, that of acting. A member of Manchester Youth Theatre since the age of thirteen, Williams enrolled in Manchester Polytechnic School of Theatre. While he appeared as a 'helper' on the irrepressible *Cheggars Plays Pop*, under the name Kevin Kennedy he then played the role of the inimitable Curly Watts in *Coronation Street* for some twenty years, one of UK TV's best-loved soap characters of all time. By 2006 Kennedy was appearing as 'The Child Catcher' in Manchester Palace Theatre's production of *Chitty Chitty Bang Bang*. It's interesting to note that Johnny repeatedly found himself in the company of other talented people who would go on to achieve fame in other spheres, or who had already done so.

Williams himself described his own period of working with Maher as a privilege. "To see that germ of genius in Johnny's bedroom," he told film maker David Nolan, made it clear that "...this guy (was) going to be brilliant."

It was the summer of 1977 that saw Johnny and Andy's first ever gig in front of a willing public on the Queen's Silver Jubilee Day. The band played Sam Cooke's 'Bring It On Home To Me', covered a decade or so before by The Animals. Before the song was complete, the performance was halted when the singer was dragged puking from the stage – Johnny's first experience of rock 'n' roll excess! With only one other proper gig to their name, which was at The Squat, a venue near Manchester University, The Paris Valentinos came to a withering halt. Johnny's next gig, on his stripped-down Telecaster copy, *a la* Rory Gallagher, came as replacement guitarist with Manchester's Velvet Underground-inspired Sister Ray. It was a stop-gap appointment with a band that was going nowhere. With Sister Ray, Maher supported Manchester's nearly-men The Freshies.

The Freshies later reached the UK charts with their single 'I'm In Love With The Girl On The Checkout Desk Of A Certain Manchester Megastore.' The Freshies were the brain-child of Mancunian performer Chris Sievey, who also created the TV comic-book Mancunian Frank Sidebottom – he of the large *papier-mache* head. Frank was, of course, The Freshies' biggest fan, and in a wonderfully ironic turnaround, achieved far more mainstream success than The Freshies ever did themselves.

Sister Ray was a brief diversion for Maher, but one of The Freshies' former keyboard players, Paul Whittall, became part of Johnny's next, more important, career move. Whittall was working with one of Wythenshaw's more achieving musicians, Rob Allman. Allman was a friend of Billy Duffy, the Wythenshaw kid who already had great ambition as a guitarist and had joined Manchester's punk legends The Nosebleeds. Fate spiralled the future Smiths closer together, as Steven Morrissey had joined The Nosebleeds as vocalist to replace the legendary milkman/singer Ed Banger. In the meantime Allman and Whittall began working with Maher, Rourke and ex-Paris Valentino drummer Bobby Durkin, under the name White Dice.

Like The Cure, Japan and hundreds of bands before them, White Dice responded to a talent-scouting ad in the music press, spotting a chance of putting themselves before some of the real decision-makers in London pop. The cassette demo that the band sent to F-Beat

Records boss Jake Riviera – the brains behind Stiff Records and the early careers of Elvis Costello, Madness, Dr Feelgood and The Damned – won them an audition in London slated for April 1980. The band threw themselves into rehearsals at Andy's house, with Rob and Johnny sharing writing credits on new material. It was Maher's first experience of a song-writing partnership, and it was mainly their own material that they played at Nick Lowe's home studio between Shepherd's Bush and Hammersmith, where the session took place. Paul Carrack, who spent a lot of time in Lowe's studio, remembers it as "a converted front room." The band was as impressed with their meeting Lowe's then-wife, Carlene Carter, as they were with the process of making the demo, but Riviera was disappointed with the results. A phone call confirmed their worst fears a few days later – and in the melt-down that followed their initial enthusiasm, Bobby Durkin left the band. There was a handful of summer gigs, writing sessions and rehearsals, with Johnny occasionally taking the lead vocalist role but White Dice weren't to last.

Early 1981 saw Maher and Andy Rourke looking for pastures new musically. The next band, Freak Party, shook off the failures of White Dice, and – with drummer Simon Woolstencroft in tow – started earnest rehearsals. The band took a harder, more funk-driven line than White Dice had, with Andy a firm fan of heavy, driven funk bass lines. Numerous singers were rehearsed and discarded, but Freaky Party were destined, as Paris Valentinos and White Dice had done before them – to go nowhere fast. Johnny was often to be seen around some of the Manchester clubs at this time, in particular The Exit, or Berlin, behind Kendall Milne's department store. One of the DJs was Andrew Berry, who at various times lived and recorded with Johnny. Occasionally Johnny would take control of the decks himself, mixing classic Sixties tracks with current dance hits. Early fan and Hacienda regular Joanne Carroll remembers how she would often go and sit with the DJs, as she knew Andrew Berry well, and recalls how more often than not Johnny would have a spliff on the go while he was spinning records.

For Marr this was a formative period, his months before the dawn of The Smiths when a number of important elements in his life came together. Musically, something needed to happen. It was clear that a new direction would have to be taken. At the same time as this became ever-more clear, three people entered Johnny's world who would go on to have a profound influence upon his life.

The first of these was his girlfriend. Two years younger than Johnny, although they shared the same birthday, Angie Brown was firmly established as his constant companion. Angie and Johnny would later marry and raise a family together.

On a professional level, the second was Manchester businessman Joe Moss. Moss had started a clothing business in Manchester in the late Sixties, and by the early Eighties had a string of shops in Manchester and Stockport that traded under the name of Crazy Face. Maher had got himself what he describes as "a job of sorts" at the shop next door. X Clothes was a boutique in Chapel Walks just off one of the city's main thoroughfares, an early Eighties honeypot for Manchester's most-stylish, a must-visit outlet for DJs and musicians. Among its customers was Mike Joyce, who was very much aware of Johnny in the store, but was still unknown to him personally. On other occasions, many of the guys who would get The Hacienda moving would come in –Tony Wilson, Mike Pickering and Peter Saville were all regulars. Maher's role was largely to hang around the shop looking cool, compiling music cassettes to play over the PA, and to generally enhance the place by bringing 'hip' people into the store.

Crucially, it was the fact that the two shops were adjacent that meant that Johnny Maher got to know Joe Moss. "He came up to me in the shop," Joe told David Cavanagh for Q magazine in 1994. "and introduced himself as a frustrated musician." Moss was a music lover, and kept a guitar in the corner of his office, which Johnny would regularly pick up and play while he hung about the older man's gaff. Ten years older than Johnny, Moss was a keen amateur player himself, interested in blues and R&B, and took naturally to the enthusiastic kid from Wythenshaw who seemed to have what it took to become a professional. The two traded skills – a little from Joe here, a little in return from Marr.

As with so many of his lasting relationships, Johnny was to get to know Joe by hanging around, chatting and playing guitars. Moss could see that all the young man needed was guidance, the right people around him, and some funding. Joe would provide elements of all three to the burgeoning Johnny Maher over time. Joe Moss was another in a long line of 'shopkeepers' who brought their retail savvy to the completely unrelated world of managing a rock group, a list that includes the revolutionary Brian Epstein and the iconoclastic Malcolm McClaren. Like his relationship with Angie, Johnny's friendship with Joe was long and lasting.

While settled in a relationship with Angie and developing his contacts around the happening Manchester scene, Maher met a third character who would go on to have an influential part in his story.

It was the winter of 1981. A friend of Johnny had recently been down to London. Wandering Soho, he had fallen into conversation with a musician he met on the street: Matt Johnson, the son of a publican, had grown up over a pub in Stratford, surrounded by East London's finest hoodlums and gangsters. Like Maher, Johnson's early imagination had been coloured by the likes of Sparks, Bolan and Bowie, and he was a confirmed John Lennon addict. The casually-established friendship brought Johnson to Manchester for a visit, and it was at the home of the mutual friend that Johnny and Matt met. Matt played Johnny stuff from his album *Blue Burning Soul*. Months before he would play the same song to Morrissey, Johnny offered up the song that would later become 'Suffer Little Children.' A life-long friendship and future professional relationship was born.

Apart from their immediately taking to one another personally, and the fact that they made a clear decision to remain in touch, Johnson's professional development stunned Johnny. Although he was only a little older, Johnson had already released a number of records, and was a *bone fide* recording artist. Among Johnny's friends, no-one had got this far this fast. As the pair sat and passed Maher's guitar back and forth, it became obvious that the unthinkable could happen. Matt Johnson was about to start on his second album, *Soul Mining*. Johnny Maher could do this too. As Billy Duffy had himself recently packed in his job to pursue music full time, so did Johnny. While Freak Party floundered, Johnny put X Clothes behind him, and wandered off to create the best British band since The Beatles.

CHAPTER 2

Smithdom

The formation of The Smiths is now the stuff of legend. Joe Moss, with no ulterior motive other than to lend something to Maher that he knew would entertain him, lent Johnny a video that told the story of Lieber and Stoller, the two American writers who had joined forces to pen some of early rock 'n' roll's greatest hits, most notably for Elvis Presley. Apart from the incredible focus and determination that the pair showed, the fact that Jerry Lieber turned up on Mike Stoller's door step, introduced himself and declared 'Let's write songs together' struck Johnny as wonderfully romantic. Linked already via Billy Duffy, it was mutual friend Stephen Pomfret who suggested that Johnny meet his mate Steven Morrissey, taking him around – in May 1982 – to a house on King's Road, Stretford, where the Morrissey family lived. The legend has it that there and then Johnny cited the American duo and indeed said "Let's write songs together." There's a nice symmetry in the idea that while Johnny Rotten met Malcolm McClaren on the King's Road, Chelsea, Johnny Marr met Morrissey on the King's Road, Stretford. How north-west playwright Shelagh Delaney, one of Morrissey's greatest influences, would have been proud. While the event has been talked up to mythical proportions since, it is clear that the pair hit it off immediately, and it was indeed a natural and immediate outcome that they should form a song-writing partnership. "I just laid this heavy jive on him," Johnny was to say many years later. "Three hundred words a second." Every name that Johnny threw at Morrissey was greeted with enthusiasm – the pair shared an incredible love of the same left-of-centre music, and from that moment on nothing would ever be the same for either of them again. The first thing that Morrissey said to Johnny was 'do you want to put a record on?" Johnny later thought that this was perhaps Morrissey "testing out where I was coming from." Johnny never missed the opportunity to put a record on: "That was out first point of contact," he said. "I went over to this shoe box with 45s in it, and pulled out 'Paper Boy' by The Marvellettes." Their first point of contact was Motown. "Right from the beginning," said Marr, "we knew it was going to be brilliant." An enterprise that would change the world was born.

The Morrisseys was another Irish family settled in Manchester. Four years older than Maher, the young Steven had spent his early years deep in artistic ferment. Naturally shy, Morrissey had pursued a novel career throughout his teens. A published author of fanzine-style booklets on the New York Dolls and James Dean by the time he met Johnny, Morrissey had submitted scripts to the producers of northern soap *Coronation Street*, and had seen his record reviews and letters published in several of the popular music papers. Steven was also an inveterate pen-pal, having a number of relationships with people via the written word in letters that flowed back and forth from his house in King's Road. Most significantly, the pair shared a musical taste somewhat at odds with the times. While they both loved the garage-glam thrash of the New York Dolls and the impassioned, poetic cool of Patti Smith, they also shared a tendency towards Sixties US girl groups, T. Rex, Sparks, and the finer points of glam. The meeting happened almost as the legend would have it, but the musical joining of hands between Marr and Morrissey was a calculated move by which each party recognised that the other could be a conduit for the other's frustrated talents.

Morrissey had more form in the Manchester music scene than Johnny. Present at the Sex Pistols' famed Lesser Free Trade Hall gig, he had auditioned for a local band around the time that Marr had started the Paris Valentinos, and by 1977 was singing with The Tee Shirts, a band which boasted Billy Duffy amongst its members.

Morrissey then went on to join Duffy in The Nosebleeds, playing support during spring 1978 to Slaughter & The Dogs and Howard Devoto's Magazine. Steven was even referenced by *NME*'s Paul Morley, who reviewed a collection of Manchester bands in June, but despite the lyrical contribution to the band that their singer was now making, their split later in the year was inevitable. Morrissey dallied briefly as vocalist for Slaughter & The Dogs, with whom Duffy stayed when the band moved to London, and was seen at almost every significant gig in Manchester. Empassioned by music and creativity, Morrissey continued to write to the music press and to support Ludus, fronted by his friend Linder Sterling. By the time of his famed meeting with John Maher, Steven had quite a *curriculum vitae* on the fringes of the Manchester music scene. A committed writer, and a lyricist with a background in a band that had done far better than Johnny's; although he played no musical instruments, Morrissey was a natural foil for the younger guitarist.

Almost immediately the pair set about writing songs together. The initial impetus was to be *song-writers*, and it only dawned on the duo gradually that what they were doing would require a band to realise the potential of their partnership. At the same time they recognised that their immediate friendship had a unique element to it. Within two days, said Johnny, he knew that "they had everything." Morrissey presented Maher with a set of lyrics that had enough shape to enthuse the musician. "Morrissey was very, very demanding of me," Johnny enthuses, still excited by the memory. "He was always looking for songs, and without him I wouldn't have written as many songs in that fashion, with such speed."

They began rehearsing with mutual friend Stephen Pomfret, who had been a member of the Tee Shirts with Morrissey. After Pomfret left and White Dice keyboardist Paul Whittal tried out, the duo joined up with drummer Simon Wolstencroft. They were so confident of 'the product' of their partnership that they booked Decibel Studios to record some demos. The studio's engineer, Dale Hibbert, joined on bass and – in nascent form – The Smiths were born, a four-piece of guitar, bass, drums and vocals, with Morrissey and Maher as the primary creative force. "When [we] got together," Maher told *Sounds* a year later, "it became immediately apparent that the songs we were writing needed bass and drums to make them work." With a basic four-piece line-up, the new-found name suggested so many things too. In essence it was a reaction against the exotic, lengthier names popular with bands current at the time (Kid Creole & The Coconuts, Grandmaster Flash & The Furious Five, Haysi Fantayzee et al) – it sounded gritty, working class, anti-pop, and interesting-by-being-not-so. If they sounded ordinary, their music would be quite the opposite. "The name doesn't mean anything," Morrisey was to tell *i-D* magazine some months later in the band's first published interview. "It's very important not to be defined in any one category."

When drummer Woolstencroft didn't last, and neither did his replacement Gary Farrell, the pair auditioned local punk sticksman Mike Joyce. Another Irish Mancunian, Joyce had already served an apprenticeship of sorts with regular gigging bands The Hoax and Victim, and was vaguely familiar with Johnny as a customer of X Clothes, where he bought his mohair sweaters. With The Hoax, he had already appeared on both John Peel's radio show and toured outside the UK, while Victim was a known band on the local Manchester circuit. Joyce joined them in a Manchester studio after receiving a demo, playing through a number of songs and getting to know the singer and guitarist quickly. "It just happened by mistake, really" Joyce told filmmaker David Nolan. "My other groups weren't just complete thrash, but Johnny's subtlety and texture when playing the guitar were different to other players I'd worked with up until that point." When Joyce joined The Smiths, he did so as by far the most experienced member. Twenty years later he described the meeting for BBC Radio. "I'd known Johnny… and seen him around town working in X Clothes. Morrissey was just walking up and down the room with a very long grey coat on, and he said hardly anything." A brief period of doubt about leaving Victim was soon abandoned. Mike Joyce was the next piece of the Smiths' jigsaw puzzle to fall into place, and his arduous vigour as their drummer was an integral part of their appeal in the years to come.

An esoteric lyricist and singer of some eccentricity; an articulate writer/guitarist raised on glam riffs and acoustic folk, and a drummer besotted with Buzzcocks and the punk ideal. The Smiths were coming. "We were put together," Marr said of The Smiths in *Designer* magazine. "We were a bunch of strangers for all intents and purposes – who then became incredible friends… We came together to make *that* music." With hindsight, it is too easy to suggest – as some cynical observers may – that Morrissey saw a musician who could help make him rich and famous, and that

Marr spotted a front man who could realise his own musical ambitions: the backroads of rock 'n' roll are littered with such relationships that never got beyond idle plans. Nevertheless there was, with Joe Moss's vital input, a calculated element to the new band's structure. Johnny and Morrissey were laying plans right from the start. According to Marr, Morrissey's plans for the group's 'aesthetic' – its financial structure and the kind of record deal it would pursue – was in place long before a note had ever been put down on tape. Following their own instincts, this was going to be a band to die for. "Right from the beginning," Marr told *NME* in 1989, "we knew it was going to be brilliant."

Morrissey's songs became the ultimate series of letters to thousands of unknown pen-pals around the world. As a young child he had been a natural writer; from the age of six he was compiling his own magazines; as a teenager he was using the pop press as a means to communicate with the outside world, placing ads in the press seeking other New York Dolls fans, and maintaining relationships through writing. In Johnny, Morrissey found a vehicle for his writing that gave his words a context: Marr's increasingly sophisticated music added weight to the structure of Morrissey's words, and formalised their content. Before finding his co-writer, Morrissey was searching for a role. Johnny had already decided that the role of vocalist/frontman was not for him. But together they knew what they had to do. "The reason why Morrissey and I got together," Maher told *Sounds* less than a year later, "was to write songs… we both felt the need to react against what we'd been hearing for the last [so many] years." The newly formed partnership was too passionate about music to allow the mundanity of the current scene to go unanswered. The key was their overwhelming optimism, the appeal of the nascent band to its first audience being the fact that they offered something to a congregation looking either for help or comradeship. While The Smiths over the years earned an undeserved reputation for glumness, Johnny's guitar lines were resplendent in their optimism, as fresh as a walk at dawn on a cool spring morning. At the same time Morrissey's lyrics leapt in an instant from the hysterically funny to the desperately heartfelt. Together, Johnny and Morrissey became the friend who one could always rely on, the shoulder to cry on or the cheesy mate to have a laugh with. With The Smiths, an audience found kindred spirits.

★

In 1982, one could be forgiven for thinking that punk had never happened. Although there were hits across the year for the likes of The Jam, XTC or Adam & The Ants, the biggest smashes of the year came from the likes of Bucks Fizz, Kool And The Gang, Nicole, Steve Miller and Survivor, with their ubiquitous movie smash 'Eye Of The Tiger.' It was an era of big hair rather than great music. For every Soft Cell there was a bunch of bands like Dollar, Bucks Fizz, Tight Fit or Bardo: either Eurovision wannabees or real Eurovision acts clinging to the charts by their fingertips. Seventies hangovers were still around, the protagonists rolling their jacket sleeves up to establish their Eighties credentials. Cliff Richard, Rod Stewart, Barry Manilow, Leo Sayer and David Essex were all still having major hits. Floppy-haired, floppy-thinking icons like Duran Duran, Haircut 100 and Wham!, alongside soft rock behemoths like Foreigner, outnumbered the genuinely entertaining acts like Madness ten to one. But The Smiths knew they had the key to an upheaval not seen since The Pistols. Johnny gushed on the subject of Morrissey, and Morrissey was equally proud of the guitarist. "Morrissey's so confident," said Johnny "that he doesn't have to cloud his lyrics in metaphor." Morrissey said that "Johnny can take the most basic, threadbare tune and you'll just cry for hours and hours and swim in the tears."

"One of the things about making records," says Marr, "is that for it to work you have to be totally and utterly in love with it for those three minutes, and you have to be able to hear that love in the tracks." While real love and true passion was missing from the pop world in 1982 and early 1983, Johnny and Morrissey knew how to love. "That might be a particular idiosyncrasy of mine," says the guitarist.

Johnny's compositional methods have been outlined piecemeal over the years. What is clear is that the song develops from feeling – what Marr has called "an uneasy feeling" that he tries to harness. When the muse is active, Johnny closes down other distracting elements. "I try not to party," he says. "I keep myself really straight and sober, which is, I guess, the opposite of what people might expect. I get up early and stay up late, sleep as little as possible and harness that disconcerting uneasiness." Marr likens the feeling to "knowing a storm is coming and [knowing] that something is going to happen." While this method served Marr best in his post-Smiths days, often during the early and heady days of the band's career the group component would overtake the individual creative element. "We were incredibly pragmatic in approach," he says. "We'd do batches of three songs at a time. We'd sit down and say, 'Let's write a song.'" The discipline of Leiber and Stoller was paramount. "Morrissey would come round to my house and we'd do three songs just like that. Then he would go away and do the lyrics, and three days later he'd be in the studio recording it." Morrissey and Marr were remarkably prolific, recording seventy songs in four years, and part of that urgency came from what Johnny calls Morrissey's "emotional and physical necessity" to write. It made the process easy. "and in that way we propelled each other towards this endless supply of songs."

Johnny has called the process "incredibly romantic." This was not, of course, in the sense of *amour*, but romance with a capital 'R.' Heightened sensation, heightened perception, heightened emotional involvement typified the Romantic poets – Keats, Shelley, Coleridge and Wordsworth – and this was the 'romance' that the two writers experienced together. "The songwriting process, and the songs we produced, are sacred," Johnny was to say after The Smiths' split. "And still are to me now." 'Suffer Little Children' and 'The Hand That Rocks The Cradle' were amongst the first, brilliant flowers of this new musical romance. Morrissey moved our hearts because his writing was so fine. Johnny moved our hearts with his passionate guitar. And they dragged us onto the dance floor too. Paraphrasing Joni Mitchell, a great song needs a little something for the heart, a bit for the mind, and something to get you on your feet. Between them, Johnny and Morrissey did that in spades.

"I have never related to the Jeff Becks of this world," says Marr. "I have never seen the guitar as a solo instrument. When I started to write songs, I wanted my guitar to sound like a whole record." Marr's comments confirm his compositional premise: "I consequently developed almost a one-man-band style." In relation to the oft-quoted comparison with the Phil Spector 'Wall Of Sound' – where Spector embellished tracks with multi-tracked drums, piano and strings – Johnny again relates his own attitude not to individual traits in the Spector sound, but to the entire package. For Johnny, as the guitar was an orchestra, so Spector was "the overall musician." "Not purely sonically, but you could hear in his records that he was completely obsessed. There were no spaces – any harmonic suggestion was realised. It's a kind of production thing." Marr's composition was a complete process from start to finish – individual songs conceived as a production exercise as much as a progression of chords or melodic structure. "If you've got four or five musicians playing then you will get loads of natural harmonics and spaces in there between the instruments. Spector was someone who would hear all these tiny suggestions and then fill every one in... [a] big, big, dense apocalyptic sound which I definitely connected with." Johnny hears 'the whole thing.' "I'll play a new song and hear piano and strings and then I try and play all that on my one guitar," he told Martin Roach.

Marr's playing style attracted attention early on. "Johnny would do interviews, and he wouldn't cite the usual guitar heroes," notes Alberto vocalist and academic CP Lee. "I specifically and distinctly remember him talking about the influence of English folk-rock. It's now very apparent – because we know more about it – but [at the time] I detected the likes of Bert Jansch and Davey Graham. And it's what made his sound unique – it's definitely not American guitar-playing." Billy Bragg spoke to me and also recalls talking to Johnny about his own guitar playing and the influences upon it. While most journalists summed up his style through analogies with The Byrds, Bragg was surprised that a British player should spring to Johnny's mind first. "I said, 'What were your influences in America?'" remembered Billy. "And he said, 'Martin Carthy.' If I would make reference points on people like Terry and Gay Woods, he would know them. It wasn't beyond him, and he's worked with Bert Jansch as well. [All that] is what he brought – that I thought was really great – to The Smiths."

Early in the history of the band, Johnny was keen to emphasise that it was *the band* that was important, not individual members of it. This was not his vehicle, nor indeed Morrissey's, but a group concept from start to finish. From that moment The Smiths were a unit. While he could not relate to self-indulgent guitar heroes, neither was he overly inspired by solo singer-songwriters. But The Smiths would represent the very best of pop music, whether it be Fifties, Sixties or Seventies. "We're trying to bring back that precious element which is, I suppose, reminiscent of an earlier time," he told Bill Black for *Sounds.* "Lots of common ground, but with separate influences to bring out something we believe to be the best we've ever heard." This would be tempered – crucially – by Johnny's own experiences. "I am a white musician," he says, "born in the Sixties, in the provinces. And that is the way it sounds." While Johnny would go on to earn respect, and an enviable reputation, for being able to walk into any studio in the world and ignite the work in hand, he never became a whingeing guitar soloist. "When that stuff is bad – it's the worst," he says.

While the general music scene was stagnant – unless you were in the hair-dressing or lace industries – there was some fun in the singles charts: Soft Cell, Culture Club, The Jam, Bow Wow Wow, ABC and XTC, Bananarama/Fun Boy Three, Adam Ant and the resplendent Associates all made serious inroads into the top twenty in 1982, along with an air of style or fun. However, a number of these were already five-years-old as acts, and pop was in perhaps its most vapid phase since the sterile months of the late Fifties and pre-Beatles Sixties. There was little heart, precious little soul, virtually no wit (Madness and Blondie aside) and equally little musicianship. The record-buying public didn't know it, but it needed The Smiths more than it needed anything: while Steven and Johnny sat head-to-head and planned their future, any discerning rock critic might have come up with a formula for a band that could shake the early Eighties up again, like punk had done six or seven years earlier. The band to re-energise the charts and the hearts and minds of the people who listened to the music would be a singles-orientated band (like the Pistols) with a predominance of guitar-driven pop. They would have both wit and wisdom, controversy but with substance: music needed punk all over again, but newly minted for the new decade.

Music needed The Smiths.

★

Morrissey and Marr knew they had what it took. Johnny's increasing versatility and accomplishment as a guitarist set against Morrissey's faith in his own concept of stardom and his proven, tried and tested ability as a writer convinced the pair that they were more than viable contenders. Put simply, they both knew what a great record should sound like, and they knew there weren't many of them around. Johnny has spoken of early singles by Sparks and Roxy Music as influencing his feel for what was right – and ironically several of these involved future Smiths producer John Porter. For Marr, the perfect equation involved a great intro, a great outro, and "something interesting in between". He cites Roxy's 'Love Is The Drug' as a perfect example: the car engine starting, the cigarette lighting.

They were controversial contenders from the outset too. Set to become probably the most notorious of all The Smiths' released songs, 'Suffer Little Children' was inspired in part by Emlyn Williams' account of Ian Brady and Myra Hindley, in his 1967 book *Beyond Belief*. One of the duo's first compositions, it could not be further from the chart pap of Shaking Stevens' 'Oh Julie' or Shakatak's 'Night Birds'. It was an astonishing accomplishment for such a new partnership, but at the same time encapsulated so much of what Smiths music would come to mean to people – stylish, melodic, mood-driven, lyrically intense and musically dense. And with a hint of the mournful. For everyone who grew up in the north-west of England in the mid-Sixties, the Moors Murders were a part of their childhood, a news story that eclipsed almost every other, a chilling reminder that, even in the day-glo Sixties, we weren't as safe and secure in our luxury as we thought we were. Williams' book contains the title of the song as one of its own chapters, and numerous references in the song – notably 'find me, find me,' the chilling call of the murdered children from their graves – are in direct reference to the best-selling book.

Another early product of the new partnership was 'The Hand That Rocks The Cradle.' According to Simon Goddard, the lyrics predated Johnny's writing partnership with Morrissey by some time. Goddard quotes Richard Boon, who knew Morrissey through Linder Sterling, having heard a home demo of the lyric as far back as 1980. 'Handsome Devil' also dates from this initial writing period. Within weeks the Smiths canon was coming together. With alarming speed, by autumn the band was ready, rehearsed and planning their first live gig.

The Smiths' first public appearance is another landmark legend in their story. They appeared as support to Blue Rondo A La Turk at a fashion show at Manchester's Ritz, on October 4, 1982. The Ritz dance hall had a history going way back in the musical past of Manchester. Only yards away from The Hacienda, Morrissey had sung there already with The Nosebleeds. Blue Rondo A La Turk represented everything that Maher and Morrissey's new band rallied against: an absurd name taken from a Dave Brubek jazz number, a ten-piece ensemble and a bubbly interpretation of the currently trendy demob style. The Smiths – Johnny, Morrissey, Mike and Dale Hibbert on bass – were determined to make a statement. With only three self-penned songs and a cover – albeit three songs soon to be established as classics – they added a temporary fifth member to their number. James Maker was a close friend of Morrissey, reportedly so like him in his manner that the pair were at the time almost inseparable. Maker is usually cited as the band's dancer for the gig, and he supplemented Joyce's rhythmic drumming with maracas and tambourine, a role that Morrissey himself would adopt on stage many times in the years to come. Maker's role was largely to grab the attention of the three hundred or so punters. "I was there to drink red wine, make extraneous hand gestures and keep well within the tight, chalked circle that Morrissey had drawn for me," Maker was to tell Simon Goddard. "My involvement was not part of any long-term plan."

Determined to make a mark, the band's initial profile and styling could easily have been perceived as 'gay'. Dale Hibbert remembered being specifically groomed for the public image. "I got carted off," he told David Nolan, "given some clothes – 'these are your clothes.' Taken to a hairdressers – 'this is your hair cut.' And they said, 'We are probably going to have an image as a gay band.'" This came as some surprise to Dale, who was very much married and a father. But the gay market was easily identified and, since Bowie's Seventies gender-bending, represented a substantial market. With the new romantic penchant for make-up and effeminate garb, it had become increasingly easy for bands to promote themselves directly to the gay audience to get noticed, without actually being gay.

There were plenty of other bands around appealing to a gay audience or promoting a gay image. Culture Club and Soft Cell both had major hits over the course of the year 1982. The Smiths might have seemed a natural choice to take the next slice of the pink pound, with Morrissey's beguiling ambiguity. But The Smiths were always too tough for that, too stylish even in this earliest incarnation, to be pigeon-holed so glibly. The Smiths had a sophistication that the above bands never achieved, their message too mixed, their dynamic too mature. Inevitably they did attract a substantial gay following, but their guitar, bass and drums drive encouraged badge-wearers from every supposed minority faction – students, gay libbers, vegetarians, animal rights activists and so on. What Hibbert's comments do reveal is a sense that Johnny and Morrissey already had a clear notion that the band would – whatever it turned out to be – have *an* agenda, a profile of their own rather than following someone else's fashion trend. The Smiths were going to *be* something.

The Ritz gig was a runaway success. Joe Moss, seeing the band for the first time before an audience, thought they were superb. In particular he thought the show was a 'showcase' for Johnny, highlighting both his songs and his ability on a live platform. If he had doubted The Smiths at all, he cast all those doubts aside. As he was to tell Q magazine more than a decade later, "there was only one place they were going."

Throughout the rest of 1982 the band continued to progress, both in terms of writing and performance, as rehearsals were stepped up. It became apparent that family man Dale Hibbert didn't quite fit. Johnny realised the natural bass player in his band should be Andy Rourke, with whom he had a natural synergy. Johnny invited Andy to join the band at a session booked at Drone Studios in Chorlton during December. One of Johnny's contacts had convinced the mighty EMI that this was a band worth an audition, and with a small advance from the record company, Dale had booked the session with the intention of producing a professional demo. It was on this evening that Andy officially replaced Hibbert in The Smiths. The Smiths proper was born, and the permanent line-up of Marr, Morrissey, Rourke and Joyce recorded three tracks: 'Miserable Lie', 'Handsome Devil' and 'What Difference Does It Make?', all destined to make it into the Smiths recording canon proper. Reunited with Johnny in a band, Andy Rourke found the transition of joining The Smiths easy. "I had a good understanding of where Johnny was coming from," he was to tell *Bass Player* magazine years later. "That was a luxury we had with The Smiths – everything just clicked."

Simon Goddard has charted the progress of 'Miserable Lie' from this early demo through to the finished, officially released version on the band's first album. What is clear is that both the songs and the band developed both lyrically and musically over the coming few months, with Johnny's guitar sound being amongst the most notable developments. The funky undertone in the Drone version of 'Miserable Lie' betrays Johnny and Andy's partnership in White Dice, while by the time later producers Troy Tate and John Porter had got hold of it, the layered guitar sound so symptomatic of The Smiths was fully evolved. Likewise, 'Handsome Devil' included a soon-to-be-discarded sax line and 'What Difference Does It Make?' featured backing vocals from Johnny, which were also dispensed with.

Visually, the band were compelling too, the antithesis of so many bands around at the time, and good-looking to boot. "It just so happens we're handsome," Johnny later told *Sounds* with endearing confidence less than a month after they signed their first contract with Rough Trade. "We didn't rope in good-looking chaps on bass and drums. It just happened that way." Great looking they were though. Morrissey's increasing penchant for outsized blouses from Evans (a high street chain catering for over-sized ladies of a certain age), Johnny's shades, Mike's chisel-cut Irish good looks and Andy's boy-next-door handsome features complemented one another perfectly.

The haircuts were an important part of the look, cut by Johnny's friend and DJ Andrew Berry. Early fan Joanne Carroll remembers the scene around the Manchester clubs with fondness, and remembers that where she used to get her barnet cut was all part of the sense of belonging to the happening Manchester scene. "Getting my hair cut at the bottom of the Hacienda, which at that time was a hairdressers," is one of Joanne's fondest memories. The atmosphere, and relationship between punters and pros was warm and friendly. "We knew [Andrew Berry] really well. I remember Johnny Marr being [in the hairdresser's chair] frequently too." On the day that Johnny and Angela got engaged, the little bunch of like-minded fans and friends from the hairdressers got together. While Joanne and her friends knew of The Smiths, it was Johnny that they got to know the best. "The day he got engaged we went out and bought a card for them," remembers Joanne. Not that the other Smiths were unfriendly, but it was Johnny who seemed to have the warmest relationships around the circuit in the early days.

Grant Showbiz was startled by the Smiths' haircuts too. Because they all went to Andrew for their 'styling', says Grant, "[that] meant they all had the same sort of haircut and it was unlike any haircut you'd seen." At the same time, their dress sense was unusual too. As well as having been shawn by the same hairdresser, Grant remembers that "they all dressed the same too. They had these beads round their neck, they had these weird clothes you had never seen before... beamed down from planet Manchester."

As a pure pop group, like The Beatles, The Smiths had something for everyone: if you didn't fancy Paul, you could always go for George. CP Lee noted the band's sartorial elegance early in their career. "Morrissey and Johnny Marr are both incredibly stylish men, but with their own absolute agenda," says Lee. "It's not quite James Dean... the leather jackets and jeans and stuff. When they first started out – the quiffs – I think Johnny was Britpop before Britpop."

51

As Morrissey quickly became the band's front man in terms of interviews, so his charming features established his own appeal. Drawing his own personal style from the cool waters of James Dean and Oscar Wilde, Morrissey looked like no other pop star before or since. The hearing aid and the flowers were to come soon enough to complete the look. Too many interviewers and reviewers over the years have speculated about Morrissey's sexuality, but in an age of effeminate, dolled-up pop stars, Morrissey was actually visually very masculine. His confident jaw would be held thrust out at the audience, his bushy eyebrows gloriously unplucked. At the same time Morrissey's visual accoutrements – the hearing aid, the flowers, the collars tucked inside his shirt – undermined that apparent masculine confidence, and made him irresistible, intriguing.

Alongside him, Johnny was the epitome of a new kind of retro cool – the blackest shades, the coolest haircut, a red Rickenbacker slung around his neck like a weapon, and his slender frame as rock 'n' roll hip as Keith or Brian Jones ever were. For Morrissey, being 'handsome' was absolutely crucial to The Smiths, and he playfully demanded "a handsome audience" to go with the band's own aesthetic. For Johnny "it just [finished] the package off nicely!"

1982 ended with everything in place for an assault on the music-listening public. 1983 would see the band established as perhaps the most important band in the UK. For a short while, Johnny moved into digs, and had a significant local figure as his landlady. Shelley Rohde was a journalist and TV presenter on Granada TV, Manchester's local independent station. She was also a well-respected author, the biographer of LS Lowry, her book being the standard work of reference on the Salford painter's life. As a result, Johnny even found his way on to a couple of Granada TV debate shows. While his stay *chez* Rohde was not long – he moved out in early 1983 – Rohde was another of Johnny's contacts who brought him closer to the centre of the Manchester scene. Even at this early point in his career, Johnny was connecting with some influential local people. Amongst the friends and acquaintances he had made over the last couple of years, several were talented enough to make it independently as successful musicians – Matt Johnson and Billy Duffy being amongst the most notable. Even at the age of eleven, he had found in Andy Rourke not only a lifelong friend but a man with the talent and the tenacity to survive being a Smith, and in Morrissey he had instinctively linked up with one of the era's biggest talents. Even former band members such as Kevin Williams were destined to stardom, despite their musical torches not burning for long. Johnny was attracted to talent — he instinctively knew which people were right for him to be around. There is no suggestion of any Machiavellian manoeuvring, but it is clear that Johnny's ambitions were fired by the quality of the people amongst whom he found himself.

The new year 1983 started with Joe Moss officially installed as The Smith's manager. Joe's friendship with Maher was firmly established, and was to be as long lasting as any within the band itself. Not only did Joe become manager to The Smiths, but at the same time he became Johnny's landlord. Johnny moved out of Shelley Rohde's house early in the New Year and into digs at Joe's house in Marple, a sedate suburb of Stockport on the fringes of the Peak District, only a few miles east of Manchester itself. By the end of the year, Johnny had moved back out of Marple and into another house owned by Joe in Heaton Moor, again closer to Stockport than to Manchester city centre. Johnny wrote the music for many of the early Smiths songs here, and his home became a focal point for band members and friends to congregate until Johnny moved to London on a more permanent basis.

Moss was the band's manager, although a lot of the issues relating to the band continued to be decided upon by Morrissey and Johnny. Financially, Morrissey took the wheel. "His motto was 'What we make we put in our pockets and pay everybody else from our pocket,'" is how Johnny described Morrissey's attitude from day one, speaking to *Record Collector*. This was never going to be a band led by a frontman with no involvement behind the scenes. In charge of more immediate matters, Joe's first actions were practical, securing the band rehearsal space above his Portland Street premises, where the band could really hone their live skills and develop musically around Morrissey's vocals. In early January, the band played their second official gig, this time with the Marr/Morrisey/Joyce/Rourke line-up that would remain largely settled through the rest of their career. James Maker graced the stage a second and last time, and with an audience of a few hundred packed into Manchester's Manhattan Sound, the band expanded upon their original four-song set. In February, *i-D* magazine was the first to run a feature on the group, interestingly featuring Dale Hibbert as the bassist, indicating that the interview was conducted before the turn of the year. The band talked of how, in the wake of Joy Division, Manchester bands ran the risk of being patronised by the media, but at the same time admitted that the Manchester scene had helped them develop quickly.

"Bands need to be more positive, and stop limiting themselves" said Johnny. "If people don't like us [it'll be] because we're The Smiths, and not because of what we wear." Before Morrissey began to proclaim on 'big' subjects such as vegetarianism, The Smiths were very anti-image in their projection. Their concerns were voiced in this very first interview; that bands should be open and positive, and shouldn't limit their work according to received patterns of predetermined behaviour, that fashion had nothing to do with music but that music was the 'major influence on life.' Interestingly, on the subject of their sound as a band, Maher noted that too many bands were trying to innovate, and that in the wake of the work of Brian Eno and David Byrne (whose hugely influential *My Life In The Bush Of Ghosts* was released in 1981) people should give up trying to be original and should get back to the basics of simply making great music.

As media interest in the band began to ferment, so their live schedule began to pick up speed. Their first Hacienda gig took place in early February, the stage strewn with flowers in an attempt to – as Morrissey was later to explain – re-introduce 'human gestures' into stage performance. By now the band had a full set, and most of the songs that were to grace their first album were integrated into the show. Later in the month, at Manchester's Rafters they supported ex-Television and Voidoid legend Richard Hell, a major event for the band so influenced by both Richard himself and fellow New Yorker Patti Smith. In March, Joe Moss provided the couple of hundred quid needed for the band to enter Stockport's Strawberry Studios, a famed enterprise owned by 10cc, to record their first single. 'Hand In Glove' was the result of the session, the lyrics to the song recently penned by Morrissey to a track provided by Johnny. Marr was to explain that he came up with the riff on "a crappy old guitar." "We [Angie and he] were visiting my parents... Then I got the idea for the riff, but because I had moved out there was nothing to record it on." Angie borrowed her parents' VW Beetle, "and drove this live riff over to Morrissey's house," says Johnny. "On the way, she said 'Make it sound more like Iggy.' And bang! 'Hand In Glove'!" Although three versions of the song were recorded over the coming months (not including the later version with Sandy Shaw on vocals) it was actually a remix of this recording that made its way onto the band's first album.

54

Fired up, the foursome travelled down to London later in March to play their first gig in the capital, accompanied by a coterie of friends and fans from the north-west, who supported the band at The Rock Garden in Covent Garden. Within days, Johnny took control of the band's future, travelling back to London to present a cassette of 'Hand In Glove' into the hands of the man who would secure their future. The Smiths were getting nearer.

CHAPTER 3

Not Rough,
But Trading

R ough Trade began life as a record store in 1977, soon
becoming one of the UK's most influential independent
record labels. Independence was not a new thing in the
record business – right back to the early Sun releases in the USA,
rock music had relied upon selective independents to find and
represent some of the most influential and interesting of bands.
At the end of the Seventies, recording companies were beginning the
drift towards conglomeration that meant perhaps half a dozen or so
labels ran almost the entire business. The fact that The Sex Pistols had
courted EMI and A&M so fiercely, illustrated the fact that the so-
called independence of punk was in fact often merely an attempt to
extricate as big an advance as possible from one of the majors. Punk's
self-help ethic, however, was instrumental in people like Geoff Travis
forming Rough Trade, and the company consistently maintained
extremely high aesthetic standards. The bands that joined the young
label – and indeed went on be a part of its future – were almost
without exception interesting and entertaining. Aztec Camera,
Stiff Little Fingers, Cabaret Voltaire, Scritti Politti and The Fall were
typical examples of bands moving from very small or self-run labels
into the Rough Trade stable, where they could attract the attention

of the media and develop a consistent fan base, and that the latter were on Rough Trade attracted Morrissey and Marr. As the music revolution that was MTV began to take a grip on the industry, it was harder and harder for bands that didn't have the pop sheen and lip-gloss look to find a home that would give them a major profile: Rough Trade was ideal for The Smiths.

Johnny travelled to London and introduced himself to Travis with immense charm and unlimited enthusiasm for the featureless little cassette tape containing such a gem. "I remember Johnny glowing with pride, saying 'This is it! Just listen to this,'" Travis recalled of their meeting in the Rough Trade canteen, when speaking to *The Face*. "I knew inside me that no-one had ever heard music like this before," says Johnny. During the trip, Johnny kipped with Matt Johnson, and this was the period for The The when Johnson was writing *Soul Mining*. The whole trip was enlightening for Marr – a glimpse into Matt Johnson's creative work cementing the friendship that was already well-established, and an inherent knowledge that the time had come for his own band too.

For Travis' part, unlike many label bosses in a similar situation, the Rough Trade supremo gave the tape an unbiased listen. "I was helplessly won over," he glowed afterwards. Deciding to release 'Hand In Glove' as a single, the label boss made one of the most important decisions on behalf of Rough Trade that he could have made. "I listened to it all weekend," he told Q in 1994, "and absolutely loved it." Travis called Johnny on the Monday, and – according to his account of 1994 – the band were in the Rough Trade offices on the Tuesday.

For Morrissey, the decision to take The Smiths on board was the label's "best-ever deal." Ultimately achieving the status as Rough Trade's most successful band, future income from The Smiths allowed Travis to invest in more bands that would otherwise perhaps have been outside of the label's grasp, such as Pere Ubu, Woodentops and Easterhouse. The label gained experience in charting successful singles bands and promoting major acts as well as minority ones, and enabled the company to expand into the US market with record stores and distribution deals. For The Smiths themselves, signing to Rough Trade was a blessing and, as would transpire later, a deep complication.

The blessing was that, from the very beginning, Johnny and Morrissey had wanted to control as much of their own business as possible. While rumours that the band would sign with Manchester's

Factory Records abounded, and other labels were reported to be interested, Rough Trade offered them the opportunity to retain a much larger share of their record deal than might otherwise have been possible, and left the success or failure of the band more than partially in the hands of the artists themselves. In short, although the advance paid to the band was considerable in Rough Trade's own terms, it was significantly less than might have been gleaned from a deal with, for instance, EMI. Instead, the deal with Rough Trade would be a profit-sharing offer whereby the company and the band split the income from The Smiths fifty-fifty. If the band were hugely successful, their income would be considerably higher than if they were signed on a lower percentage/royalty deal. "We like Rough Trade as people," Morrissey told *Melody Maker* in the autumn. "And they like us. That has to be the most important thing. And if people want to buy the records, Rough Trade will supply them." Such implicit confidence in such a simple process was endearing. Both Johnny and Morrissey trusted that the route to immense success was inevitable. People would hear The Smiths. People would like The Smiths. People would buy their records. Nothing could be more simple for a duo who had etched out the steps to success from day one. "I want to be heard and I want to be seen by as many people as possible," explained the singer. How he would be proven right, time after time.

The complication of the contract was that – while they waited until the early summer to formalise the deal – only Morrissey and Maher appeared as signatories on it, and this would come back to haunt them and many of the people around the band in the future. Although Rourke and Joyce were reportedly present at the signing, their names did not appear on The Smiths' contract with Rough Trade, and so – contractually at least – they were not officially/ technically 'Smiths'. The situation was, much later, to cause Morrissey, Maher, Rourke and Joyce great problems and lead to one of the most acrimonious court cases in rock history, as well as to public vilification at the hands of the ever-considerate British tabloid press who had waited decades to dig their teeth into the band.

For now though, the deal enabled Johnny to take the band into the studio and start work on the much-discussed, much-anticipated debut album. There were gigs to play, now with the knowledge that the future of The Smiths was in part secured, and it was a heady and exciting time for Maher. Dave McCullough, writing for *Sounds* a

month or so after the contract was sealed, wondered whether Rough
Trade were in a position to really do justice to the inevitable potential
that the band had. One of the first journalists to try and get to grips
with what the band were *really* about, McCullough noted their
confidence – "they KNOW the talent that The Smiths possess."
Morrissey, for his part was confident in the deal. "Obviously we
wouldn't say no to Warners, but Rough Trade can do it too," he told
the journalist. Johnny was keen to stress that one of the reasons that
they had not signed to Factory was that they might forever be tagged
a 'Manchester band.' "What we're thinking of isn't even in terms of
national success. It's more like worldwide!" Super-confident they may
have seemed but, over the year to come, interviews with all the
band members would demonstrate one thing – whether it be Johnny,
Andy, or whoever, the thing that was important to all of them was
The Smiths, and what The Smiths could achieve, almost as though
they were the unwitting owners of a patent on a remarkable product
that could not fail to succeed in a barren marketplace.

Smiths' sound engineer Grant Showbiz confirms that the
example of The Fall was key to The Smiths' choosing to join Rough
Trade. Grant himself got to know the band very soon after they
joined the label, and was with them effectively the whole time, from
their fifth gig to the end. "I did the sound for a hippy band called
Here And Now," recalls Grant. "We lived in a bus and we played free
concerts, which at the end of the gig we would ask for a collection
for food and petrol for the next gig." Manchester was one of Here
And Now's biggest gigs, a valuable contribution to the hippy funding.
"Andy and Johnny came to one of those gigs, and I guess probably
saw me cavorting!" Self-described as " a fairly loud and shouty sort of
person," Showbiz's careering back and forth was noticed by the pair
of Smiths.

Showbiz's second link to The Smiths came via Mark E Smith's
band. "I was working for The Fall at Rough Trade," Grant remembers,
"And Morrissey knew of The Fall, so I think from Morrissey's end he
knew my name and liked what The Fall were doing, in that they were
slightly sort of angular and different to what was going on then."
So when Rough Trade found themselves with The Smiths on their
hands, they also found they had someone who they felt could handle
this odd bunch of lads from up north. Morrissey, Andy and Johnny all
knew of Grant, and he soon became one of the most 'inside' of The
Smiths' insiders.

"The third thing," Grant told me, as he looks back on how he came to know the band so well, "was that Geoff or Scott Piering at Rough Trade knew me and could see [that The Smiths were] a young band from Manchester. At that point they did seem a little bit like aliens from another planet." Scott Piering was another member of the team to be on the inside from early in The Smiths' story. Piering was Travis' natural choice to promote The Smiths, with a history of working with some of the less mainstream acts that came his way. "Scott had been many things, but he was 'indie man,'" recalls Showbiz. "He was a promo who was up against other plugging companies." As a result, Piering often found himself working with 'interesting bands' in the early days of their career when – as Grant Showbiz puts it – "they couldn't afford a 'proper' plugger." But a 'proper plugger' Piering certainly was, as he proved over his time pushing The Smiths.

"My own feeling was that people like Scott and Geoff [Travis] realised that they could talk to me – and I made sense," said Grant. "I wasn't a lunatic, and I could get on with weird bands from Manchester," he laughs. Showbiz, Piering and The Smiths were put together by Rough Trade, and it was a long and lasting relationship. Indeed, Showbiz continued to work with Johnny outside of the band, when the pair both worked with Billy Bragg much later. For now though, Showbiz's input was first employed to clean up the live sound of the band. The sound that they produced was often rough-cut at best, recalls Grant. "I started on their fifth gig, and they had *echo* on Morrissey's voice." To illustrate, Grant does a fantastic impression of Morrissey's voice with too much echo on it which does not transmit to print. But the point is made clearly enough – overloaded echo "wasn't what you wanted with a band like The Smiths."

As the team came together, one more major change took place which confirmed the identity of The Smiths proper. While Steven had long-abandoned his Christian name for the iconic-sounding moniker 'Morrissey', John Maher decided that it was time to distance himself from any potential confusion regarding his name and his background in the Manchester music scene. It is hard to see how anyone would have confused the rake-thin, stylish guitarist with newcomers The Smiths with the frenetic blaster behind the kit in the six-years-in-the-public-eye Buzzcocks, but while John Maher remained a member of the highest-profile Manchester punk band, Johnny decided to change his name to Marr. The song-writing partnership that was Morrissey and Marr was officially born.

61

'Hand In Glove' backed with a live recording of 'Handsome Devil' was released in May. The band had briefly considered releasing it on their own independent label – according to Morrissey very much at Johnny and Moss's instigation. May also saw a series of gigs that pushed the band more firmly into the limelight.

Fewer debut singles have sounded better. Live, the song was an electrifying beast too: Johnny's cyclical riffs carried the rhythmic attack as presciently as that of Joyce and Andy. Early in their career there was a unique lyricism in the playing, a melodic onslaught as well as a metronomic tempo. Behind Johnny, Rourke's bass playing was equally incisive, his funk background not lost amongst the darker clouds of Morrissey's lyric. "I tried to do a tune within a tune," Andy explained retrospectively in *Bass Player* in March, 2006. "I wouldn't be happy with a bass line unless you could hum it." On top of this exquisite mix, Morrissey – in the band's first two officially released songs – revealed himself as a unique lyricist and vocalist, as new and fresh as could be. His vocal both bland and tantalising, his lyric mundane and intriguing, the mix of desperation and urbane wit was irresistible.

'Handsome Devil' contained the same lyrical polarity. Not many bands aiming at the top of the singles charts would have dared blend a Velvets-like hint of sado-masochism with a cod-music hall lyric. Johnny's aggressive intro recalled early-Sixties Joe Meek recordings, as well as the repeating-riff influence of Pretenders guitarist James Honeyman-Scott and The Byrds' Roger McGuinn. All with a swagger that The Ants could never achieve however charming their own Prince tried to be. Like so many later Smiths singles, both tracks carried storming introductory bars, relentless and punishing passages that would grab the listeners lapels and drag them in. Part of the appeal of The Smiths sound was born of practical necessities. Morrissey's vocal worked best in a lower key than the band were often happy playing in, and so both Andy and Johnny employed capos across much of the material on the band's first album, raising their own pitch but lowering the key, setting the musical tone higher and the vocal range lower. So was born one integral part of The Smiths' sound.

The moment was ripe for The Smiths, as pure as pure could be. "The debut affair of the year," said *i-D* magazine of the single. For *NME* there was an "indestructible self-belief and irresistible intent," while Irish mag *Trouser Press* noted two "punchy numbers of great promise." The band themselves were aware of the record's sensational feel. "It really was a landmark," Morrissey was to tell

Jamming the following year, while to another interviewer he described it as "searingly poetic... and yet jubilant at the same time." "I felt my life was leading up to 'Hand In Glove'," agreed Joyce. "My life began." For Johnny it was a dream come true, the fulfilment of a decade-long dream fuelled by practice after practice, rehearsal after dreary rehearsal in bands going nowhere. Recalling his own tactile love of the collectible seven-inch single, he proudly boasted "it was a fantastic piece of vinyl." For Joe Moss, the reason why the band hit so hard and so fast was because of the absolute freshness of everything they did, the urgency and energy bounding through every bar.

On May 6, a meeting took place that was to shove the nascent Smiths into another gear in terms of reputation and profile. As Ken Garner recounts in *The Peel Sessions,* BBC producer John Walters was tipped off about the band's gig at the University Of London Student's Union by Rough Trade promoter Scott Piering. The Smiths were supporting – from well down the bill – The Sisters Of Mercy, and Waters was impressed not only by the reputation that the band had brought down from the frozen north but also by their stage charisma. While Waters later claimed to have merely recognised the band as "a lead worth following", it was definitely the enthusiasm of his colleague back at 'the Beeb' who picked up and carried Johnny Marr and his band to the nation. Waters was, of course, famed as the producer of John Peel's radio show, and he offered the band their first Radio One session on the spot. The session – which took place less than two weeks later, on May 18 – was produced by BBC legend Roger Pusey and engineered by Nick Gomm, and immediately set a standard that – even to this day – both fans and band members feel was rarely bettered on tape. Tracks recorded were 'What Difference Does It Make?', 'Miserable Lie', 'Reel Around The Fountain' and 'Handsome Devil.' All four songs – and these versions of them – became firm favourites for many fans over and above the official album-released versions.

May also saw the band's first interview with *NME,* a second London gig at The Electric Ballroom, and unfounded rumours that Mike Joyce might be replaced by Simon Woolstencroft on drums. It is difficult, throughout the story of The Smiths, to ignore the relentless parallels with The Beatles. But just as Ringo was – by snooty music heads in the Sixties – often dismissed as a tub thumper who, had he never met John, Paul and George, would be on the club circuit, so did Mike Joyce often get a very rough and unfair ride.

In fact, Ringo's drumming was revolutionary and to the discerning ear one of the *best* things about The Beatles. Likewise, without Mike Joyce's punk input, The Smiths would have been a very different band, and assuredly not the one we all fell in love with.

Grant Showbiz recalls Joyce's live input fondly. "A more technically proficient drummer might have really fiddled with [The Smiths' sound], and taken it in a different direction," says Grant. "Whereas Mike would just nail the beat and fly through it." The sound of The Smiths in full flight is – whether you were in the audience or listening to live tapes – exhilarating. For Grant, the meat in this resolutely vegetarian band came from the drum kit, and he acknowledges the comparison with Ringo's input in The Beatles: "It's silly to say The Beatles thing – but there was an element of this guy just bashing the fuck out of the drums at the back." It wasn't just the 'bashing the fuck out of it' though. The beauty in the performance came via the incongruous meeting of Mike's drumming with the rather more esoteric thing happening out front. To Grant, while Johnny's instrumentalism and Morrissey's lyric was "sometimes quite a pretty, fey thing," the key to the blend came from Mike "nailing it, and making it dirty and hard."

The band were most definitely on a roll. The John Peel session aired at the end of the month, and immediately there was a major response from Peel's listeners. "You couldn't buy pre-publicity like that" said newly appointed promotions man Scott Piering. The immediate demand for the band was such that the session was twice repeated on Peel's programme within six months. The Smiths were becoming well known nationally, and back at home in Manchester the flames of their developing notoriety burned high across the city. "I was aware of them emerging, and the people in Manchester talking about them," says CP Lee, then the notorious singer of Manchester's wonderful and anarchic post-punks Albertos Y Los Trios Paranoias. "In fact, there were more people talking about Mr Moss – in that he was doing something." Lee's point, that it was Joe Moss having a band that was getting somewhere that was attracting much of the attention locally, demonstrates the surprise amongst much of the Manchester music community that The Smiths were now leading the game. "None of them were known, as musicians," says CP. "The only real contender was Morrissey because he had sung with The Nosebleeds... and was known as a character around Manchester. But the rest of them were really unknown entities, so there was more talk about [Moss] managing them more than anything else." CP Lee was a close friend of Richard Boon, then involved with Rough Trade distribution, and was regularly in the Rough Trade office himself. He remembers the buzz there too. "To me they were such an unknown quantity. They appeared like a little nova – a super-nova – bursting out of nowhere. It was very, very noticeable."

Back in Manchester, the post-punk hierarchy was surprised by the rapid ascension of The Smiths. The inner circle of the tribe, or the 'elderly members of the village' as Lee describes the generation that had emerged from punk, hadn't spotted this little outfit sneaking through the door. "You had a lot of people who had had a crack at it – Buzzcocks had made it, and I suppose you could say Mark E Smith made it," says Lee, "but a lot of people like The Distractions and The Blue Orchids hadn't. Suddenly here was this upstart team with no punk credentials. In a sense, anti-punk, you might say, who appeared from nowhere and [were] doing sell-out tours." There was a certain amount of professional jealousy in Manchester about that, that led to a kind of dismissal of Morrissey and of The Smiths. It wasn't that they were seen as a flash in the pan, but Lee believes that this is where the disparaging 'Oh it's all miserable... heaven knows it's miserable...' mockery of The Smiths started, to cut the band down to size in their home city. Twenty years on, it still surprises CP Lee that the band's ascendance was so rapid. "It *does* amaze me," he says. "When I listen to the stuff... where *did* they come from to *play* like that?" Where indeed!

Grant Showbiz also recalls how it was the live Smiths that really shook him, how their musicianship was spectacular right from the start. "I saw them on their fifth gig, and... in a funny sort of way they were more formed live [than in the studio]." Grant found 'Hand In Glove' difficult to get a handle on, to quite understand where they were coming from. "(It) always sounded like a rush to me, and then seeing them live – it was suddenly nailed." As sound engineer on virtually every concert The Smiths played, it is natural that he should find their live shows the more exhilerating, but it was more than that. For Grant, the live band was the key to understanding the albums and the singles. Having seen the way the songs worked live one could, then – as Grant puts it – "file back into the record."

Manchester got a chance to try and figure this conundrum out when the band lined up at The Hacienda in early July for their first gig there at the top of the bill. It was a major night for the band, but also for The Hacienda itself. Over the course of the summer, the band began the recording sessions with Troy Tate that were to evolve slowly into the first album. Ensconced in Wapping's Elephant Studios, the sessions were intense and the work was focused and dedicated. "It was very exciting," Johnny told Johnny Rogan for *Record Collector* in November 1992. "Troy was a really nice guy."

The Smiths were riding high on the success of their debut single (number 25), had a clear agenda for their sound and for their image, and were honing a style and an ethos that would see out their career. Johnny was excited to be working on the album, and while he had reservations about the sound evolving on certain tracks, for a while he was happy to go along with the work. Introduced to the band by Rough Trade, Troy Tate had even produced his own single, 'Love Is', for the label; however, the sound of the album received mixed responses from the group themselves. According to Johnny's 1992 interview with Rogan, Morrissey was more disappointed than himself, but the implication is that the dissatisfaction came from both the senior partners, while manager Joe Moss reportedly preferred the Tate sessions to the finally released product. Mike Joyce has also expressed a fondness for those recordings, telling *Select* magazine that he thought it had more atmosphere than the final version. What is clear is that Tate's album captured a very different Smiths to the one finally released in the spring of the following year.

There's certainly a different feel to the album in its 'Wapping state.' Various bootleg versions of the numerous takes that the band produced have circulated over the years. What is consistently obvious is that, as a studio band, The Smiths were more primitive than they would become with only a few more month' recording experience. The sessions have a 'demo' feel about them, inevitably, as they were never completed as ready for release. Most notably, Marr's guitar work is less developed. In terms of the writing process, some of the tracks were composed in full by Johnny, who would then present them to Morrissey for lyrics to be added, or Morrissey would present a set of lyrics to Johnny for the reverse process. By whichever method a particular song was composed, the band as a whole would often put down much of the music and then hand over to Morrissey, who would add his vocals as the last act on each track. That process was, according to Mike Joyce "one of the most fantastic things about working with The Smiths," waiting with immense anticipation for Morrissey to finish the songs off. They were never disappointed. "He'd just *spring* this lyric on you," remembered Mike.

Everyone surrounding the band was hyped up. This was clearly a band going somewhere fast. But what is interesting about the process was how much each individual member of the band fell in love with The Smiths themselves: without undue lack of modesty, Rourke, Joyce, Morrissey and Marr became the biggest fans The Smiths had, or would ever have. That desperate passion was one of the most significant elements in the band that was passed on to their expanding fan base.

By the end of the summer, the sessions with Tate had been put on hold, with Tate taking a back-step into Smiths legend. The band were immersed in gigs that would further cement their live reputation around the UK, while their radio presence was improved even further. With gigs in the Midlands and London under their belts, the BBC decided to invite the band in for a second session, this time for *The Kid Jensen Show* in June. The session was broadcast in early July. Back in Manchester, the band returned to top the bill at The Hacienda. In August, a third BBC session was produced by the man who would, over the coming months, have a huge influence on The Smiths as a recording band, and on Johnny in particular.

John Porter, a former member of Roxy Music, produced the session at the legendary Maida Vale studio on August 12, taping versions of 'I Don't Owe You Anything', 'Accept Yourself', Pretty Girls Make Graves' and 'Reel Around The Fountain' – tracks that he would become much more familiar with in the coming months. While the session would be broadcast on the Jensen show in early September, events of the late summer gave the band a vital but essentially unwelcome slice of tabloid publicity when *The Sun* newspaper began attacking Morrissey's lyrics. The band were suddenly headline news, and while the focus was very much upon Morrissey, the misinformation and scandal caused by the controversy – based upon the lyrics of 'Handsome Devil' and the notion that the BBC had banned a Smiths song from its airwaves (it had actually decided not to broadcast the version of 'Reel Around The Fountain' for the next Jensen session) – gave the foursome a taste of things to come in terms of tabloid sensationalism.

In September, yet another session was recorded for Peel, featuring the first recording of 'This Charming Man'. As the autumn progressed Johnny and the band had played in all corners of the UK, been interviewed or reviewed by the majority of the British music press and were back in the studio at work on the album. This time

John Porter was in charge of the sessions, having agreed with Rough Trade to take over the production of the debut album. While the initial intention was that Porter would essentially just remix the album and knock it into shape, it became clear to all the parties concerned that a re-recording would be a preferable option. "Through a mutual friend," Porter said in 1994, "Geoff asked me if I'd take a listen to the tapes."

Johnny had been working on new material, and over September and October the band settled, with Porter now officially on the books, into Pluto Studios in Manchester. 'This Charming Man' was one of the first tracks to be recorded – slated to be the Smiths' second single after Geoff Travis had heard it in session at Maida Vale. The music had been written by Marr on the same night as he penned 'Pretty Girls Make Graves' and 'Still Ill' – typifying his batch-writing of songs in groups of three to present to Morrissey – all born of the wandering Marr imagination on the train journey back to Manchester after recording a session for Radio 1. Fortunately for all of us, Johnny has always been able to keep his musical ideas in mind should they occur to him away from a recording or writing environment. According to Ken Garner's book, *In Session Tonight*, it was a "happy, casual but serious decision" by Travis and the band that led to 'This Charming Man' being chosen as the single, and the Peel take was broadcast three times before the re-recorded version was released officially in the late autumn. Simon Goddard has noted the "near jazz-like complexity" of the chord progressions that define the song's chorus, the Tamla feel to the verses, its "impossibly captivating" feel. The track is indeed one of finest moments in The Smiths' canon. Famed for its fifteen tracks of guitar overdub, the main instrument used was not the supposed trademark Rickenbacker, but a thirty year-old Fender Telecaster, with several tracks of acoustic guitar mixed up for good measure. Constantly looking for ways to add both polish and the sense of impetuous creativity, Porter also included – at the end of the chorus – the sound of Johnny dropping knives onto the instrument – adding to the vibrant colours that the record invented.

The single was released on October 28, 1983, in both seven- and twelve- inch formats. Morrissey's lyrics were inimitably complex – his perfect mixture of the mundane, arcane and emotionally compelling. While Johnny's guitar work was stunning, the vocalist too proved himself by now completely in control of his work both as a writer and a singer. Promoter Scott Piering realised there and then

68

that the blistering debut of 'Hand In Glove' was no fluke, and Travis too was hugely impressed with what his new signings had on board. Mike Joyce found himself immensely enthused by the experience of watching his own band develop so beautifully, so quickly. As he recalled, in Q magazine's 1994 retrospective article, "we'd have the music finished, and Morrissey would come in and sing... It was just so moving... such an experience to hear your singer singing like that over a track that you have just done."

Back in London's Matrix Studios, the band continued with album sessions which hopped between there and Pluto in Manchester. At times Rourke and Joyce reportedly felt over-awed by Porter's presence, his wealth of experience as a producer and bass player often making them uncomfortable, but for Johnny the experience was a learning curve of the highest order, and as Marr developed his studio-awareness, so the entire band benefited. John Porter taught the band more about the production process than anyone to date had, taking Johnny under his wing almost as though he were a younger brother needing guidance. He recognised a stunning talent in Johnny, and felt almost beholden to help develop it. "He showed me how to make a record," Johnny told *Record Collector* in 1992, and while Marr has clearly admitted that the album did not have the finish and the completeness that it might, The Smiths nevertheless arrived as a recording band under Porter's guidance. Indeed a large part of the album was played on Porter's 1954 Fender Telecaster, as well as on a Les Paul and Rickenbacker 12-string. After the rest of the band went home, John and Johnny would often spend the entire night in the studio, layering guitar parts and piecing together the various pieces of the sonic jigsaw. By morning they would stagger from the studio exhausted, but with finished tapes to hand. It was a lesson in how to manage one's time and concentration in the studio that would remain with Johnny throughout his career.

As the tracks came together, while working at Eden Studios in Chiswick, Porter decided to bring in one of his contacts to add a little extra colour to some of the songs. Paul Carrack knew John Porter through the mid-Seventies band Kokomo, and received the call from The Smiths' producer out of the blue, as often happened to the increasingly in-demand ex-Ace and Squeeze player. "I used to do quite a bit of stuff in Chiswick when anyone needed any keyboards doing," remembers Paul. Bands would be in urgent need of some piano or organ work, and Carrack would get the call. "John [Porter] said he was producing these guys, and that they had this real sort of cult following," Carrack recalls. "And he said that it was a bit unusual." Carrack remembers receiving a cassette from Porter, containing the Troy Tate tracks – "some sort of demos or tracks on cassette to get accustomed to," as he describes them. Having listened over a few times, Carrack "just went up one evening and overdubbed," appearing on three of the albums' songs – 'I Don't Owe You Anything', 'Reel Around The Fountain' and 'You've Got Everything Now'. "They'd recorded the tracks and just said 'feel free,'" remembers Paul. "I just instinctively played what happened, and I doubt if it was more than one or two takes per song." The band relaxed around the studio as Carrack added what he describes as "the icing – a little bit of colour." Morrissey was, famously, impressed with Carrack's trademark swirling Hammond organ sound on 'You've Got Everything Now', noting with typical dry wit that it sounded like 'Reginald Dixon on acid,' which Carrack took as "a huge compliment! I remember him just sort of huddled in the corner, quite shy," says Paul.

Carrack remembers Johnny as being open and friendly throughout the sessions – as indeed were the whole band: "I don't remember it being arduous… they were really nice." Johnny in particular struck Paul as a little bit different to the usual punky guitarist with whom he often found himself working. "I thought Johnny was a nice guy – he talked about his parents, who were music lovers," Carrack remembers, being impressed when Johnny engaged him in a conversation about the legendary country artist Jim Reeves. "We often used to find that, when you're with the younger bands, they would be very 'anti-' anything like that. Going back twenty years, we were old farts then, and to be talking to this young guy about things like Jim Reeves… I thought, *well – they must have something.*"

This intriguing band made a big impression on this seasoned session player. "I do remember thinking it was unusual. It definitely had a very strange vibe about it – that sounds wrong – a very strong atmosphere." More than twenty years later, with an astounding list of credits to his name that includes working with every major artist on the planet, and enjoying a burgeoning and ever-developing solo career, Paul is reminded of his few hours' work with The Smiths on an almost daily basis. "I've got a bit of a CV, I suppose," he laughs now. "And [after] two or three hours with them, it's amazing how many people will jump on that and say, 'You played with The Smiths!!'"

Legends were certainly being born in the autumn of 1983. Lennon and McCartney. Jagger and Richards. Leiber and Stoller. Bacharach and David. Morrissey and Marr had arrived.

A mighty night for Johnny, and indeed for the entire band, came on November 24, as The Smiths made their first historic appearance on *Top Of The Pops*, still [just] the UK's premier pop show. While for many acts *TOTP* was a huge stepping stone to the big time, The Smiths were becoming successful despite the media interest in them rather than as a result of it. But every so often an act appears on *Top Of The Pops* that changes the world. Bowie's appearance singing 'Starman' in July 1972 was one such instance. The Smiths' first appearance was another. "I didn't take [contemporary pop music] at all seriously until I saw Johnny Marr," Noel Gallagher said of the show. "When The Smiths came on *Top Of The Pops*, that was it for me. I wanted to *be* Johnny Marr." The Smiths records and sessions were being played on the radio *because* people wanted to hear them, rather than the other way round, but the band were understandably excited, as they took the stage following gender-bender extraordinaire Marilyn. Johnny was nervous, and so intent on not making a fool of himself that his tactic of self-preservation was to root his feet firmly to the floor and to stay put. Rocking while Morrissey's flowers and a stage-full of balloons lent a festive exuberance to the proceedings, Johnny was very visible on *Top Of The Pops*, and it was not only Noel Gallagher who was watching – a generation of indie guitarists were inspired too.

Immediately after *Top Of The Pops* – on the same night – the band were met outside The Hacienda by Mike Pickering. Two thousand punters had managed to get in, while a thousand more thronged along Whitworth Street outside. To a fanatical audience the band played a fourteen-song set that concluded with a rousing 'Hand In Glove'. What Johnny called "three years of *A Hard Day's Night*," had begun.

As Christmas approached, the band took off for their first visit to the USA, booked to make their first appearance at The Danceteria, New York's leading dance club, on New Year's Eve. It should have been the start of a significant assault on America's eastern seaboard. While Morrissey had family in America and had visited them a number of times in his teenage years, for the rest of the band it was their first time on an aeroplane. To be heading out west to the Big Apple was as exciting as it got – "having our dreams come true," as Johnny described it. In fact it was the start of a careering course for

The Smiths and for Johnny in particular. While the band appeared to gather speed along some pre-determined racetrack to success, in fact it was more as though they were beginning to lose control of the steering. The Smiths suddenly – and not for the first time – found themselves without a manager on the very day that they left for New York. So close to the band's departure that several members of the party were surprised not to find him at the airport, Joe Moss decided to hang up his managerial hat and let go his connection with the band he had been so instrumental in getting going.

Over the years there has been much speculation about why Joe made this decision. Sound man Grant Showbiz, speaking to Q magazine many years later, felt that Moss got out to avoid having to deal with the pressures of the increasing numbers of people who wanted a slice of the band. Showbiz personally believes that that the fact that he was not 'music biz' didn't help him. Rough Trade, he believes, would have preferred their own management. They definitely "had a sniff that they'd got 'the big one.'" If that was the case, it was perhaps understandable that the company putting in so much money into The Smiths – regardless of whether the sums were modest compared to a major label – would have preferred the man at the business helm to be someone they were more familiar with.

"What actually happened I don't know," says Grant – reinforcing the air of mystery that still surrounds the matter. "I've always imagined it was that way inclined. We went to America for the first time and Joe wasn't with us." Others have speculated that Morrissey and Moss did not see eye to eye, or that Johnny's friendship with Joe got in the way of the creative relationship between the two writers. To whatever degree any of the above unproven rumour is true, it only influenced Joe's actual decision to leave, which was actually for a completely different reason. Joe had earlier separated from his first wife, and had young children both from that relationship and his new partner, so family priorities were naturally high on his agenda. Moss himself was forty years old, and dealing with a bunch of teenagers in the fastest-moving, most destructive industry on the planet. Exciting it might have been to witness the birth of The Smiths, but the birth of a daughter took precedence. Joe Moss left the band because – whatever the pressures that were or were or not upon him – his family was more important to him than The Smiths.

One thing is sure: the band missed his guidance. "They were so lucky to have that year or so with Joe," Grant remembers again.

"That really defined what they did afterwards. It was all done 'Joe-less' after that."

Landing in the USA without Moss, Johnny and the band were met in New York by a limousine organised by the woman who had booked them for The Danceteria, Ruth Polski. Polski specialised in coming over to the UK, identifying new and exciting bands, and being the first person in the USA to book them there. She had a good track record too –The Fall, New Order and – according to Grant Showbiz – Echo And The Bunnymen were amongst her conquests. Grant remembers Ruth as "a wonderful, wonderful woman." Polski is remembered as an opportunist, "in the most delightful way," says Grant. "Obviously we were very happy that an American promoter was all over us, and was being very lovely to us."

Arriving in the States without a manager, Johnny and Morrissey did their best to keep their hands on the wheel. While they may not have had a manager – and the fact was not missed by Ms Polski – they had brought *something* with them; a virus. Within days Mike Joyce hit the deck with a major dose of chicken pox, and while publicist Scott Piering began to take on some of the managerial responsibilities it was – as it proved for much of the rest of the life of the band – Johnny and Morrissey who also tried to keep hold of the reins. The gig at the Danceteria went down very well, but because of Mike's illness the remaining dates had to be cancelled. Disappointed in New York, Johnny and Morrissey's response was to pen 'Heaven Knows I'm Miserable Now' in their hotel room, reflecting a low point for the band as a major opportunity to cement their profile in America was lost. Silver linings and all that…

★

Back in the UK in the early days of the New Year, Johnny settled into the upstairs rooms of Joe's house, where he was still living, and Morrissey became the first Smith to move to a flat in London, in the elegant surroundings of Cadogan Square. While the pressures of taking care of the band continued to increase, issues in Johnny's private life took a turn for the worse.

First of all, Marr's relationship with Angie Brown had shuddered to (an albeit) temporary halt. Angie had not travelled to New York, and it was virtually the first time they had been apart during their already long relationship. The split lasted about two weeks. The effect on Johnny was dramatic. "That was the point when my heart went out to Johnny," Grant Showbiz remembers. "[I thought]… if he's lost Angie what's he gonna *do?*"

Johnny's other problem was Andy Rourke. Andy was developing a classic rock 'n' roll habit, heroin, and in a gesture of support alongside Johnny's friendship, Joe Moss offered Rourke his basement to live in while he tried to sort himself out. It was important both for him and his role within the band that Johnny and Joe were there to help. Several people close to The Smiths remained unaware of Rourke's problems, and all around him felt that – especially with the anti-drug manifesto that the band had developed – his problems should remain (excusing the pun) under wraps.

★

While the juggernaut of publicity and notoriety continued to nudge them forward, the New Year of 1984 would prove to be the biggest yet for The Smiths. This was the year of Sade, the Nigerian-born sister of all things cool through the mid-Eighties. Britain sat back and chilled out to her 'Your Love Is King', wore sunglasses in the early hours of the morning, grooved to The Thompson Twins and waited for the Next Big Thing while Billy Ocean's 'Caribbean Queen' gently rocked the elevators of the world. The singles charts were crying out for new blood – something iconoclastic, stylish, dashing and irresistible.

It was fitting then, that January saw the release of 'What Difference Does It Make?', backed with the gently finger-picked 'Back To The Old House', a song written with Angie in mind. The single did very well for the band, proving to be their second-highest chart placing when it stalled prematurely at number twelve. The band appeared on *Top Of The Pops* to promote it. The same show featured the first appearance on a UK stage by a young upstart singer and dancer from New York, who harboured a mighty talent and an even mightier ambition. The following night the twenty-five year old from Bay City, Michegan, appeared at The Hacienda. She earned fifty quid for her troubles, and – unable to gain access to her digs at Mike Pickering's house – spent the cold January night on his front door step. By the same time next year, Madonna's rise to the top of the pop ladder would be almost complete.

The Smiths were quite clearly in line to be 'the next big thing,' but they were pipped to the crown over the course of the year by a

74

bunch of Scousers from down the M62. While Morrissey's lyrics *hinted* at sexual uncertainty, and while Johnny, Andy and Mike were undoubtedly the best guitar and rhythm section going, it was Frankie Goes To Hollywood's all-out sado-masochistic and highly produced pyrotechnics that actually stole the show.

While The Smiths' production sound was fantastic – they were a dream waiting to come true in a hundred thousand bedsits – Frankie Goes To Hollywood had a sheen and gloss that made their material irresistible. While The Smiths were the next big singles band who were going to break internationally and be huge, in the course of the year the Frankies broke all records with their three number one hits 'Relax', 'Two Tribes' and 'The Power Of Love'. Commercially at least, they did in twelve months what The Smiths failed to do in five years. The key was that The Smiths rallied against the increasing importance of the pop video in the age of MTV. Frankie Goes To Hollywood grasped the nettle of publicity firmly, and their videos were superb advertisements for their material. The first British act to hit the number one slot with their first three singles since Gerry and The Pacemakers, their success was secured with stunning promotion from Manchester journalist Paul Morley and, with 'Two Tribes', a video directed by Godley and Crème, formerly of 10cc. If Liverpool won three-nil against The Smiths, it was ironically with Manchester's help.

Undeterred, Johnny and the band soldiered on, and 1984 was in many ways the year of The Smiths too. February saw the release of the eponymous debut, *The Smiths.* The band's first album opens at stately pace. 'Reel Around The Fountain' is a graceful, haunting piece, introduced not by Marr's guitar or Morrissey's memorable croon, but with Mike Joyce's metronomic snare and hi-hat. Lyrically, the song opens on a dialogue between writer, audience and band apparently already half-run. Although this was a brand new band with a brand new album, the listener is invited into a myth all ready to be unravelled. Johnny's guitar plays courtly arpeggios around a cyclical central motif based upon traditional folk structures. While the lyric speaks of tale-telling, the folk tradition is extant in Johnny's chord structure that mirrors the Scottish standard 'Auld Lang Syne.'You can easily sing the Scottish melody over Marr's A, E, F-sharp minor, D routine, and Johnny imposes a melancholy into this traditionally rousing, major key format. Notably, Johnny adds a series of major seventh and sixth notes into the phrasing – accents which were to become a trademark of his playing. The central lyrical and thematic motif of the song measures the movement from major to minor perfectly. If the tone rather than the content recalled Joy Division, Marr has also linked the song's development to James Taylor's gentle acoustic sing-along 'Handy Man' – a far cry from the rented rooms in Whalley Range, the childhood victims of Ian Brady and the pretty girls making graves found elsewhere on the album.

'Reel Around The Fountain' is one of the greatest debut album openers in rock history. When the first complete rhyme of the song – 'told/old' – falls onto the first minor third it is a wonderful moment. The lyric's theme of a childhood debased drops suddenly onto this most telling note, suggesting much about the music that was to come from Marr and The Smiths over the years to come. Paul Carrack's gentle, enigmatic contribution underpins the guitar phrasing subtly and perfectly too. Traditional structures are enlivened by delicate touches of harmonic and melodic detail, as closely fused to the lyrical content as is possible. The Smiths' sound was born.

The second track, 'You've Got Everything Now' runs at a nervy, bass-led punk pace, with Morrissey's phrasing desperately trying to pull the pace of the song back, but instead – as the band hit the choruses – the track takes on a perfect beat as Johnny's tumbling riffs quickly establish another trademark. 'Miserable Lie', despite its mournful opening, soon kicks into a savagery and energy that caught the flavour of the early live Smiths perfectly. On 'Pretty Girls Make Graves', the song's circuitous minor chord sequence is set firmly against Johnny's jaunty, acoustic strumming on the half-notes and Rourke's walking bass. The jangling electric picking is typical of what would become synonymous with Smiths' music, the feel of the song would reappear later in songs such as 'Frankly Mr Shankly', but the dichotomy between the mournfulness of Morrissey's vocal and the optimism of the electric guitar, between the jolly strumming and the minor key is perfect Smiths, the ability to maintain two or more concepts at one moment within the same song.

Similar phrasing is picked up early in the next track and reflected throughout the sinuous course of 'The Hand That Rocks The Cradle', which Simon Goddard cleverly notes throws a nod to Patti Smith's 'Kimberly'. 'Still Ill' is one of Marr's most effective riffs, 'Paperback Writer'-like and as fresh as the day. One of the great things about Johnny's work – especially on early songs like 'Still Ill' – is that, rather than simply defining an introduction, shatteringly good riffs run throughout, and define the entire song.

'Hand In Glove' and 'What Difference Does It Make?' sit together on the album as if the last ten years of pop music had been waiting for this moment alone – two pieces of such perfect pop, crafted and presented with a devastating confidence and bravado that belies the youthfulness of the band. Then 'I Don't Owe You Anything', with Johnny's Burt Bacharach-like stabs and jazzy linking chords works perfectly to slow the album down before its big finish. 'Suffer Little Children' was dropped from the band's live sets quite early in their career. The version immortalised as the closing track on *The Smiths* was one of the few songs on the album with which Marr was happy in retrospect, but outside the band the response to the song was phenomenal and routinely sensational. Rarely has a song snuck into the back end of a relatively unknown act's debut album caused so much fuss: Morrissey was laughably virtually branded an associate of the Moors Murderers himself in the hysterical UK tabloids, as the crimes of Ian Brady and Myra Hindley were raked over by newspapers happy to make headlines out of misrepresenting an artistic statement. For Smiths fans overseas, the track may have meant less, but for anyone growing up in the North West of England in the mid-Sixties, the story remained one of the most affecting of that decade.

While the press tried desperately to kick up a fuss, Morrissey retained a dignity in his own responses to the furore. To informed, intelligent listeners, the song was a desperately moving collection of images, literate and haunting, indeed infinitely less offensive than many of the books and articles already written on the subject. The entire piece is like a movie, plot unfolding, character developing, drama ensuing. Marr's guitar modulates between A and D major seventh chords for much of the track – a fragile and graceful tone, the same structure as Erik Satie's delicate piano piece *Gymnopedie No 1*. Johnny's arpeggio'd chords recall a similar delicate and elegant tone. As Morrissey's vocal becomes more and more haunting, Johnny's sense of drama and mood drops quickly into a minor key as the voice of Brady's accomplice takes the stage. The disarming laugh of Myra Hindley was provided by Morrissey's friend Annalisa Jablonska.

The Smiths is like one of those grainy kitchen sink movies so beloved of Morrissey, *Saturday Night, Sunday Morning* on vinyl. Its tone is conversational, earthen, but its themes are elevated and troublesome. Musically it is articulate and sensitive but at the same time kick-arse rollicking good fun. It remains one of the best debut albums of all, and – if it wasn't perfect – it was better than anything else around at the time by a long way.

The album's cover 'starred' Warhol cohort Joe Dallesandro, and caused almost as much concern for some of the band members as it caused excitement with reviewers. Designed by Morrissey and Caryn Gough, the artwork set the standard for Smiths releases to come: a very careful selection of images that portrayed both the concept behind the band and some of the artistic influence and ethos behind the conception of the album itself. Here, of course, the cropping of the original still from Warhol's movie *Flesh* masked some of the homo-eroticism of the image, but implied enough to encourage speculation regarding the band's sexual stance.

Looking back on the album a couple of years later, Marr told *Melody Maker* that he was "not as madly keen on it" as he had been. He felt that the attack and 'fire' was missing from the record, and reflected the feeling of many of the fans that perhaps the later *Hatful Of Hollow* captured this early Smiths sound better. Morrissey was also said to be not entirely happy with the production, although he too recognised that it was better than anything else around. Although the album had now been recorded twice, with two different producers, bizarrely rumours circulated that there were moves afoot to re-do it again. Idealism was one thing however, and having reportedly cost Rough Trade £60,000 – a sizeable sum for an independent label – the chances of The Smiths' debut album being re-recorded or re-mixed yet again were probably nil.

Johnny proudly called The Smiths music "rock from a housing estate", and indeed they categorically made fundamental pop music. They spliced liberally from the music that influenced them, juiced it up with lashings of their own flavouring, and passed the unique result on to a new generation. The key trick was that they never allowed those influences to drown their own musical voice. In the same way, The Beatles had blended Buddy Holly and Carl Perkins influences with Motown and skiffle to come up with 'Beatles' music. CP Lee calls this process "pop lore" and likens it to the folk tradition of passing traditional songs and formats through the generations. The process applies equally to all pop formats, however, and not just traditional folk. "It just refers to popular formats or popular music, whether it's folk music or pop music," says Lee. "Or blues music. But you can see [how Marr] dips into and carries on a tradition, by amending it." While those influences remain submerged within the musical phrasing, and the lyrical concerns, the music is nevertheless new. As much as Morrissey continued a tradition of Northern writers and performers from George Formby and Gracie Fields to Shelagh Delaney and Alan Bennett, so Johnny's music had mixed up the glam of T. Rex with the finger-picking folk of Bert Jansch and Davey Graham, the raunch of the New York Dolls with the pristine production ethics of Sixties girl groups, yet the music of *The Smiths* was unassailably Smiths' music, unique and new.

A tour to support the album took in Sheffield University, North Staffs Poly, Coventry and Loughborough, but came to a grinding halt when Morrissey developed throat problems. Gigs were cancelled in advance, but a series of TV and media appearances kept the Smiths flame alive. Speaking to *NME*, Johnny spoke of the differences between himself and Morrissey as personalities, and clearly flagged his happiness that Morrissey remained the spokesman for the band while he generally kept out of the public eye. A second appearance on *Top Of The Pops* promoted 'What Difference Does It Make?' – shown again later in the month as the single made its way up the charts. Then more TV, more radio, more magazines. With the tour back on track, the void left by the departed Joe Moss was finally filled after a fashion, albeit a somewhat confusing fashion.

Ruth Polski, late of the New York Danceteria gig, re-appeared on the scene in the UK claiming to be the band's manager, and a disagreement with Scott Piering, who said he was in charge, ensued. "I don't think she ever was 'the manager'," recalls Grant Showbiz "She was one of a number of people who may or may not have had a conversation at four in the morning, and woke up imagining she *was* the manager." She wasn't the first to do that – in the business as a whole – and, according to Grant "not the last."

Ruth Polski returned to the USA, and was tragically killed in a car accident some time later. As far as The Smiths' sound-man was concerned, she never caused any hassle. "She was just a kind of fun-loving creature," he recalls. But issues of money and organisation continued to rear their ugly heads as the tour proceeded, while the pressures on Johnny and Morrissey increased. To whatever extent Polski and Scott Piering did argue, it was Piering who took the upper hand in the management issues at stake. Nobody really filled Joe Moss's role like-for-like. "No-one ever said to me, 'Joe's gone – *he's* looking after us,' or 'He's gone – *they're* looking after us,'" Grant told me. Rather, Piering was one of a whole group of people who, over time, contributed. "Everyone at that point – they were just going 'Fucking hell – this band is going to be massive," says Showbiz.

Grant Showbiz remembers the late Scott Piering fondly, and knows that his management of the band was always well-intentioned. "Close up he could see the disarray because he was travelling with us," Grant notes today. "He thought '[These people have] had a go. Why don't I step in and see what happens?'" What happened of course was that the Smiths continued to be too hot to handle. "It was great," says Grant, "watching Scott trying to be a bit more corporate and a bit more organised." But corporate and organised was not what The Smiths were about.

The band charged through all corners of the UK before coming to earth in London in mid-March. At the Hammersmith Palais, Sandie Shaw became the only other singer to front The Smiths besides Morrissey, previewing her own version of 'Hand In Glove.'

Shaw's version of the song was recorded at Matrix studios in London, in February 1984. The band included 'Jeane' and 'I Don't Owe You Anything' in the same sessions. Although the single only scraped into the Top Thirty on its spring release, Sandie was of course no stranger to the higher reaches of the UK charts. Over the course of the Sixties, she established herself as both the coolest woman in British pop and the first of the UK's occasional winners of the Eurovision song contest, in an era when participation in that event was not seen to be quite as naff as it is today. Sandie's high cheekbones and long, dark fringe made her as much a visual icon of the time as a musical one, and her trademark barefooted TV appearances guaranteed her column inches in the press too. Her chart debut, '(There's) Always Something There To Remind Me' was an iconic snapshot of 1964 power pop; her stylish follow-up 'Girl Don't Come' was exactly the kind of melancholic-yet-breezy tune to appeal to both Morrissey and Marr. By 1984 Sandie was a long way away from being a chart regular, but while it may have been fifteen years since her last lowly chart placing, she was only thirty seven – hardly a pop star dragged from her pensionable years! She was the perfect partner for Morrissey and Marr.

By now, Johnny and the rest of the band had joined Morrissey living in London, with Marr a resident of Earl's Court. Before recording with The Smiths, Shaw had been badgered over several months by Johnny and Morrissey, and it was a novel experience for Johnny, Andy and Mike to have a girl singer up front. Simon Goddard

80

recounts the frequent visits to the local veggie restaurant enlivening what was an enjoyable set amidst the turmoil of the current tour. While the live schedule floundered on, the three instrumental Smiths backed Sandie on an entertaining *Top Of The Pops* appearance during which Johnny, Andy and Mike – in homage to Sandie's Sixties predilection for shoelessness – performed barefoot while Sandie herself delivered Morrissey's lyric whilst rolling, impassioned, across the studio floor. It was a memorable appearance for Smiths fans.

The tour had taken in various dates in Europe – several concerts were cancelled – and the tour manager had parted company with the band, increasing the sense of disarray around the entire operation. The role was taken over by Stuart James, before the release in April of 'Heaven Knows I'm Miserable Now' offered some respite and continued the band's chart onslaught, reaching (unbelievably) their highest chart placing at Number 10. Written, as noted, immediately after the New York debacle, the track had been recorded with John Porter at Island Studios in London in February. While opinions of the song among band members have varied over the years, 'Heaven Knows…' remains one of the best loved songs in the Smiths' catalogue, combining both Johnny's sophisticated, articulate guitar and some of Morrissey's funniest and most heart-wrenching lyrics, perhaps better than any other early single. Another two appearances on *Top Of The Pops* saw, in the latter of the two, Johnny wearing some rather splendid bling around his neck, while Morrissey paraded handsomely with a large branch hanging from his back pocket. Stylish and funny and miserable and cool were The Smiths in 1984.

TV shows and gigs in Europe were resumed for a few days, followed by a similar handful of dates in Ireland, before returning to the heady heights of Carlisle, Glasgow and Scotland. June saw the band play at Glastonbury. As a sideline for Smiths watchers, there was the release of one of Johnny's first projects outside The Smiths, the Quando Quango single 'Atom Rock.' Quando Quango was an Anglo–Dutch electro dance set-up, formed in Rotterdam in 1980. By 1982 they had moved to Manchester, combining synths and saxophone to forge electro dance tracks way ahead of their time. Signed to Factory, Quando Quango included Mike Pickering alongside the bass of Barry Johnson, late of chart successes Sweet Sensation (and later of Aswad), A Certain Ratio's Simon Topping, and an ever-changing list of contributors. They were produced by the extra-curricular Bernard Sumner of New Order, and it was via

Quando Quango that Johnny first got to know Sumner, with whom, of course, he would come to be inextricably linked for a decade. The band had had significant success in the USA already – a market far more ready for their sound – with their single 'Love Tempo.' By the time Johnny was involved, playing guitar on both tracks from their 1984 single, his reputation as a Smith was established and the connection turned a few heads. The King Of The Indie Guitar liking dance music – that wasn't on.

Johnny has spoken entertainingly of how he fell in love with dance music at the same time as he learned to be a red-hot guitar player. Back in the day, Johnny would hang out in his bedroom with his guitar-playing mates, "skinning up and being serious," as he described it to *Guitar Magazine*. "My sister would be in the next bedroom listening to dance music," Johnny continued. "Getting ready to go out with her friends. And they just sounded like they were having a better time… They'd say to me 'What are you listening to this miserable crap for?'" At that point Johnny turned to Chic, The Fatback Band and War, and fell in love with dance music for life.

Johnny also joined in with future bedsit king and queen Everything But The Girl on their single 'Native Land', a pairing more likely to be approved of by Smiths fans. Rather than adding Smiths-style guitar crash to the record however, Johnny actually appeared on harmonica – a role that he would adopt on several collaborations over the years to come. Although he did not appear on the follow-up album *Love Not Money*, it was noted in several circles just how much influence The Smiths had on that collection of songs.

The appearance at Glastonbury was followed by a much-needed break. Grant Showbiz remembers the hectic schedule, and notes that – especially without Moss's input – the band flew by the seat of their pants much of the time. At Jam Studios in London, The Smiths reconvened for the taping of their next single, 'William, It Was Really Nothing', again with John Porter twiddling the knobs. 'Please, Please, Please Let Me Get What I Want', 'Nowhere Fast' (held for the release of the next album) and 'William, It Was Really Nothing' were composed one after the other very quickly in Johnny's Earl's Court apartment, the former a perfect example of a song almost spilling out of Marr despite himself. In the creative meltdown after finishing 'William…' came 'How Soon Is Now?', almost as an afterthought. "Because you are relaxed," explained Johnny to Martin Roach, "you carry on noodling, and that way you write another good track immediately afterwards." He described 'Please Please Please...' as a "Del Shannon song. After about a minute and a half of writing it," Johnny recalls, "[it] had a Del Shannon feel, so I continued to write that with my mother in mind, because she listened to so much of [that music]."

Johnny was clearly on a creative roll in the spring and summer of 1984, and could have expected the success of 'Heaven Knows I'm Miserable Now' to have been followed by even higher chart placings. Despite the ongoing confusion surrounding the band's affairs, the quality of his writing – and Morrissey's – was undiminished. But 'William...' only reached number seventeen in the UK singles chart, a crushing disappointment to be followed by an extended period without a major chart hit. The single illustrates the increasing complexity of Johnny's work with Porter, as guitars were overdubbed one after another. It is one of The Smiths' most exuberant tracks, played at a breakneck speed that even Johnny himself later marvelled at. The capo on the fingerboard allowed Johnny to take the dazzling chord progressions out of the standard fingering and to really kick out. It is a wonderful record that should have been a top five hit.

CHAPTER FOUR

A Band To Die For.

In August, Morrissey moved back to the affluent suburbs of Cheshire, south of Manchester and near to the city's international airport, a well-heeled domicile for a gentleman of increasing means. Peel sessions were broadcast in August, showcasing some of the tracks to be heard on the next Smiths' album, and in September 'Native Land' was released by Everything But The Girl. It was intended that the band would tour the USA in October, with rafts of new material to be gigged and recorded too.

Many of the songs were 'premiered' during the short mini-tour of the south-west and south Wales, with gigs in Gloucester, Cardiff and Swansea. These gigs were scheduled as warm-up dates for the US tour, but instead, with the release of compilation album *Hatful Of Hollow* imminent (more of which later), The Smiths held off until November, where they played a series of dates in Ireland.

By the early autumn the tank was being filled for the limo rides to Liverpool where the new Smiths album was to be recorded. John Porter was not involved with the album sessions this time. As far as Johnny was concerned, despite *Hatful Of Hollow* having been "banged out", it was a fantastic record, and he decided to do the production job himself with the band. With Stephen Street firmly established as engineer, the band booked Amazon studios, hidden in the midst of one of Liverpool's nastiest industrial estates, a fitting venue for Britain's at-once most glamorous and most modest band to record. While the group was established in London, they had decided to move back north to record the album. "It was clear that we needed to come back to Manchester and get rained on," Johnny said in retrospect. "It's good for creativity." The idea of a limo being The Smiths' chosen mode of transport might have appeared somewhat at odds with their down-to-earth image, but in fact the ageing Mercedes was an ex-undertaker's vehicle... much more fitting for the band's profile. While the demands of publicity, tour requests, TV and radio continued to increase, there was an element of a siege mentality in the studio, strengthening the band's resolve. Morrissey spoke publicly about the album's progress as Christmas approach, enthusing that the songs were stronger than ever.

Meat Is Murder was touted by Johnny at the time as The Smiths' *Revolver* – while the album hasn't quite lived up to that reputation, it was to be one of their most influential releases. Not only did half the population of under twenty-year olds appear to take up Morrissey's plea for vegetarianism in the wake of *Meat Is Murder,* but so did The Smiths. In later interviews, Joyce and Rourke have spoken about how much Morrissey's influence was felt throughout the band on the subject, who were often torn between the need for a good fish and chip supper and an ideological premise that they all supported. Johnny, of course, remains a vegetarian – in fact, with a largely vegan diet – to this day.

Musically, the sessions that comprised *Meat Is Murder* produced a complex piece of work, in a little under two months. Slated for release the following February, the band wasted no time, and Johnny and Morrissey were at the peak of their game in terms of writing. However, the pressure was on in terms of managing the band and without close friend Moss at the helm and with the world clamouring ever more for interviews, tours, sessions, radio, TV etc, all this fell squarely on the shoulders of Morrissey and Marr. It was, simply put, exhausting. It is eternally to Morrissey's credit that, within such an environment, he also managed to make his role as the band's main spokesperson appear so easy. For Johnny, who would avoid interviews like the plague if he possibly could, it was hard enough, but Morrissey was appearing in every magazine, newspaper and music weekly in the land. The pressures "strengthened our resolve," Johnny told *Select.* "We were driven. Morrissey and I would never sleep... It was just me, Morrissey and Angie... all the time."

One track not on the original album but included on the re-mastered editions later (and, indeed, included on the original US release) did not emerge from the Liverpool sessions. 'How Soon Is Now?' has become, of course, another of the most notable Smiths tracks, covered and sampled across the years a number of times by other acts, most notably – and entertainingly perhaps – by Russian 'lesbian combo' Tatu. The song was written in February and recorded with John Porter in July at Jam studios in Finsbury Park. It was one of Johnny and Porter's all-nighter sessions, with the pair locked together in the studio over the small hours of a Saturday night. John Porter tells of how the tape was posted through Morrissey's letter box on the way home, and how the singer turned up at the studio the following day with the incredible lyrics complete. The track was nailed in no more than a couple of takes.

Everyone around the band recognised something special in 'How Soon Is Now?', but a decision was made at Rough Trade to only release it as the B-side of the twelve-inch version of 'William, It Was Really Nothing.' It was the wrong decision, and by the time the track was released as an A-side in its own right early in 1985, the song had been released so many times that it did well to reach a lowly number 24 in the chart. The argument has been put forward that Marr was 'guilty' of being too prolific, almost that there were simply *too many* potential A-side singles knocking around in this golden period of writing, but that sounds a bit like Manchester City supporters complaining that their team had won the Premiership by scoring too many goals. The failure to capitalise on 'How Soon Is Now?' earlier was perhaps a tactical flop that may have cost the band the major international hit they deserved. While there had been four single releases in the year from May 1983 to May 1984, it was six months before 'How Soon Is Now?' came out as an A-side. Touring would occupy the band when they were not in the studio, of course, but it was a surprising hiatus. The experience was disappointing for all concerned. "That's where it all, sadly, started to fall apart," said Porter. In fact 'How Soon Is Now?' proved to be Porter's only appearance on the album, and he did not work with the band again for some considerable time. *Meat Is Murder* was credited for its production to 'The Smiths', and was 'engineered' by Stephen Street.

Trying to keep the customers satisfied, in November Rough Trade released the aforementioned *Hatful Of Hollow*. The band's second official album release, the mid-price compilation (a sticker signalled that the maximum recommended retail price should be £3.99) enjoyed full-on design criteria and a fantastic selection of tracks culled from a variety of B-side sources, and including the superb sessions for the BBC. One track, 'This Night Has Opened My Eyes', was available for the first time on vinyl, and the band chose the Peel-session version over a studio track recorded at the same time as 'William, It Was Really Nothing'. The blue sleeve featured a shot of an uncredited Cocteau model, not Joe Orton as it has often been said, with the band's name proudly emblazoned in large-face type to pull casual listeners in from across the biggest record store. The album boasted a gatefold sleeve and a proper laminated card inner sleeve bearing the lyrics of each song. If Rough Trade had arguably stumbled on 'How Soon Is Now?' then – under Morrissey's art-directing eye – they made up for it in spades with this unusual package. *Hatful of Hollow* drew in thousands of new listeners to The Smiths, who had maybe read about the band, heard a couple of tracks on the radio, and were curious to see what this new phenomenon consisted of. The album allowed instant easy access to the information required, and *Hatful Of Hollow* probably did more in the early years to broaden the band's fan base than any other release. It remains a benchmark for many Smiths fans. Marr was unsure about the album before its release. While he knew how good many of the recordings were, and had the fondest memories of all the BBC sessions, the project was an unusual strategy for a band already planning their next studio album. But it worked.

The opening track was the resplendent single 'William, It Was Really Nothing', the whole band sounding wonderful. Johnny's picking over meaty acoustic strumming, Mike Joyce's drums high in the mix and Rourke's punching bass providing a superb harmony to the guitar parts. The album was the door opener to thousands of new Smiths fans. Between Morrissey's impassioned voice and Johnny's fabulous arrangement there couldn't have been a listener in the land who didn't want to know more about this entertaining, enigmatic and enthusing four-piece. For the established fans who had studiously taped the Radio One sessions on their crackling cassette recorders, the release was a vindication of the quality of those sessions. After the familiar single came a track from the May 1983 Peel session,

'What Difference Does It Make?' Again, the track has an irresistible drive and panache, both in the band's performance and in Morrissey's vocal. Mike's lilting beat and punishing fills complement the guitar and bass parts perfectly as Morrissey's vocal sails off into the stratosphere. It was a significantly different version to that released as a single, more compact and with a far more prominent 'live' feel, and for many fans this version remains the beloved one.

'These Things Take Time' had a similar feel – a rough diamond with all its facets evident to the jeweller's eye before the stone is cut. The track was lifted from the BBC session of July 1983 recorded for David Jensen's radio show, and again Joyce and Marr drive the track along with immense style and urgency. Sequenced into an album format, the pace at which each superb track followed the previous one was astonishing: these songs felt as though they had forever been destined to appear in such a format. More jaunty, and maintaining the fabulous pace of the album so far, 'This Charming Man' – from the September 1983 Peel session – is a highlight of the album, a permanent testament to the song's first appearance on tape. The now-familiar opening chords of 'How Soon Is Now?' drift in with Johnny's open-tuned Epiphone presenting one of rock's most simple and immediately identifiable riffs, slowing the pace of the album down. By now the casual listener was hooked and the committed fan entranced. While the melody and lyric suggest a downbeat, sober wistfulness, the emotional tug of the track comes from it being musically in a major key but lyrically in a minor one. Joyce's drums have some of the mechanical urgency of early Joy Division, while Rourke's bass complements the 'Faux Diddley' guitar line. The jigsawing of the guitar parts together was a remarkable and inventive bit of studio trickery, as each burst of vibrato from the Fender amps was recorded individually, and track after track built up one at a time.

'Handsome Devil' was another lift from May's Peel session. Redolent of the earlier Troy Tate version, but laced with an urgency and poison in Morrissey's delivery, Johnny preferred this version, all three instrumentalists lashing out on the track. 'Hand In Glove' was blistering, 'Still Ill''s punchy harmonica intro and exquisite guitar provided the perfect foil for Morrissey's vocal, and 'Heaven Knows I'm Miserable Now' opened up side two with as much carefree abandon as The Smiths could muster. 'This Night Has Opened My Eyes' was claustrophobic and dark, while 'You've Got everything Now' and 'Accept Yourself' were abrasive and perfectly enunciated.

The album came to a close through lovely versions of 'Girl Afraid', a gorgeous version of 'Back To The Old House', 'Reel Around The Fountain' and the poignant 'Please Please Please Let Me Get What I Want'. Johnny's heart-wrenching mandolin finish to the song, included at the suggestion of John Porter, was one of his most distinctive pieces to date, and it drifts off the end of the album with one clear message: 'watch this space.'

Released on November 24 in the UK, the gatefold sleeve showed a relaxed but serious side to the band, a shot taken backstage at Glastonbury. Morrissey wore his hearing aid, spectacles and boldly-striped shirt, a near-smile of irony on his lips. Looking drained and staring directly into the camera, Mike Joyce sits with a cigarette burning through his finger-tips. Andy Rourke is in mid bass-line, and – half-hidden in the background – Johnny is strapped up to his guitar too, his right hand poised mid-pick over the strings. Grainy, insular, involved – the picture of The Smiths at work. Reviewers in general loved the album. Adrian Thrills noted Marr's considerable contribution, referencing his "multi-tracked barrage", the "splendour in simplicity" and the "magnificence... of misery." Thrills referred to Marr as "one of the era's truly great instrumentalists" – this in effect only months into their career. For *Sounds*, Bill Black wrote of the "economy and excitement" of the package, and for many listeners the album not only filled the gap between *bona fide* studio albums, but cemented all that was wonderful about the band both in the studio and live – the fired-up musical attack, the lyrical splendour, the professionalism and the naivety combined. A taste of honey mixed with a spoonful of some harder medicine to ward off the winter ills of November 1984. The album spent almost a year in the UK charts, peaking at number seven – a considerable achievement for a compilation record from a band who had still to prove themselves.

The Irish concerts which immediately followed the album's release saw a set comprised of established favourites, to which the audiences sang along valiantly, and new songs destined for the next all-new studio album. Replacing Cilla's Beatles' song 'Love Of The Loved' as the introductory music for the gigs, the band took the stage to the strains of Prokoviev's 'March Of The Capulets' from *Romeo And Juliet*, a brash and dramatic change of tone that the band retained for much of the rest of its career as a live act. With the single 'William, It Was Really Nothing' still in the hearts of the fans, the band's profile was high, and the reception from the audiences was without exception fantastic. The new tracks that the band played went down as well as the established favourites. 'I Want The One I Can't Have', 'What She Said', 'Nowhere Fast', 'Barbarism Begins At Home'– which was originally introduced as 'Fascism Begins At Home' – and 'Rusholme Ruffians' all got an outing. 'Barbarism Begins At Home' was to become a favoured set-opener, sometimes extending to a work-out of more than fifteen minutes as the band blitzed audience after audience. On occasion Johnny would throw lines from The Beatles' 'Day Tripper' into his own riffs. Reports from the concerts recall Morrissey admonishing latter-day punks for spitting at the band from the audience with the words "If you don't like us… *leave!*"

Sea-sickness was rife on the journey over from Holyhead, and Johnny was briefly hospitalised on arrival, but he was soon reunited with the rest of the band at their Dublin hotel. After the last gig in Belfast, the band played their final live date of the year in Paris. The set list was pretty much as in Ireland, including the *Meat Is Murder* songs, but 'Please Please Please Let Me Get What I Want' – which had opened a number of the Irish concerts – was dropped.

The pop year came to an end with Band Aid's 'Do They Know It's Christmas?', the biggest of all charity singles, as pop egos were apparently 'left at the door' in the recording of the best-selling seven-inch of all time. The Smiths were not involved. For Johnny, the end of the year brought reflection. 1984 was one hell of a year for the twenty-one year old. Back in the previous December, he had had two singles and a handful of gigs to look back on in the previous year. Now, there had been three more hit singles, two successful albums, tours that would have made Keith Richards think twice about getting out of bed, a partnership with Sandie Shaw, collaborations with like-minded peers, the continuation of his relationship, despite interruption, with girlfriend Angie, and a move to London. Johnny Marr had the world at his feet.

Weeks into the new year, a Valentine's card to the world, *Meat Is Murder* was finally released to an ecstatic reception. Doubling the Smiths' visibility, the band appeared on *Top Of The Pops* the same night, presenting the new single 'How Soon Is Now?' to the world on February 14. The band (almost) swept the board in the *NME* Reader's Poll. As well as being voted the 'Best Group', Johnny was voted 'Best Instrumentalist' and he and Morrissey took the gong for 'Best Songwriter', while Morrissey was runner-up as 'Best Vocalist'.

The new album declared a more sophisticated Marr sound, broader in scope, from Fifties-influenced rockabilly to spaced-out funk. The opening track 'The Headmaster Ritual' was written on an acoustic guitar in open D tuning, its expressive chords influenced by Joni Mitchell's innovative tunings. Johnny jigsawed various unfinished pieces into the final song, the guitar parts – played largely on Martins and Rickenbackers – planned with military precision. It remains one of his personal favourites, dating so far back that it was almost three years from the initial concept to the finished vocal track. 'The Headmaster Ritual' was another track on the receiving end of tabloid attention in the UK, with Morrissey's scathing and specific lyrics about 'Manchester schools' inspiring interviews with the current headmaster of his *alma mater*.

The band had already tried out 'Rusholme Ruffians' a number of times since September. If the London media thought they had The Smiths by the scruff of the neck, here was another song to nail the band firmly in Manchester, Rusholme lying a mile to the south of the city centre. The song, introduced by the sound of a fairground ride, was a beautiful homage by Morrissey to "the last night of the fair", and by Johnny to Elvis Presley's '(Marie's The Name) His Latest Flame', into which the band would regularly segue in live performances. Marr's lightness of touch on the song's two-chord lick is delightful, but Andy particularly lit up the track with one of his 'hum this too' bass lines.

'I Want The One I Can't Have' kept the pace of the album up, one of Johnny's most brisk and sprightly tracks, the blend of acoustic and electric guitars and bass as sharp as a nettle sting. The track was mooted as the next Smiths single, but was supplanted by 'How Soon Is Now?' 'What She Said' combined punishing riffs from Marr with Joyce's part-glam, part-metal drums into a savage piece, while 'That Joke Isn't Funny Anymore' took the foot off the accelerator for a slow waltz around the ballroom. Johnny coloured the track with several layers of treated guitars that howl alongside Morrissey's emotional fade out, only to fade back in after the vocal has drifted away. The arrangement was superb, Morrissey's performance one of his very best in the canon of Smiths releases, and Johnny's guitar a delight. The track was one of Marr's favourite Smiths tracks, and Morrissey's vocals one of his favourites too.

'Nowhere Fast', another song commercial enough to have been released as a single, was actually only released as a live version on the

B-side of the twelve inch issue of 'That Joke Isn't Funny Anymore.' Introduced with a Sun-classic bit of rockabilly, the upbeat nature of the song, and Morrissey's 'on the beat' vocal were an irresistible blend. Morrissey develops a number of themes in the lyric that re-appear often within The Smiths' canon. With the relative chart stalling of some of the recent singles, it seemed a shame that the song wasn't used more productively. 'Well I Wonder' ran like a pedigree horse tightly reined in by its rider, a beautifully arranged, discretely played song loaded with understated emotion, literally washed clean at the close by the sounds of a shower of rain from a soundtrack album. The song was imbued with a simplicity and spirit that defined the best of the band. It's interesting to note that while Johnny had berated other bands for trying to innovate too much in the wake of Byrne and Eno's *My Life In The Bush Of Ghosts,* many Smiths songs were enlivened by dubbed-in sound effects and pre-recorded samples. The difference is that where Byrne and Eno used the insertion of sound sources to establish themes and develop observational criteria, The Smiths used them more like watercolour washes dropped into or over a completed song, thereby adding grace or atmosphere. 'Well I Wonder' was one lovely example of this process at work.

'Barbarism Begins At Home' had been a staple of the live Smiths since way back in December 1993, an astonishingly long time for such a track to have lain un-used [it was released as a limited promo disc in January, flagging up the 'new' sound of the band]. If heads were turned by the funk workout, anyone who knew Andy's background or Johnny's penchant for stomping disco should not have been surprised. Live, the song was often an extended wig-out for the band, and used to stamp an immediate authority as a set-opener on wild and expectant audiences.

The album's final, and most controversial track was 'Meat Is Murder' itself. This song defined Morrissey's stance at the time: trenchant, passionate and uncompromising. The sound picture of Johnny's reversed guitar and dubbed effects captured the spinning blades of the slaughterhouse and the plaintive cries of heavily-reverbed cattle introduced the slow, desolate pace of the song. As on 'Suffer Little Children', the death of the beautiful creatures of the song are hauntingly painted by Morrissey's lyric and delivery in a musical landscape bleaker than anything else in The Smiths' repertoire.

The critics loved the album, finding a density and panache in Johnny's writing and a new outward-looking Morrissey, less introspective and addressing issues broader in perspective than on *The Smiths*. Danny Kelly, writing for *NME* noted Johnny's "unnervingly evocative and beautiful" playing, while Bill Black wrote of Johnny's "aural heartburn," "screeching, preaching guitar" and "raucous rockouts" (he also, wonderfully, called The Smiths "Rough Trade's very own Red Cross parcel"). "Johnny Marr's music and production embraces Sun-era rock 'n' roll, quasi-HM, folk and psychedelia" wrote Matt Snow, while Paul du Noyer observed "major league greatness" in Johnny's work. It was a triumph all round, an album on which Johnny shone brightly and was mirrored by the input of all the other band members. In particular Rourke's bass contribution was fantastic. Morrissey's performances, of course, were spectacular. A little over a fortnight after its release, *Meat Is Murder* became The Smiths' first (and last) number one album. The Smiths had raised the stakes. By contrast, over time Johnny came to think of the album as the least successful Smiths album from an artistic point of view.

Before the tour to promote the album, personal pressures again intruded on Johnny's role within the band. Andy had dabbled with drugs since high school, but by the time of *Meat Is Murder,* Andy's use had become a serious issue both for Johnny and for the rest of the band. With an anti-drugs profile high on The Smiths' public agenda, the matter had been kept hidden even from people within the inner circle of the band. In later interviews, and still displaying a loyalty to his writing and business partner ten years on that was quite moving, Johnny admitted that, to a degree, he found himself protecting and helping not only Andy but Morrissey too. Not because of any drug use on the singer's part, but because if Rourke's problems were made public, in all likelihood it would have been Morrissey who would have had to face the press. Yet while the needs of the band were one thing, Andy was also Johnny's oldest friend, and the troubles that he endured hurt Marr too. Engagingly, Marr told Johnny Rogan in 1992 that while his thoughts were with Andy he also was worried about the effect that any scandal would have on his family as the band were becoming more and more successful. "It was the first time the family had something to be proud of," Johnny told Rogan. "[And] no-one wanted to screw that up for Andy."

As the pressures on Johnny increased, one of The Smith's most successful tours got under way in March, a series of dates that cemented the band's reputation across the UK and which remains for many fans the perfect memory of the band, and of Johnny – by now deeply into a Keith Richards look. Rock 'n' roll is littered with front-men who adopt a persona behind which they can both keep themselves sane and also hide. Bowie was one perfect example, and the educated, articulate and well-spoken Mick Jagger of the early Sixties stood quite to one side of the arrogant, preening cockerel of the Rolling Stones. But with guitarists it's perhaps less common and with Johnny quite subtle. "I was guilty of that," he said later on. "What was happening to me made it easy to confuse the public persona and the private one." In a modest way, Johnny was – perhaps inadvertently as so many pop stars do – protecting himself from the hurt and constant intrusion from the outside.

Much of the hectic abandon of the previous year's trawl around America seemed behind the band this time out. When they returned to Manchester's elegant Palace Theatre in March, Rough Trade had released the new single 'Shakespeare's Sister', backed with 'What She Said' from the new album. The record only reached 26 in chart, a disappointment both for Johnny and Morrissey who both loved it. Morrissey called it "the record of my life", while claiming that "Rough Trade had no faith in it whatsoever... they didn't service it or market it in any way." As far as Johnny was concerned, the song was a culmination of the aspirations he had at the time, and he claimed in *Melody Maker* that, on the evidence of this track alone, if Elvis had had Rourke and Joyce in his band he would have been "even bigger!"

By early April, the tour wound to a halt at London's Royal Albert Hall, a mighty venue for the increasingly gargantuan band. A few more dates preceded Johnny's third trip to the United States with The Smiths, under the watchful gaze of a new manager. Matthew Sztumph, already managing Madness, took the reins and attempted to manage the increasing complexity that was The Smiths on tour. Including their first visit to Canada in the schedule, the band was fantastic on the *Meat Is Murder* tour of America, who took to The Smiths big time, turning out in droves for the big dates and selling out almost everywhere.

On June 20, Johnny married the girl who had – the odd temporary separation notwithstanding – been at his side constantly throughout and before the momentous months since The Smiths broke big. While Angie was never 'a Smith' in the sense that Linda McCartney was 'a Wing', she had been amongst the band and there to support Johnny from the start. Several times over the years Johnny has implied that his experience of The Smiths was himself, Angie and Morrissey set against the world. Grant Showbiz agrees: "The key to Johnny is Angie," he told me, remembering how the pair were inseparable. "Johnny had the dual power of Angie on one side and Morrissey on the other." When things got tough for Johnny, he could lean either way and know that there was support: "Those two people, kind of saying 'what you are doing is great, carry on,' or 'I know it's hard, but you can do it.'" Like a three-sided pyramid, with Angie by his side, he 'had the power.' Showbiz is also quick to note that, should Morrissey ever become more distant in the relationship, Angie was always there, and so Johnny could cope because he always had somewhere to go.

Marr clearly considered his partner as crucial a part of his make-up as a musician and a band member as he considered her a part of his life outside of music (although at the time it didn't appear that Johnny actually had such a thing). He has said that had they been able, the pair would have married when they were sixteen, but it was at San Francisco's Unitarian Church that – with Andy as a witness – they finally tied the knot, slotting the quiet ceremony between gigs in New York and Oakland.

By the time the tour came to a close at the end of June, everyone agreed that it had been a rousing success. Logistically it had been an improvement on previous tours, but musically Johnny was already wondering whether his 'one man orchestra' style of guitar could continue to work in a live context: the more overdubs in the studio, the more gaps in the sound on stage. Johnny was beginning to think that a second guitarist was needed in the band, to allow him the freedom to play the way he increasingly wanted to.

The eastern gigs of the US tour was supplemented by support from The Bard of Barking, Billy Bragg. "Johnny," says Grant Showbiz, a friend of both men, "was very matey with Billy." Their friendship was based upon "great chumminess." Grant tells the entertaining story of how Billy came to join the travelling circus that was The Smiths on tour.

"We had this whole thing where we were using transvestites to open the show," says Grant, who enjoys recounting the heady days of the early Eighties. "Although that was a really good idea in Morrissey's head, actually when you get a transvestite lip-synching to Madonna, or whatever it is, and you've got a whole heap of American jocks who – for some unknown reason – really love The Smiths and don't quite understand what's going on *within* The Smiths… they're just going to throw bottles at them. Thousands and thousands of people throwing bottles at the stage," remembers Grant, turned out to be "a really bad thing! So we were like, 'we've gotta get rid of the transvestite – who can we get?'"

Billy Bragg was staying in America at the time, trying – as Grant puts it – "to hit a tour." Billy would get on a tour and run with it until it finished, looking for another one to join immediately – simply putting himself about on American stages. He might hit a tour in New Orleans, and pick up another in Chicago. When The Smiths decided to ditch the transvestites, Billy was in the right place at the right time. As Grant Showbiz puts it, "the call went out… send over Billy."

Billy's twelve performances were the perfect warm-up for the band – solo electric folk from a man with a mission, whose monologues and political songs blended with yearning love songs and set the audience up nicely for the careering headliners. They also confirmed to Bragg that his work could carry an American audience as well as a British one. It was here that a long-term friendship was formed between Billy and Johnny.

"I didn't know them," explained Bragg to this author of the time leading up to the tour. "They were in Manchester and I was in London. I didn't cross paths with them much except for GLC gigs and working with them in America. But I like to think I got on really well with Johnny when we were on tour." Marr was equally taken with Bragg. "I used to like watching him from the side of the stage," Johnny recalled in April 2006 for *Uncut*. "He would have most of them really cheering, a lot of them laughing, and some of them well-riled." By the time The Smiths hit the stage, said Marr, the crowd was filled with exactly the right energy. "There was a palpable tension… so we could take it up a gear. It was a brilliant package."

While Billy was later to record and release the Morrissey/Marr song 'Jeane' himself, he also included it in his set from time to time while touring with the band. "'Jeane' was a great song," says Billy today. "When they weren't playing it on the American tour, I would stick it in." For his own website, Billy also wrote that working with The Smiths had influenced him a great deal. "I felt that they were my comrades," he wrote, "in a struggle to bring the focus of song-writing away from production and videos, and back to good tunes and great lyrics." For Bragg and Marr there was a long relationship ahead, and many great records to be made.

Over the summer, all matters 'pop' were focussed on Live Aid, the first rock festival since Woodstock to really engage the world's imagination. The Smiths were not involved, as they had not been with the previous Yuletide's Band Aid single. Morrissey was typically scathing on the subject of Live Aid and the yawning gap between the egotistical rock star and the needs of the average African child. Instead, The Smiths released their next single, 'That Joke Isn't Funny Any More', which continued the band's frustrating stumblings in the singles chart, reaching a lowly forty-nine. Johnny was disappointed with the result, particularly singling out Morrissey's contribution as "brilliant." For the time being, The Smiths continued to release 'proper singles,' in other words songs not simply taken from the current album, but too many times the records failed to deliver in terms of chart placings and sales, though the band were selling out dates in both the UK and the USA and would ultimately reach the number one album slot. Johnny has noted that perhaps the band – while so patently a singles-orientated group for much of their career – were too divorced from the needs of the radio playlisters. Great records to own, but not necessarily great for radio play. It seems bizarre to say this in hindsight, but such great tracks as are detailed in The Smiths' chart listings did not shift millions of singles.

During July, the band were booked onto the then high-profile *Wogan* TV chat show, a major bandstand for anyone from the latest celebrity chef to the saddest, 'movie-star' fitness video/salesman. An appearance on *Wogan* guaranteed an audience of millions, but while Johnny sat in the studio with Andy and Mike, waiting for Morrissey to arrive, there was no warning at all of the fact that the singer would not appear. The band never appeared on *Wogan*, and we'll never know whether its comfortable, middle-class, knee-touching format was the wrong environment for the band or whether Morrissey and Marr would have charmed the grannies of the nation as they had charmed its youth. This was in many ways typical of a band lacking long-term management, and came on top of a history of changing live schedules and cancelled gigs. Rough Trade and the rest of the band were philosophical about the *Wogan* incident, but it cast a light upon a general air around The Smiths. While bands such as U2 enjoyed the support of one manager throughout their career, what might The Smiths have achieved had they had their own version of Paul McGuinness? But then they simply may never have been The Smiths that we all fell in love with, and might have become stadium-plodding complacents rather than the dangerous, fun and exciting band they always were.

Grant Showbiz believes that on the one hand they could have been a huge band if they'd had long-term management, but agrees that, at the same time, what defined The Smiths as great was something that would have possibly been lost in the process. "Joe just stayed with them long enough to set up a way [that] things were done," he says today. That gave the band a blueprint from which to work after Moss left. "We were either doing it the way Joe used to do it, or we were doing it the way Joe didn't do it – but there was *something* to react to. But when I think of how we stumbled through…!"

Looking at their near contemporaries, such as U2, Grant has mixed feelings that the band never quite got the album/tour/ merchandise mix right and missed commercial opportunities that could have made them immensely rich. "In some respects you would wish it upon them that they would have had that," he says, "but at the same time it means that they [remained] unique." Indeed, as testified to throughout Johnny's career, what they wrote, played and sang came first, before anything, and that too was a defining feature of The Smiths' career, whoever was at the helm. Put quite simply, the music was the most important thing. "I imagined," says Grant, "that there would be some sort of corporate meetings going on. But it seemed like they were just hanging out with one another. [It was] the best way, these things always are… it just happened." While The Smiths were rapidly becoming a wild horse that needed reining in before it disappeared over the horizon altogether, it seemed this arrangement at least kept them hungry and creative.

Rumours abounded that Rough Trade were about to 'lose' The Smiths. Apparently dissatisfied with the level of promotion they were receiving, and burying themselves in the studio for a few weeks the band laid low while Rough Trade countered the rumours. The group set about recording 'The Boy With The Thorn In His Side' at Manchester's Drone Studios, where they had recorded their first, ill-fated demo for EMI. The song was polished up at London's RAK studios, *sans* producer, as the band took the production credit themselves.

Similarly, the sessions for the new album which began at RAK in mid-summer were also 'produced by Morrissey and Marr' and engineered by Stephen Street. The first track for the album committed to tape was 'Bigmouth Strikes Again', a behemoth of a track and one that consistently justifies Marr's reputation as *the* best guitarist/one-of-the-best-producers of his generation. As the sessions progressed, it was clear that both Johnny and Morrissey were struggling, trying to work through studio sessions and record track after track while at the same time dealing with the minutae of the band's growing business empire. Matthew Sztumph had moved out of the revolving door of The Smith's management and the business of being The Smiths was becoming increasingly intolerable for Johnny, as more and more of it fell once again on his and Morrissey's shoulders. The continuing irony was that the camaraderie between the four members of the band was still good and Johnny's relationship with Morrissey unharmed despite the pressure, but it seems obvious in retrospect that if The Smiths had retained a long-term manager they might have enjoyed more longevity.

Like a prodigious child, too bright for its own good, The Smiths were hard to handle. Back in the Sixties, the death of Brian Epstein left the Beatles' ship rudderless and the band began to dissolve almost immediately. For The Smiths, it was almost as though Epstein had died on them before they even got going.

Out of the studio by the late summer, Marr *et al* headed off on a short tour of Scotland, while 'The Boy With The Thorn In His Side' was released at the same time. Musically it was one of the band's more exuberant recent single releases, Johnny's bright acoustic strumming gently coloured by electric overdubs. Increasingly, as tour followed album, and singles that should have been top ten failed to make the top twenty, the Ultimate Singles Band-elect appeared to be turning into a traditional album/tour/album outfit, against all the odds.

In September, Johnny made another appearance on a record away from his own band, on The Impossible Dreamers' single 'August Avenue'. While that record failed to set the world alight, more significantly 'The Boy With The Thorn In His Side' disappointed again. The top ten was unthreatened by the release, which made a lowly appearance at number twenty six. As well as the single, a number of new songs were premiered on the tour, songs that would be heard on the album to be released after Christmas, amongst them 'Bigmouth' and 'Frankly Mr Shankly'. The reception from most of the Scottish audiences was fabulous. The band were again very much on form live, and continuity was maintained on the tour as Stuart James stayed in the role of tour manager. A gig at Glasgow's Barrowlands was televised for Channel 4's *The Tube* and dates at Aberdeen and Inverness were augmented by a trip way off the traditional rock 'n' roll tour map when the band played in Lerwick, Shetland.

After the Scottish gigs, the band returned to London. Over the autumn Johnny was virtually a resident at Jacob's Studios in London. Having been listening extensively to The Beatles' *White Album* during the previous tours, he knew from the outset that the next album, to be called *The Queen Is Dead*, had to have something of the same eclecticism, the same air of seriousness in the music, and capture the variety of a certain moment within a certain band. The songs were getting better, and Marr knew that he had something significant on his hands. Johnny was rarely to be seen outside the studio, working harder on these tracks than on any other Smiths album. But the pressure was definitely on. And it showed. "We were under a lot of pressure to come up with something really strong," Marr was to say. "And we knew it."

The sessions were spread between RAK and Jacob's. More and more Johnny found himself alone in there, still grafting the incredibly long hours that had become his working practice. While the music of *The Queen Is Dead* developed, an iconic image of the band was taken by photographer Steve Wright. The famous photos of The Smiths at the end of Coronation Street (not the actual street of the TV soap), outside Salford Lads Club, remain one of the band's most-loved legacies. It was the 'lads' element rather than the famous street name that attracted Morrissey, who devised the shoot. While at once cementing the image of The Smiths as a bunch of 'lads,' a gang of four inextricably bonded together for all-time, there was also a heady sense of irony in the notion. While Morrissey later became something of a boxing aficionado, the entire concept of a 'lads club' – with its inherent intimations of sweaty nights at the table tennis table, and trips to the seaside in a rented charabanc – must surely have jarred with the singer's sensibilities in the months of 1985 and 1986, though might have appealed to his fictionalised concept of life in a northern town. Just as Beatles fans from around the world flock to be photographed stepping over Abbey Road's famed pedestrian crossing, so now Smiths fans from San Fransisco to Tokyo clamour to be shot outside The Lads' Club.

If accident could contribute to the recorded versions of a song, this concept was grabbed with relish. The intense, wailing feedback that declares the album's opening was indeed a glorious accident that was retained, adding immense drama to the sense of anticipation that the record would have. Throughout the sessions Johnny dipped into the Detroit songbook of the MC5 and the mighty Stooges for influence. Studio trickery was at hand for the recording of the backing vocals of 'Ann Coats' who was in fact Morrissey, his voice run at double speed (Ancoats is a tough suburb of city centre Manchester). On 'Bigmouth Strikes Again' Johnny used a Fender Stratocaster for the first time on a recorded track, and while he avoided simple Hank Marvin twang, he instead introduced another mixture of African highlife and English folk. The recording sessions were the most exploratory and innovative for the band so far, and without the guiding hand of a producer or manager it was a remarkable achievement.

But Johnny was beginning to feel out of it. "I try to take care of myself and live in the real world," Johnny said of the process of recording what he described as the best LP the band made. "But some of my best work has been produced when I wasn't." While the responsibility of production was shared with Morrissey, and the decisions of direction were always shared, the responsibility for the most time-consuming elements of the recording process – the musical tracks – fell largely on Johnny's shoulders.

"[He] was never out of the studio," Mike Joyce remembered. "He worked hardest on that album out of everything we did." Working unbelievable hours, Johnny quite simply made himself ill, as he continued to deal with Rough Trade, to speak to or dodge the press, and help handle the financial affairs of the band. Grant Showbiz still marvels at what he achieved. Johnny Marr, 'guitar hero', arch-producer and iconic musician, was at this juncture, just 22 years old.

CHAPTER FIVE

The Pleasure,
The Privilege

19 86 was a pivotal year for The Smiths and for Johnny Marr. While all things around him seemed under increasing pressure he produced what many observers still rate as his finest work, not only the most likely contender for 'best Smiths album', but also a heavyweight in the stakes as one of the best rock or pop albums ever made. The year began with the band appearing as part of the Red Wedge tour at the invitation of its progenitor Billy Bragg, who had of course toured with them in the States. The band also played a gig in Liverpool alongside The Fall and New Order in support of a group of the city's councillors who were head-to-head with the Thatcher government over their failing to establish legal rates for the city. While Rourke and Joyce had already appeared in a Smith-free role earlier in the Red Wedge tour, this was the first appearance of The Smiths proper as part of the dates, their first direct alignment to a political party cause.

Red Wedge was pop music's answer to another year of stifling Thatcherite brutality being administered to the British public like a dose of vile medicine that promised to heal the nation but only made the ailing populace sicker than ever. Johnny has only occasionally issued forth on matters political, but he was clearly no lover of The Iron Lady.

"We felt pretty fucked over by Thatcher's government," he was to say later. "And the environment was pretty crap." Johnny highlighted the creative process as his means of coping with such anger and frustration. "We had to escape from that environment," he said. "Morrissey turned it into poetry. I turned it into music." Bragg's rationale was to fuse the messages of the Labour Party with the passion and pulling power of pop, and to tour the nation waving the flag of truth and political veracity, increasing the visibility of Labour policy while partying hard from venue to venue. It was rock 'n' roll with a conscience and working-class ethic that, in retrospect, was a worthy attempt to revitalise a Labour Party that took another ten years to finish the job from within.

Within The Smiths however, there were problems afoot, that would almost put an end to the original line-up. A handful of dates in Ireland confirmed that even while Andy was making the biggest effort of his life to clean up, whether on or off the drug the effect was the same: he simply wasn't always able to contribute to The Smiths what had become his trademark fluency, beat and passion. It was decided that, for better or worse, Rourke could no longer remain a permanent member of The Smiths. The legend is that Morrissey, unable to confront the bassist face to face, left a simple note under the windscreen wiper of Andy's car, informing him of his having been thrown out. In February the band was to all intents and purposes a trio.

This perhaps paints a negative picture of Morrissey, but in truth his sympathies were apparently more with his band mate than against him. Both Marr and Morrissey appear to have felt that it was more in Andy's own interests to *not* be in The Smiths than to continue to be. Johnny was to talk of Andy's being ousted as "a necessity" amidst the turmoil of his having to act as substitute bassist, producer, manager. It was simply too much to deal with one's best friend struggling as he was, within a band itself always teetering on the edge of chaos. Celebrity addiction was very much in the news, as Boy George's own heroin issues made the front pages of the tabloids across the UK. To keep the attention off The Smiths, and to try and bring some sense of order to the band, a quick fix was needed.

Teenager Craig Gannon had a sound CV, having graced the line-ups of a number of bands all to some degree bearing the influence of The Smiths. He had played in Roddy Frame's Aztec Camera, another beautifully electro-acoustic guitar-driven pop band, in The

Colourfield with ex-Special Terry Hall, and with The Bluebells. "We just had a few rehearsals – me and Johnny mainly, learning the guitar parts," said Craig. "Everybody made me feel really welcome – everybody was really nice to me and made me feel at home."

While Craig joined the band with undoubted experience and a healthy pedigree, he was welcomed with a somewhat confusing message. Craig was told that Andy was out, and so Johnny would like him to step in on bass guitar, but should Rourke come back then he would like him to stay on second guitar. Still only nineteen, when Andy did return Gannon found that Rourke and Joyce were his natural allies in the band, while Johnny and Morrissey were always more at a distance. Johnny in fact later admitted that he felt that he didn't get to know Gannon as well as he might have. For Gannon though, eventually he and the band just found that "we didn't like each other…" The key relationship within the band itself remained between Marr and Morrissey.

Over the course of the spring, The Smiths were once again recognised in the polls of the various music papers. *NME* voted them 'Best Group', with *Meat Is Murder* the 'Best Album'. Johnny and Morrissey were voted 'Best Song-writers', Morrissey coming top in the poll for 'Best Male Vocalist', 'Best Hair-do' and 'Best-dressed Man'. *Melody Maker's* poll dumped The Smiths second to U2 in the categories for 'Best Band' and 'Best Live Act', and Robert Smith and The Cure's *Head On The Door* took the 'Best Album' gong, with *Meat Is Murder* cantering in second. Johnny, however, was recognised as 'Best Instrumentalist'.

Matters of band management came to a head when, with Andy re-instated and Gannon established in the line-up, Morrissey and Marr began a renegotiation of their contracts with Rough Trade and Sire, and reinstalled Matthew Sztumph in the role of manager. After the May release of 'Bigmouth Strikes Again' as the new single (backed with the instrumental 'Money Changes Everything') and a later appearance on Channel 4's *The Tube*, the band hit the road, their first tour as a five-piece. As mentioned, Johnny's increasing studio savvy meant that his guitar parts were getting harder and harder to reproduce on stage, and Gannon most certainly helped the band to progress live, allowing Johnny more space sonically. Gigs in Glasgow, Newcastle and Manchester prepared them for a further onslaught on the North American market, determined as they were to break the US open. The tour that opened in Ontario, Canada in July came to a halt in mid-September when the band cancelled the few remaining gigs in the south-eastern states.

Much has been made over the years of the fact that Johnny Marr took to drinking in a big way during the American tour of 1986. Johnny Rogan recounted Johnny's memories of the experience: "All I remember is really bad times, like laying on the end of a bed with Angie saying, 'Someone's got to do something about this.'" It was the pressure of the tour that put the strain on Johnny and saw his intake increase – rather than his drinking causing him a problem that affected the tour. Looking back on the period, Grant Showbiz thinks that Johnny's consumption was high, but no higher than perhaps the average guy in his early twenties under the sort of immense pressure Marr was subject to. Young kids who leave home and suddenly find no-body behind the door when they crawl home from the pub do tend to overdo it, and Johnny's drinking was more that of a young man under pressure than that of a potential alcoholic.

"Courvoisier did seem to suddenly arrive in our lives and make itself known to us," says Showbiz. "But given the excesses that we *could* have got into... I mean, there *were* moments, and they were crazy moments. But it didn't go *that* insane."

"[I've] been around a fair amount of gnarled old rockers," Showbiz says, adding to the picture of The Smiths carousing through the USA in the summer of 1986. "It wasn't as if... it was never... you know, naked people on top of pianos, knocking over tables or accosting strangers and trying to beat up their girlfriends." Showbiz's memories don't include seeing Johnny losing the plot at any time. "None of that," he says. "I can't honestly remember Johnny being out of control."

There were high jinks, of course. Grant recalls that members of the crew did occasionally spend a couple of hours behind bars to sober up, or were booted out of clubs for the same reason, but in general the tour was well-behaved. Compared to other bands, although they weren't saints, The Smiths were well-behaved. "I'm used to getting singers, or whoever it is, out of the hotel room at eleven o'clock," says Grant. "And they're drunk. and it's just a matter of trying to keep the level of alcohol in them sufficient so that they can perform, but not enough that they fall over. But Johnny was never like that." Morrissey's general habit of retiring early, and the fact that Johnny was accompanied by his wife were, again, key. "I think a lot of that again is down to the fact that Angie was there, and that

Morrissey wasn't that interested either. So that in some respects the two pivotal members of the band were never going to party hard."

The Queen Is Dead was released in May, reaching the tantalising peak of number two in the album charts. For its guitarist it was, and remains, "a fantastic piece of vinyl." The title track bore all the hallmarks of Johnny at his most creative, the punishing schedule reflected in the murderous, strident chords and thunderous drumming from Joyce. As noted, the feedback howl that runs throughout the track, and the rigorous wah-wah of Marr's guitar, recall The Stooges, or MC5, Johnny and Morrissey's blueprint for proper rock 'n' roll. Rourke's bass lines are equally lapel-grabbing, the entire track a *tour de force* of the very highest quality. As the song was completed, Johnny was to say in retrospect, that he "came out shaking." For the opening track alone the album was worth its price, but of course virtually every song defined something vital and invigorating in The Smiths at their best.

'Frankly Mr Shankly', with Morrissey's splendid lyrics and vocal delivery was written on acoustic guitar from start to finish at Johnny's house, an early delight on the album and an all-time favourite for fans. The track shifts melodically through Johnny and Andy's jaunty interplay on the bouncing half-note, the song presented simply with bass, acoustic guitar and drums. While the vaudeville snigger of the song is irresistible, the target of the song's ire was reputed to be (according to Simon Goddard) Rough Trade supremo Geoff Travis, who had presented a distinctly unimpressed Morrissey with one of his own poems. 'Frankly Mr Shankly' stands as one of the enduring reasons why people have loved The Smiths so much for so many years. The rush from 'The Queen Is Dead' into the stumbling music hall comedy of the track that follows it sums up so much about a band with a heart as big as an ox, a brain (to borrow from Douglas Adams) the size of a planet, and a belly-laugh sense of humour that few of their peers could counter. God bless Mr Shankly.

'I Know It's Over' continued the emotional rollercoaster of the album, and was an immensely moving song for Johnny too. Morrissey's lyrics hit the emotion of the track perfectly in synch with Johnny's own feel. Rarely has such deep sorrow been so deftly expressed in pop. 'Never Had No-one Ever' continues the sense of desolation and desperation, once again set up simply by Johnny's simple chording. Simon Goddard relates how in initial takes of the song it was, unsuccessfully, augmented with trumpet that, according to Mike Joyce, was "quite ridiculous." Instead, the emotional torch of the song is ignited by Johnny's own electric guitar.

'Cemetry Gates' came to Johnny on a train journey back from London. Repeatedly hailed as one of the country's best new songwriters, he decided to specifically set himself a test. "I was on the train, thinking… 'If you're so great, first thing in the morning sit down and write A Great Song.' I started with Cemetry Gates; B minor to G change in open G." The breezy open-tuned strumming jigsawed perfectly into Morrissey's equally warming lyric, filled with references to the movie *Guess Who's Coming To Dinner*.

'Bigmouth Strikes Again', like 'The Queen Is Dead' is one of the muscular armatures that roots the album. Flagged by Johnny as his own 'Jumpin' Jack Flask', the irrepressible pace of the song and the Stones-like backing vocals can clearly be linked to that inspirational track. The song kicks off on unaccompanied, pacey acoustic guitar, soon hoofed into action by Rourke and Joyce's rhythm section. On record the track was impressive, but live recordings demonstrate the power of the song in The Smiths' live show, a fabulous piece of music.

'Bigmouth' was followed by 'The Boy With The Thorn In His Side', one of Johnny's most glorious riff-based songs combined with ecstatic non-verbal crooning from Morrissey, a natural choice for a single from the album. 'Vicar In A Tutu' trotted along, rockabilly style, to more of Morrissey's Kenneth Williams-meets-*Private Eye* observation, ridiculing the church while painting a vulgar picture of clergymen in ballet garb.

While 'Vicar In A Tutu' is relatively lightweight amongst the album's best songs, the track that followed it was sublime, perhaps the most-loved of all the band's anthems. The gorgeous, repeated closing refrain summed up The Smith's legacy in eight simple words: 'There Is A Light That Never Goes Out'. This and 'Frankly Mr Shankly' were both written at Marr's house on acoustic guitar, with Morrissey and Johnny working together on ideas that had been knocking around in Johnny's head for some time. 'There Is A Light…' became an instant Smiths classic, one of the best-loved of all their songs. There was an instinctive ability in the duo to each complement the other's ideas quickly and accurately. Whereas Lennon and McCartney had abandoned the face-to-face writing technique that spawned so many hits very early in their career, Marr and Morrissey were able, right to the end of The Smiths, to sit down together and come away with a perfectly crafted and finished song that would be polished and perfected in the studio. Johnny was moved when he heard the first playback of the finished piece. "I thought it was the best song I'd ever heard," he said.

The album opened with a nod to The Stooges or the Stones. It ended on a note more out of *Carry On* than *Raw Power*. 'Some Girls Are Bigger Than Others' is one of Morrissey's most entertaining lyrics and one of Johnny's most infectious riffs, knocked off one night while sat watching TV with friends. Constantly picking away at the fret board until the complex little gem was completed, the beautifully turned picking is one of Johnny's most delightful pieces. Linked to Morrissey's lyric (Morrissey told *NME* that "the fact that I've scuttled through twenty-six years of life without ever noticing that the contours of the body are different is an outrageous farce") the song is a delight.

★

In July and October respectively, the fabulous singles 'Panic' and 'Ask' were released. 'Panic' – recorded in May, well after the sessions for *The Queen Is Dead* were over, remains one of the band's most-loved records, a live favourite and the one most likely to encourage a sing-along. Glam-heavy, 'Panic' was one of the rare songs that Johnny wrote in response to a Morrissey lyric composed first, rather than other way round, or by the pair sitting and working together. "I'd been over to his house," Marr recalls, "and I knew he had a new idea with a hook that was 'Hang the DJ'. So I basically wrote 'Metal Guru'!" The band even approached legendary Bolan producer Tony Visconti to record the track with them, but the plan never got off the ground, while film-maker Derek Jarman shot an entertaining, Smith-free video. The song – successful in reaching number eleven in the charts – has the same glorious, descending riff, the same heavy drumming, and the same rousing feel of a teenage night out with the boys – so ironic, given the content of the lyric.

'Ask' was a joyful, gentle song both musically and lyrically, with Steve Lillywhite's wife Kirsty MacColl on backing vocals. Johnny's perfect picking sounded as though he'd trip up, but of course he never does. In October it reached an almost satisfying number fourteen on the singles chart. Back in the UK, worn from the hugely successful US tour, Marr remained largely tight-lipped when news leaked out that – with only one album remaining due on their contract with Rough Trade – The Smiths were signing to EMI, the most major of the major labels. If this was, as reported, the beginning of the end for independent record labels, it didn't stop Johnny's work rate getting back up to speed. They did indeed sign with EMI in September 1986, with the leviathan record company admitting that there were ends for The Smiths to tie up with Rough Trade before their deal would kick in. While Rough Trade and EMI slugged it out in the music press, further dates were lined up around the UK through the autumn, taking in the faithful of Carlisle, Middlesbrough, Wolverhampton, Cornwall, Newport, Nottingham and Kilburn in London. At Brixton the band were supplemented by an extra drummer for two songs. The tour wound up with a quick rush – a sell-out at the London Palladium, a riotous gig in Preston, and a finale back in the home town at the end of October. The concert at the Free Trade Hall proved to be Craig Gannon's last although his exit from the group was not announced officially until November. Marr has spoken since of not thinking Gannon would "fit in" with any new recordings and how Johnny's writing partnership with Morrissey was essentially not added to by the now-former band-mate. The Smiths were a four-piece once more.

Winding down towards the end of a hectic year, Johnny came closer to catastrophe than any of the recent rock 'n' roll excess could have meted out when, in November, he was involved in a near-fatal car accident. Spinning out of control, the Manchester rain lifted Johnny's tyres off the road, and within seconds he had endured and survived a serious crash, wrecking the car but walking away from the incident virtually unscathed. The following day he was fitted with a neck brace at a Manchester hospital, but thankfully there was no permanent damage, though the experience was a major wake-up call. The immediate result was that the band cancelled an imminent gig with The Fall at The Royal Albert Hall, re-scheduling it for later in December at Brixton Academy.

Bootleg recordings of this gig reveal a band at the peak of its powers: aggressive, thrashy, perfect. From opener 'The Queen Is Dead' to the closing song 'Bigmouth...' the pace is frenetic and everyone completely on song. It was appropriate that it should be so, for, though nobody could have realised it at the time, this would be the last time Johnny Marr and The Smiths would play together live in the UK.

★

Meanwhile, as the summer of 1986 drifted into autumn, various pieces of work appeared that Johnny had worked on with Billy Bragg. Much of it was amongst Marr's best work to date, and all of it demonstrated his incredible work rate and ability to hit the nail on the head in terms of song-writing, playing and production. The first was a beautiful version – where Johnny played acoustic guitar to Bragg's spoken word voice-over – of the Four Tops'/Left Banke's 'Walk Away Renee', which appeared as the B-side to Billy's own 'Levi Stubbs Tears'.

Bragg was working on his third album *Talking With The Taxman About Poetry* with John Porter producing. "What I had in common with The Smiths, was that I didn't come through the big record company mainstream route. I hadn't been 'found' and 'groomed,'" explains Billy. Like The Smiths, Bragg had found early champions in John Peel and John Waters, and had had his first sessions for Radio One in 1983, as had The Smiths. John Porter had been the natural producer for Billy: "We didn't really know any record producers. So in the end we worked with the producers – the only ones we'd ever been in the studio with, the ones on the Peel sessions. That was my experience," says Bragg today. "John's reputation of working with The Smiths had gone before him and was pretty good." The influence of The Smiths on Billy's work was subtle, more in terms of his career than in his own writing. He had, of course, toured with the band in the United States, and his career path followed a similar trajectory, albeit as a solo artist. Bragg compares his own experience of independent labels in the Eighties to that of The Smiths, noting that being on Go Discs was "a little bit like being on Rough Trade" but without 'the baggage' that came with it.

Marr had come into the sessions via John Porter to add guitar to a number of tracks. "I was going up to Wood Green every day to make the record," recalls Billy fondly. "While the engineer was miking up Johnny's acoustic for the overdub on 'Greetings To The New Brunette', he was playing 'Walk Away Renee' on the guitar." The purity and perfection of Johnny's quiet picking struck Bragg immediately, and he spotted something special. "I said out of the corner of my mouth to Porter, 'Roll the tape, roll the tape.' So we taped him playing it." On the tube journey home, Billy chewed over the performance he had witnessed of the classic song. It didn't seem right to simply cover the track as such. "He was just sat there playing while they put mics around him... sat there in the way that he does, unself-consciously (sic) playing. It was just beautiful," he remembers today. "I sort of went home on the tube that night, and on the way back in the morning wrote the lyric." It was a spoken monologue inspired by Johnny's rendition of 'Walk Away Renee' that Billy brought to the studio rooms, and therefore has a completely different identity to the original song. The concept struck Johnny too as worth pursuing. "When I explained what I was doing he did a proper take for me," says Billy, "and put those nice opaque chords at the start. And off we went! It was just a wonderful backdrop to my monologue."

Billy Bragg's experience of working with Johnny Marr is one of joy and of evident companionship. The pair worked really well together, and it is all too clearly heard in the work that the sessions produced. In terms of what Marr brings to the studio with him, Billy talks of Johnny's 'folk sensitivity.' "That hadn't really been heard since the early Sixties when people were coming out of folk music and forming bands like the Byrds," he says. Quick to avoid linking Johnny's playing style with that of Roger McGuinn of The Byrds, Billy explains further: "I don't wish to make that comparison and say 'he sounds all Byrds-y like' – because it's not the sound of what he was *doing* but more the style, the picking style. That's what made it flow. He followed his intuition. That's what made him so great." For Marr, it was an equally productive friendship. "We were Manchester pot-smokers," he told *Uncut*. "and talking to (ex-army man) Billy, it was a little bit like 'Stand by your beds,'" but the relationship was clearly warm and long-lasting.

Talking With The Taxman About Poetry contained two other tracks on which Johnny's playing is evident – 'The Passion' and the resplendent 'Greetings To The New Brunette.' From the punched-out opening major chords on an acoustic guitar, via Kirsty MacColl backing vocals to die for, to the sustained outro on electric, the latter is one of Bragg's best loved songs, and one of the most engaging singles in pop history. It is also quintessential Johnny Marr. As this book was being finished, Billy was writing his own treatise on the nature of 'Englishness', watching the World Cup with both the eyes of a football fan and a writer on nationalism: what better time to ask him about the song with the timeless lyric 'how can you lie there and think of England/When you don't even know who's in the team?'? The song, he feels, reveals more about Johnny's roots. "My experience of him is he must have been a folk music fan when he was growing up," says Billy, "because he knows a lot about folk music." Despite being the king of the Rickenbackers, outside of his own band Johnny clearly was happy to indulge his other musical interests and explore some of the music that had been so important to his own development.

The B-side of 'Greetings...' included a cover of The Smiths' 'Jeane', which of course Billy had fallen in love with, and played live several times to audiences who had come to see The Smiths in the first place. When re-released on *Reaching To The Converted*, Billy wrote that because The Smiths had stopped playing the song, "I picked it up and looked after it."

Talking To The Taxman About Poetry appeared in September, while 'Greetings To The New Brunette' was released as a single in early November, all set for the UK top five. Stunningly, it made it barely into the top fifty, spending a disappointing three weeks on the chart, despite being credited to 'Billy Bragg with Johnny Marr and Kirsty MacColl' – three of the hottest names around. A week after its release, in concert in Leeds, Billy introduced it as "a song which deals deftly and swiftly with the subjects of stealing cars, having sex and dyeing your hair. Three things linked only by the fact that they make your fingers smell funny afterwards." Probably a good job that they didn't enjoy repeated appearances on *Top Of The Pops*! Some years later the pair revisited the song for *Reaching To The Converted*, re-titling the song 'Shirley' "because that's what everyone calls it anyway."

At the same time Johnny and Billy also worked together, albeit at a distance, on 'The Boy Done Good'. "That had been stuff that had been knocking around, a tune that he'd given me the music to during *Don't Try This At Home*, up at his house," says Billy. "I finally wrote some lyrics to it. But it all happened too late to get on the album so we put it out as a single subsequently." Billy explained the genesis of the song further on his website: "Johnny put this tune on a tape for me and I wrote the lyrics shortly after his beloved Manchester City were relegated from the Premiership." The song was originally entitled 'Big Mal', after the legendary Malcolm Allison, former boss at Maine Road. Pulling all the various references around the song together, Smiths' sound-man Grant Showbiz – still working with Billy today – nicknamed it 'Big Mal Strikes Again'. While Billy decided against naming the song after the Smiths' classic, he did keep the reference to 'the sky blues' when the song was released on the 1996 collection *William Bloke*.

Meanwhile, the career of The Smiths nearing its end, the band kept close to their roots by recording, early in December, their last John Peel session. The four songs that were broadcast on December 17 were 'Is It Really So Strange', 'London', 'Half a Person' and 'Sweet & Tender Hooligan.'

It was another closing door.

CHAPTER SIX

The End Of
A Perfect Day

19 87 was another year of Thatcherite frustration for anyone in the UK with a social conscience. In an interview published the following year, but recorded before the dissolution of The Smiths, Johnny spoke of his anger at the increasing sense of hopelessness among the nation's young. "My generation of school kids – they're the ones who have been hit by it the most. It is literally as bleak as people imagine it to be. It has changed a lot of British society… social attitudes have changed remarkably. There's no-one who can stand for working people in England any more – it's a Conservative dream." Musical distraction came from the shambling, rambling Pogues, whose If I Should Fall From Grace With God featured their timeless duet with Kirsty MacColl, 'Fairytale of New York.' While disaffection continued to infect Britain's cities, a new Manchester band was packing out the venues in their home town and finding themselves almost routinely ignored by the suits down south. 1987 was a good year for The Stone Roses, the local reputation of Ian Brown, John Squire et al building up a head of steam comparable to that of The Smiths in their early days.

But time was running out for Manchester's finest, despite their remaining deep in the hearts of the record-buying public. In the

Valentine's Day Reader's Poll for *NME* The Smiths once again walked off with the awards for 'Best Group', 'Best Male Singer', 'Best Album' for *The Queen Is Dead* and Morrissey was voted 'Most Wonderful Human Being'. 'Panic' was not only voted 'Best Single' but also came in the top handful of songs voted 'Best Dance Track' – a long way from the disco-unfriendly early Smiths.

Sessions for the new single 'Sheila Take A Bow' were problematic, with rumours of studio no-shows and frequently tense atmospheres. The recordings were not altogether productive. Early in the New Year 'Shoplifters Of The World Unite' was released, a majestic blend of Morrissey and Marr magic that got to number twelve in the singles chart. Johnny's parts were compared to Brian May, while the guitarist himself was more keen to credit the influence of Nils Lofgren on the track. The band got back to work, this time inviting Sandie Shaw back for another crack at 'Sheila...', only to eventually not use her contribution. Eventually John Porter had a final mix of the song, but even that was not used. The band re-recorded it at Tony Visconti's studio, this time with Stephen Street at the desk. As history sorted these matters out for itself, John Porter was never to work with The Smiths again.

March brought the release of *The World Won't Listen*, the band's second compilation-cum-sampler album, that re-visited the format of *Hatful Of Hollow*. The album again came close to the number one slot but stalled at the last hurdle; like *The Queen Is Dead* it made it to number two. For the fans on the other side of the Atlantic Rough Trade/Sire released the closely related compilation *Louder Than Bombs*. As *Hatful Of Hollow* gave everyone a taste of great things to come, so these two albums reminded everyone of just what a fantastic band The Smiths had become.

The band itself was concentrating on the future, though, not the past. The sessions at Visconti's Good Earth studio also produced the next single, 'Girlfriend In A Coma'. In effect this was also the start of sessions for the fourth and what would prove to be the final Smiths studio album. The *Strangeways* sessions were unusual, in that right up to the last moment, as Stephen Street remembered, even Johnny didn't know exactly what Morrissey would bring to the studio in terms of lyrical input. "We were putting the backing tracks down totally blind," he remembered. "Just making sure the key was okay with him." Johnny was keen to clean up some of the working practices that had become *de rigour* for him in the studio. There were fewer guitar overdubs – in fact no guitar at all on the opening track – and in general his work is heavier, more concentrated. "I wanted to make sure my main guitar parts really counted and stayed on the record," he told an interviewer much later. Not content with simplifying and re-assessing the process of putting the album together, Johnny also – for the first time on a Smiths record – included a traditional solo on 'Paint A Vulgar Picture', so momentous that he marched everyone out of the studio before committing it to tape.

When the sessions ended and the band celebrated with art co-ordinator Jo Slee and Geoff Travis, the latter sensed that there was an air of finality around everyone, as though something more than just the latest album was finished.

'Sheila Take a Bow' reached number ten in the singles chart, and thus became the equal-highest chart position of any Smiths single. Classic glam *homage*, the track reeked of the early Seventies pop charts, when the stomp of The Glitter Band would play next to the parading guitar pop of T. Rex on the radio. Both influences are evident in the recording, that was of course made at the studio of Tony Visconti, T. Rex's own producer.

Then, in the summer, it was formally announced that Johnny Marr had left The Smiths.

★

Early in August, *NME* ran the headline 'Smiths To Split' to break the news to the world, announcing that the band was "likely to call it a day after the release of their next album." While Morrissey denied the story, and famously threatened to spank with a wet plimsoll anyone who said the band had split, by the next issue of *NME*, Johnny confirmed that he had left. The article had appeared in *NME* while Johnny was in Los Angeles. "I don't know where that story came from," Grant Showbiz told film maker David Nolan. "The thing that *pushed* Johnny into leaving was that article." Nobody quite knows who released the information to the magazine, and with what motive. "[Johnny] was that pissed off about it, and where it might have come from, that he said, 'Right –I've had enough anyway – and I *have* left.'"

The final Smiths sessions had been a miserable affair. Johnny had already decided to leave the group, but had done the last session although perhaps he didn't want to be there. Grant Showbiz – as almost the last gasp in his relationship with The Smiths as a coherent band – produced a version of Cilla Black's 'Work Is A Four Letter Word', that Johnny always looked back on with disaffection, at his own Firehouse studios in Streatham. Along with 'Keep Mine Hidden' – their very last recorded track as a group – these songs were destined to be sent out to the world as a goodbye note on the B-side of 'Girlfriend In A Coma.' Those final few days in the studio were a strange affair.

Rourke and Joyce have both attested to the fact that Johnny was working far too hard, trying to better *The Queen Is Dead* with *Strangeways*. "[He] really needed to take a lot of time off," said Andy, noting that when everyone else took time out Johnny had just kept on working. While it was Johnny himself who had suggested that everyone take a holiday, he couldn't leave the job behind himself, and Johnny was clearly pushed over the edge in August 1997. The album, for Joyce, was "a white knuckle ride" and just because the music was so great didn't mean that the pressures on Marr were any the less. Geoff Travis also felt that an extended break, after which everyone reconvened, might have been enough to rekindle Johnny's enthusiasm for The Smiths. Maybe if Johnny had gone away for six months or so, they may have come back revitalised and ready for more. "Fame," said John Peel, who knew a thing or to about it himself, "is such a bastard!"

So many people seem to think a split could have been avoided if the band members had just avoided one another for a while and taken a holiday. Grant Showbiz mentions the same thing, even now. He feels that the band stayed together as long as it did because of the bond of friendship between the group. Once that starts to break down, you've had it. "[If] you don't have the backbone of good smart management – to just say 'Go away, you don't *have* to make another record!'" then Grant thinks you're on the rocks. A good manager can stop the group and say, "Forget about records. Go away and think about it for six months, and *don't talk to one another*!" Sadly, for Johnny and The Smiths, nobody was there to say this to them.

On the announcement of Johnny's departure, the press, and fans, had a field day. To all intents and purposes, the end of The Smiths was presented as Johnny's 'fault.' When Johnny and Morrissey had formed The Smiths, Marr was 19-years-old. By the time he left the band he was still only 23. But now he was a legend, a voice, a face, a songwriter and guitar player who had saved a generation, a lionized figure. As with John Lennon and The Beatles, both external pressures and internal strains confirmed that Marr had in fact outgrown both the band and his own personal need for it. One of the biggest problems had been the ongoing managerial issues, the business of the business of being The Smiths. "The practicalities faced by Morrissey and me when we had to try and run that kind of organisation really got me down" Johnny admitted later.

Ironically, the rising level of success in America was a contributing factor. More tours, more albums, more press, more intrusion – it would have been too much. Morrissey and Johnny had both considered moving to America to live for a while, consolidating their success there, but with the constant expectations of the entire Smiths organisation that Johnny be there to sort things out, the idea became intolerable. While the band seemed to have everything they ever dreamed of, the stresses placed on Johnny and Morrissey to handle the financial end of this were enormous.

On leaving the band, Johnny was able to start cleaning up his own issues, telling interviewers that he would never allow a band to put so much pressure on him, or upon the relationships that he had enjoyed with friends. One of these relationships was that with long-time friend Joe Moss, who still had an outstanding issue with the band that he had left years previously. Moss has kept a dignified near-silence on the subject over the years, but on his leaving the band there had been an outstanding debt incurred in the early days of The Smiths, when Joe had coughed up for a PA system for the band. One of Johnny's first actions was to try and clear the air over this with his friend, manager and mentor. As Johnny explained to Johnny Rogan in an interview much later, he paid Moss the outstanding monies due out of his own money, and that matter, at least, was closed.

"Towards the end of The Smiths," Marr told *NME* journalist Dave Haslam in 1989, "I realised that the records I was listening to with my friends were more exciting than the records I was listening to with the group." Marr retained a cautious air in interviews immediately following the group's disbandment, but this didn't stop people from continuing to blame him for the break up of the band. "Some people are never going to forgive,' he told *NME* in 1989. 'They didn't know anything about the way things were. They'd have preferred me to have died rather than split the group up."

As well as the pressures of the business, it is clear that general musical issues were another reason for Johnny hanging up his guitar picks for a while. Although over the years he has wavered between citing *Strangeways* or *The Queen Is Dead* as his favourite Smiths album, despite the quality of the former, there were clear issues about where the band could possibly go next. They were, in his own words, a long way down a musical *cul-de-sac* where the expectations of the audience no longer met with the aspirations of the guitarist. A long time disco and soul fan, Johnny was listening more and more to types of music that – if he had decided to implement the influence in The Smiths' own sound – would have brought about mass revolt amongst the fan base, many of whom felt technology and innovation weren't allowed, so while the electronica of his future work with Bernard Sumner beckoned, to stay in The Smiths seemed to mean that jangly guitar was all that was expected of him.

In short, the excitement, the *joi de vivre,* had gone from Johnny's experience with the band. There is an irony in Johnny's name that – translated into French – sums up his situation at this point nicely. There's even been a hit record bearing the title. In 2003 there was a single named 'J'En Ai Marre', in French, by a singer called Alizee. *J'en ai marre* (pronounced almost exactly as is Johnny's name), roughly translated into English, means 'I've had enough,' or 'I am fed up.'

Personally, while he continued to get on well with the group members, he had to escape the pressures that were affecting his health and his happiness. Professionally he felt the group had run its course if it could not meet the demands upon it that its audience maintained. Musically he had other fish to fry. As far as Marr was concerned, to continue, and to promote *Strangeways* via the inevitable world tour and all that it entailed would have served only to worsen the situation and completely destroy the relationships that he still enjoyed with Morrissey, Rourke and Joyce, and perhaps kill him too. Like a marriage doomed to failure from the start, he had enjoyed great times and was rightly proud of the band, but had never been completely happy as the hectic world around him worsened and worsened.

Of course, Johnny received hate mail. For the bedsit lost and lonely, Marr had destroyed the dream that was The Smiths. Astonishingly, it appeared at first that The Smiths would try and continue without him. Various replacement guitarists were mooted – Aztec Camera's Roddy Frame and Ivor Perry from Easterhouse amongst them. There was even a recording session booked for a Morrissey, Rourke, Gannon and Perry line-up of The Smiths. It lasted two days, and produced two tracks – one of them a rudimentary version of 'Bengali In Platforms' that would appear on Morrisey's *Viva Hate*. But without Johnny it simply wasn't The Smiths. After two days the session foundered, and Ivor Perry no longer stood in for Johnny Marr.

However much the image of the band had become more and more centred upon Morrissey's role as spokesperson and front-man, if Johnny wasn't there, this band was not The Smiths any more. Of course a replacement guitarist could learn Johnny's parts for live shows, and undoubtedly could have contributed to the writing process (both Perry and Frame are without doubt exceptionally good players and writers), but The Smiths music was the creative hub of two particular individuals – the loss of one meant the end of the band.

There were, of course, the conspiracy theories blaming everybody. Morrissey disapproved of Johnny's 'freelancing', Morrissey wouldn't tour, Johnny wanted to tour the world and live the life of the rock 'n' roll superstar etc, all rumour, nothing proven. It was said that manager Ken Friedman had deliberately driven a wedge between the two. Of course the truth was more simple than any of these... The Smiths had run their course. "It had nothing to do with how I feel about Morrissey, and how he feels about me," Johnny told Dave Haslam. "We had a good time recording the last LP, and I was unhappy before that. And I was unhappy after that... If we had to go off on tour and try to promote the record with the bad atmosphere that was around, the situation would have got even more hideous."

The band was over long before the split actually came, and once the decision was made there was no going back. As Ziggy had exhausted Bowie both personally and creatively, and as The Beatles had been left behind by the Yoko-influenced new creativity of John Lennon by 1969, so Johnny had tired of being 'a Smith.' He was suffocating. It was time for pastures new.

Rather than dwell on the split, it was probably more remarkable that The Smiths lasted as long as they did. The band was born of two very diverse talents and a remarkably concise vision. That that partnership produced work of such quality and lasted for five full years was a major achievement in itself. They came, they saw and they conquered, and regardless of who was to blame for the split, when the job was done they went their separate ways. Johnny was then, and remains to this day proud of what The Smiths achieved. The love of the seven-inch single that fired him so fiercely as a child was still with him as an adult, and he is proud to have released such gems that remain as treasured objects in the hearts and minds of record buyers even now.

That ought to be that, but years after the split Johnny was still troubled by its manner. He represented the break up as the biggest failure of his life, as he revealed to author Martin Roach in *The Right To Imagination And Madness*: "We *should* have split when we did," he reflected. "Simply because we had lost touch with basic emotional values which we all possessed." He felt they were all "perverted by our egos," which by then had turned the band into caricatures. "We were good people," he says. "But we did the split wrong."

In the wake of the split, Mike and Andy went on to work with Sinead O'Connor. Mike joined his early heroes Buzzcocks for a while, and worked with both Julian Cope and PiL. Both Rourke and Joyce worked with Pete Wylie, while Rourke joined ex-Happy Mondays drummer Gaz Whelan in a band called Delicious, later coming together in the band Aziz. Most significantly, the pair continued with Morrissey for a short while in his solo capacity, later playing a remarkable concert in Wolverhampton that also included Craig Gannon in Morrissey's band. The gig was both valediction and the beginning of a new era, and – if you wore a Smiths T-shirt, the first 1700 punters to arrive got in for free.

★

Released in early September 1987, *Strangeways Here We Come* gave a clear impression of the creative crossroads that The Smiths had reached as they shuddered to a halt. It was a fitting finale. Lyrically the album mined familiar seams yet musically searched for something new, a two-headed snake. It was a heavy-duty piece of work. Johnny has always been extremely fond of the album, periodically claiming it as his favourite Smiths release of all. While he struggled to find a new direction for the band, the stripped down atmosphere still appeals to him today. For Andy, the album did indeed point to a different future for the band had they stayed together, but Mike found it hard to listen to, even long after the band was done. "You don't put that one on when you fancy some nice easy listening," he observed dryly.

'A Rush And A Push And The Land Is Ours' opens with Morrissey's reverbed voice hauntingly 'coming inside' over jaunty piano chords. If Johnny was looking for pastures new musically for The Smiths, then he could have made no more radical statement of intent from his own point of view than to open the album with a track void of guitar. Instead, it is Johnny on vamping piano, clearly relishing the simplicity of the bouncing chords against Joyce's military percussion.

'I Started Something I Couldn't Finish' was one of *Strangeways'* best tracks, a glammed-up rocker that kicked off with a musical quote from Bolan's '20th Century Boy', big, expressive Keith Richards' chords and a stomping drum track that wasn't pretty but is a killer part of the song. The 'horn section' was another diversion for The Smiths, but on 'Death Of A Disco Dancer' there was a real treat, a rare instrumental outing for Morrissey, who had been playing the studio piano and who added his own solo contribution to the song. The descending B minor riff around which the song was based – like 'Dear Prudence' or 'Tales Of Brave Ulysees' – gradually fell into an open, grungy jam, some of the most visceral moments committed to tape by The Smiths. Whether Morrissey's piano piece was rehearsed or not, he certainly played in key and included a number of jazz rolls that suggest there was a little more than mere happy accident. After the repeated descending chords, at the end Johnny plays a mini-Sergeant Pepper coda of rising chords to finish the song off.

This was definitely a new Smiths – no clipped, jangling siroccos of guitar, but mayhem, improvisation. If the songs to date had been surprising, 'Girlfriend In A Coma' harked back to *The Queen Is Dead*, with Johnny's half-beat acoustic guitar recalling 'Frankly Mr Shankly'. This was one of Morrissey's finest moments, at once absurd, hysterical, and deeply, deeply moving. If the attempt was to be as audacious as possible, then simply by the refrain of the title the song succeeded, but the clarity and honesty of Morrissey's vocal is very moving. Set that against the cheeriness of Johnny's guitar and Andy and Mike's rhythm, and the song could not fail to bring a smile. With lyrics about a girl in a coma... The Smiths were at their devilish best and most contradictory.

'Stop Me If You Think You've Heard This One Before' was an instant classic: so much more sophisticated than the early records, this was a band at the height of their powers – Johnny's trick of throwing cutlery at a heavily-reverbed guitar, the innocent-punk solo, and again Morrissey at his very best. 'Last Night I Dreamt That Somebody Loved Me' was one of Morrissey's most dramatic – but not quite melodramatic – performances. The minor piano chords over the sound of chaotic crowd noises was reminiscent of 'Meat Is Murder', and it was two minutes before what might be called 'the song' proper came into the mix. The effect was of a movie soundtrack to an emotion about to break, and when Morrissey appeared, suddenly, it was stunning. Johnny's arpeggios, the artificially concocted strings and mandolin... pure wonderful Smiths at their best.

'Unhappy Birthday' was an unusual song, a mixture of the jazz-inspired chords of 'Heaven Knows I'm Miserable Now' and the regular acoustic strumming of something like 'Cemetry Gates'. At once it can be the least satisfying track on the album, and at the same time perhaps the one most interesting to stop and listen to for the musical track alone, with Johnny's echoing solo notes that slide the song in and out. While it contained elements of the same kind of juxtaposition that invigorates 'Girlfriend In A Coma', it lacked the suggested irony of that song, yet retained something else irresistible and eminently The Smiths. 'Paint A Vulgar Picture' was another difficult track – Marr's music is dense and circuitous, hitting changes off the beat, and Morrissey's melody shifting at every turn.

By 'Death At One's Elbow' the transformation of The Smiths was complete. Only two years ago this track would have been a pure pastiche of Sun Records rock 'n' roll. By *Strangeways* however, the trick didn't work any more, and the song is probably the weakest point on the album. Compare this song to 'Last Night I Dreamt...' or 'Death Of A Disco Dancer' – it's a joke that isn't funny any more, and these two songs show where The Smiths were heading by the time their day was run. 'Death At One's Elbow' was a redundant piece of work. And, as an album band, their day was running out fast. The gentle, entrancing 'I Won't Share You' – plucked on a studio autoharp, Johnny pressing down the keys to damp the strings into pre-defined chords – was the last song on the last Smiths album proper. And of course, its lyrical content is loaded with irony and metaphor and could be a dozen different things to a dozen different people, but the key element was that this intriguing new album ended on a note of almost adolescent adoration... something that The Smiths had spent five years defining.

The critics reaction was mixed. For some observers it was a dismal album, the sound of a band in disarray. For others it was better than *The Queen Is Dead*. *I-D* magazine described the album as "as good as *The Queen Is Dead,* but probably not better." *NME* referenced Johnny's "beatific melodies" as establishing The Smiths' final greatness, and noted that – whoever Johnny and Morrissey chose to work with in the future – theirs was perhaps "a once-in-a-lifetime partnership." *Rolling Stone* picked out some of Johnny's "emotional highlights" from the album, observing that the band were right to pack up rather than continue without him, while among the negative reactions, for Suzan Cohen in *Star Hits* this was "not exactly the way I [want] to remember them."

As the year came to an end, so The Smiths' discography of original releases began to run out, as singles were released from *Strangeways.* In October 'I Started Something I Couldn't Finish/Pretty Girls Make Graves' reached a disappointing number twenty-three on the singles chart, while in December 'Last Night I Dreamt That Somebody Loved Me' coupled with the Elvis-inspired 'Rusholme Ruffians' just scraped into the singles chart at number thirty. For the ultimate singles band it was a disappointing climax to the year, cheered by Melvyn Bragg's *South Bank Show* TV special on The Smiths, perhaps a more fitting farewell.

Johnny Rogan wrote an article for *Record Collector* magazine suggesting that the joining together of Morrissey and Marr was "a unity of opposites." It has become easy to distinguish between the articulate, witty, controversial front-man Morrissey and his musician partner. Johnny the Keef-clone party boy with a penchant for disco seems entirely at odds with his more literary partner. In fact, Morrissey and Johnny are much more alike than the media myth and polarised images suggest. To a degree there was a deliberate distancing of their roles in the band. Grant Showbiz worked with them almost constantly during the life of The Smiths. "In some respects they are much closer than people see them," Grant confirmed to this author. He feels that they were easily and quickly characterised by the press, and as a result there was an easy role for each of them to fall into. Johnny too has indicated that it was the similarities, not the differences, that bonded the song-writing pair. "[When we met] he knew we were different in the way we expressed ourselves," said Johnny recently. "But the most important thing to him was the most important thing to me spiritually. You can't be that close with someone for that length of time... without having the ultimate connection." Living up to the images that developed through interviews and under the public's gaze, each seemed to fit the expected role as it made the band easier to 'read.' Showbiz sums the dichotomy up thus: "Morrissey's like 'I'll be more elaborate and I'll be more embroidered,' and Johnny's like 'Well, I'll be less elaborate [then], and less embroidered than you ever said I am.'"

Because Morrissey wrote the lyrics, it was his interest in literature, theatre and film that was profiled in the press, while Johnny's most obvious asset is his practical, musical input. Oscar Wilde and Keith Richards. But it is vital not to forget that Johnny is a highly intelligent, literary-inclined man with an interest in esoteric literatures and cultures too. Over the years, his declared interest in Native American culture, the writings of Eastern mystics, his constant assimilation of cultural values and mores betrays a man as articulate in the languages of the higher arts as his partner. Similar misrepresentation have smudged the reality of dozens of bands over the years. Socialite Mick Jagger, cricket buff and friend of royalty, and Keith the heroin-addicted, Jack Daniels-quaffing survivor ignores Keith Richards' highly articulate and well-spoken actual self. The image of acerbic John the wit, and Macca the thumbs-up tunesmith, ignores the fact that while Lennon was sat at home watching *Meet The Wife* and putting on weight, it was McCartney who was trawling the London theatres for inspiration, compiling tape loops and listening to Stockhausen. Morrissey and Marr was a successful creative partnership of equals because they were in so many ways very much alike. Both men are softly-spoken, articulate and intelligent book lovers, fans of inspiring pop, each with a fabulous sense of humour and fun. It was only in the media that their characters were drawn so differently. Anyone making the mistake of seeing The Smiths as the product of literary Morrissey and artisan craftsman Marr, beware. Johnny Marr is, as Grant Showbiz puts it, "a sharp cookie!"

Johnny Marr retained great memories of The Smiths, and like all four band members, remained very much a fan of the band that he had created. Asked what his fondest memories were, Johnny remembered the recording sessions, the first exciting thrill of success, and the never-diminishing humour that the band always enjoyed. While his own memories of the group were clouded by his reasons for leaving, Johnny has never had anything other than great things to say about the band itself or its output. It's touching to note again that – despite all – the four biggest fans of The Smiths have always remained Johnny Marr, Morrissey, Andy Rourke and Mike Joyce. They were truly a wonderful thing.

From bedsit strummer, to world-ranked superstar, Johnny Marr was free of The Smiths, and ready to go out and engage the world on his own. The whole world seemed to want him.

★

Constantly asked to look over his shoulder, Johnny threw himself immediately forwards into his work as a jobbing guitar player. Distracting attention away from *Strangeways,* September had also seen the first fruits of Johnny's work on Bryan Ferry's album *Bete Noir* when the single 'The Right Stuff' was released. Based on the Smiths instrumental, 'Money Changes Everything', it was born of studio trickery when Johnny re-learned a riff played backwards on his four-track cassette recorder. With Ferry's lyrics added to create a totally new song, the repeated influence of Bo Diddley in Johnny's work is heard again.

"Someone at Warners thought it would be a good idea for me to work with Johnny," said Ferry. "[They] sent me a cassette of some of his music, and I liked it very much." Ferry liked Marr very much too. "When I met him we got on very well," said Bryan. From the north of England himself, albeit the other side of the Pennines, Ferry found Johnny lively and genuine. "There's a kind of Northern honesty about the cut of his jib, which I liked very much," he said.

"That song is very much phonetic and rhythmic," Johnny reflects. "The fact that Bryan didn't write anything radical didn't worry me because phonetically he got it right, and with those really high backing vocals it sounded perfect." With Andy Newmark, late of Sly Stone's band on drums, Ferry's band nailed the track to Johnny's eternal delight. The album was a critical and commercial success on its release in November. *Melody Maker's* Chris Roberts chastised Ferry for roping in "some dickhead indie guitarist" as a cynical move to endear himself to a younger audience than his traditional one, but the comment was entirely in keeping with the tongue-in-cheek article that in fact praised the album highly as "the sophistry of old-style 'romantic bluff.'" Despite Johnny's typically in-and-out, job-done role, the album was actually a year and a half in the making, though of course Johnny's contribution lasted nowhere near as long. Typically enthused by whatever he has worked on since The Smiths, Johnny thoroughly enjoyed the experience and the vibe of being in Ferry's band, which he joined in the USA for an appearance on *Saturday Night Live.* As with Marr's work with Talking Heads, yet to be released, the guitarist had been brought in to add something new to a project that Ferry was carrying around the studios of the world as he tried to refine new ideas and develop new moods for his own work.

If the jingle-jangle moaning of The Smiths was to be put to bed, then there was – as always – more work to be done. Fulfilling what might have been a lifelong ambition – he had loved the early guitar sound of James Honeyman-Scott and had used their guitar lines as warm-up routines for years – Johnny Marr joined The Pretenders. Gun-slinging band-hopping is nothing new – Mick Ronson's joining Mott The Hoople and Robert Smith's temporary membership of Siouxsie And The Banshees are just two examples of guitarists filling a necessary slot in an established band when needs must. Both Johnny and The Pretenders were at the time managed by Ken Friedman, and joining Chrissie Hynde's band gave Marr a professional continuity, and while his presence helped the Pretenders out on tour it also gave him an immediate working relationship with a profoundly talented performer and writer in Hynde herself, who became a life-long friend. Better working than not – better a US tour with a top band than moping around South Manchester bemoaning the demise of his own.

Johnny looked back on his relationship with Chrissie Hynde years later. "One of the things that people don't know..." he said of his time in the band, "[was] that my part in The Pretenders is ten per cent about the band and ninety per cent about my relationship to that woman." Battered by the press and by the experience of leaving The Smiths, Johnny was brought down to earth with a bump when he opened up to Chrissie. "I'm going 'Oh things are tough... Oh I left my band,' and her vibe was 'Well, two of my fucking band died... and I don't even really know who your band are. Let's go see some life.'" It was exactly what Johnny needed to help him get back out in the world.

The only published fruit of Johnny's time with The Pretenders is his appearance on their single 'Windows Of The World', released in April of 1989. With Hynde's vocal as characteristic as any in rock, and the 'Pretenders sound' certainly as distinctive as The Smiths', it's no surprise that the track sounds far more 'Pretenders' than 'Johnny,' but beautifully arranged and as emotionally compelling as can be.

*

As the dust settled on his independent status in 1988, Morrissey was quickly out of the traps with his first solo single 'Suedehead'. With fellow Mancunian Vinni Reilly on board, and Stephen Street

Young and beautiful: The Smiths in 1983. *Paul Slattery / Retna UK*

Johnny and Sandie, 1984. *Paul Slattery / Retna UK*

One man and his guitar. *Paul Slattery / Retna UK*

Johnny with Chrissie at the Nelson Mandela benefit, Wembley 1988. *Richard Young / Rex Features*

The Right Stuff – Johnr... ...an chill out. *Andre Csillag / Rex Features*

Proving that two heads are better than one? Electronic, 1991. *Steve Double / Retna UK*

'Look out mate – we're on the stairs!' Johnny and Liam, the *Q awards,* 1996. *Scarlet Page / Retna UK*

'Love Will Tear Us Apart' Johnny and Morrissey in 1984. *Sipa Press / Rex Features*

The Write Stuff – Matt Johnson in 1999. *ITV / Rex Features*

Dedicated follower of fashion. Marr in 2003. *Tibor Bozi / Retna UK*

Father and son – Johnny and Bert Jansch at Patti Smith's 2005 Meltdown. *Nickie Divine / Retna UK*

The Healers, 2003: Johnny, Alonza and Zak in NYC. *David Atlas / Retna Ltd*

Johnny and Andy at the Manchester v Cancer gig, 2006. *Peter Doherty / Retna UK*

'Healing Hands' – Johnny with childhood hero Lenny Kaye, Meltdown 2005. *Ilpo Musto / Rex Features*

back in the fold, the disc was a triumph, with 'Hairdresser On Fire' soon established as a firm fan favourite too. Ironically, given the Smiths' reputation as a singles band, the track confidently sauntered into the UK top five, and Morrissey's status as a solo artist was established in a trice. *Viva Hate,* his first solo album, received similarly gushing plaudits. "Still the bees knees," said *NME,* while for *Melody Maker* it was a great album by "our last star." Nearly twenty years on, with *Ringleader Of The Tormentors,* Morrissey was still being referenced as such.

Johnny was by no means adrift himself. He exited The Smiths a better guitar player than when he started the band. After learning the ropes from John Porter, Johnny's experience as a producer was extensive and his understanding of studio and recording techniques equally so. Regularly listed in the end of year polls as 'Best Composer' Johnny's reputation as a writer was second to none, and with an increasing CV of contributions to other people's records under his belt, there was a list of people with whom he was either going to work, had worked already, or was rumoured to be working with. His name would open any studio door in the world.

On a personal level, Marr had the mettle to take advantage of these strengths. With his background hustling around the Manchester clothing scene, he had clearly learned a tough business sense that put him in good stead when it came to managing anything. Still married to Angela, he had the stability of a long-term relationship to fall back on, and the support of someone who had known him from the days before his name was famous. He had managed all this, helped friends through addiction and sorted himself out of a potentially worrying situation with alcohol too. The Johnny Marr who kicked off 1988 with a contribution to the Dennis Hopper movie *Colours* [although he wasn't happy with the way it had worked out], had one hell of a career behind him already, and he was still only twenty-five-years old.

Marr's first full year as an ex-Smith allowed him the freedom to work in any field he chose to wander, yet the shadow of his erstwhile band continued to fall across his working life. For a while, Johnny considered moving to Los Angeles or New York to escape the pressure of people in Manchester continuing to harass him for leaving The Smiths, but decided to move back to his home town permanently, where true friends and family were only minutes away. As well as personal connections, when Johnny looked around the world for the most happening place in terms of music, it was Manchester that stood head and shoulders above the rest.

Away from the day-to-day grind of co-managing the business of The Smiths, Marr also soon found he enjoyed a greater sense of security in working as a contributor on other people's projects. If The Smiths had been 'a matter of life and death' then better to concentrate on the former. "I'm happier," he said, with typical understated modesty, "now that I know where the rent is coming from."

Manchester itself was – largely down to the shadow that The Smiths had cast over the city – continuing its rebirth as the UK's premier rock city. Coming home, this was another reason for Johnny to get involved again in Manchester life. From a distance it seemed to Johnny that – wherever he looked in the world – the best music, the most inspirational stuff, was once again coming from Manchester. The city was alive again, without his band having to shine all the lights at once. Shaun Ryder's Happy Mondays' debut LP *Squirrel and G-Man Twenty Four Hour Party People Plastic Face Carnt Smile (White Out)* had been released in 1987, and their follow-up EP *Madchester Rave On* established not only the city's profile in blending rock and dance rhythms but also gave a name to the Madchester phenomenon. Factory Records released *Bummed,* their critically acclaimed second album in 1988, and by their third – *Pills And Thrills And Bellyaches* – Madchester was a firmly established cultural concept. Alongside The Mondays came The Stone Roses, whose first Silvertone album was released in 1988. An overnight success – that typically took five years to happen – The Roses had formed around the same time as The Smiths, but although they had a near-guitar-legend of their own in John Squire, it took them much longer to establish a public face. In comparison with The Smiths, these two Manchester bands were notorious: Ryder's much-publicised drug intake made for a public profile based more upon his ability to make headlines than his undoubted ability to make great records, while The Roses' various tiffs with record companies meant that there were six long years between the releases of their first and second albums.

Through the summer, Johnny made occasional trips to join New Order in the studio as they were recording their album *Technique,* cementing the friendship with Bernard Sumner that would evolve into Electronic. Ironically, it was through the Madchester scene that the true revolution in the singles chart that The Smiths had wanted to bring about actually happened. What Morrissey and Marr had wanted to do – to completely revitalise the world of the seven-inch single – came about as the phenomenon of house music seeped into clubs like The Hacienda. While the music of Detroit and Chicago slowly gained credence, and while DJ-ing became as much a celebrity activity as being in a group, it was the guitar bands like The Mondays and Roses who dipped into the cultural meld and charged their more traditional rock with an immediate and contemporary dance consciousness. When house morphed into acid house, it became a national phenomenon, and the E-scene was emblazoned across the front pages of the tabloids.

Madchester and 'baggy' deflected attention away from the legend of The Smiths and towards a new hierarchy of Manchester bands, albeit most of them heavily influenced by them. Marr was able to begin rediscovering himself, finding out what made 'Johnny Marr' happy instead of having to keep the fan-base of his former band content. Within the band Johnny had often been uncomfortable in the role of 'talking head'. As Johnny's sense of dislocation increased, he had felt able to give interviews only when he felt 'up' and it had become harder and harder to find opportunities where he felt he could actually be himself. Now, with the attention of the world focused on other Mancunian mega-stars, Johnny could quietly rebuild his sense of his own self.

One brief project was to provide the riff that acted as theme tune to the short-lived TV music show *APB*. To great critical reviews, in March the fruits of Johnny's work with Talking Heads was released. The Heads were one of the first American immediate post-punk, CBGB bands to develop a world-wide profile, due largely to their sparse instrumentation and the lyrical intrigue of nervy front man David Byrne, whose performance was an art form in itself. Enlivened by the input of Brian Eno, Talking Heads had been one of the most influential bands in the world for a decade, but as Byrne became more involved in extra-curricular work outside of the band, the sands were running out for the group. *Naked* proved to be their last studio album, and though he thoroughly enjoyed the sessions, Marr himself felt that the atmosphere within the band was "slightly odd," and perhaps their closing moments as a recording unit were hard for an outsider to penetrate.

'The Heads' themselves were delighted with Johnny's input to the album. He was brought onto the project by the album's producer Steve Lillywhite, initially to augment 'Ruby Dear', the Bo Diddley rhythm of which cried out for Johnny Marr. Johnny's input was, in fact, included on four of the released tracks. The album was one of the later-Heads' strongest, augmented by anything up to three or four extra musicians at any given time. To get away from New York, the band decamped to Paris, where day-long sessions at Studio Davout were devoted to each individual track, with melodies and lyrics to be added in New York once the tracks were down.

"What was rather amusing to us," remembers Heads' drummer Chris Frantz "was that Johnny came with a giant flight case of guitars, and a famous guitar tech that we had met before at Compass Point Studios in the Bahamas when he was working with The Rolling Stones. This guitar tech was an old pro who regaled us with stories about 'Keith' and 'Eric', 'Jimmy' and 'Pete.' Clearly Johnny had reached the big time." Chris recalls.

The first track on which Marr worked was '(Nothing But) Flowers', knocked off at lightening speed while waiting for the band to settle down for the recording of the second track 'Ruby Dear'. Johnny's twelve-string is evident throughout the middle section of the song, as well as in the distinctive introduction. '(Nothing But) Flowers' typified much of the collection, and Chris Frantz remembers that twelve-string contribution as his favourite piece of Johnny's. The track was a softer song from a band very much looking for more earthen textures than the earlier, clipped industrial sound of their previous albums. As mentioned, 'Ruby Dear' was a Bo Diddley-based track on which Johnny's trademark guitar is evident throughout the song. On 'Mommy Daddy You and I' Marr provided 'Twang Bar Guitar', giving the song a unique, antique flavour that matched the nostalgic lyric. As well as Johnny, Talking Heads had also invited Kirsty MacColl onto the album, which was produced by her husband Steve Lillywhite, and on '(Nothing But) Flowers' Marr and MacColl appeared together again. 'Cool Water', Johnny's fourth and final contribution to the album, is a sombre, atmospheric number, driven again by riffing guitars but bearing an Eastern European flavour and more than a hint of Eighties-era King Crimson in its minor key urgency. Byrne encouraged Johnny's detuned drone that characterises the song, played without traditional fingering or notation, a truly experimental bit of improvisation.

Johnny's contribution to *Naked* was brief but meaningful, his work on the four tracks that made the finished album considerable. David Byrne told this author the experience was very fruitful and enjoyable. "It was one or two days at most," he recalled. "He was so fast in the studio." Frantz remembered Johnny's cool demeanour and appearance. "At the time Johnny was wearing a little Greek fisherman's cap and loads of jewellery, certainly more than (Heads' bassist and Frantz's wife) Tina. He was cute and very chipper." Adaptable, musically articulate, understanding what was required and providing it with the minimum of fuss – Johnny's brief standing as a Talking Head was enjoyable all round. "It was a blur," remembers Byrne. "A good blur!"

Morrissey's classic summer single 'Every Day Is Like Sunday' was culled from *Viva Hate*, a fabulous record that painted a romantic picture of a lost northern seaside town against an orchestrally-weighted band that continued to establish his solo work. In the meantime, Steve Lillywhite and Kirsty MacColl came to feature large over the next few months in Johnny's life. While Kirsty had of course featured on 'Ask', and Lillywhite been brought in by Morrissey to work on that track, she and Marr had become good friends since the sessions with Billy Bragg. Kirsty's CV stretched back way before The Smiths. Famously the daughter of folk legend Ewan MacColl, who had left the family home before she was born, Kirsty's career owed as much to Beach Boys and Kinks influences as to the earthen tones of her Salford-born father. In fact, MacColl was almost a mini-Smiths herself. Her clear love of harmony, her succinct, intelligent and crafted lyrics laced with pathos and humour, musical tracks unadorned by musical diarrhoea but, like her lyrics, to the point and punchy, her work had much in common with Johnny's already. Writing her own songs since the age of seventeen, Kirsty's credits went back to late Seventies punk bands like The Addix ("I was just the token boiler on backing vocals," she said in 1981, with her typical, ironic, charming modesty). In 1981 she skirted the dangerous waters of one-hit-wonderdom with 'There's A Guy Works Down The Chip Shop Swears He's Elvis', and released her debut album *Desperate Characters,* returning with a hit for Tracey Ullman on 'They Don't Know', on which Kirsty's backing vocals were the clearest sound on the single. By 1988 she was working on singles and tracks that would lead to *Kite*, her first solo album for seven years, which was released the following year. "I didn't write anything for a couple of years when I was having kids," she said in 1989. "It took a long time to start up again." Increasingly free of what she admitted was writer's block, Kirsty produced a fantastic batch of songs for the assembled troupe of musicians to work upon. Typically generous, describing Johnny as "very energetic, a very 'up' person to be around," Kirsty was happy to name-check Johnny as one of the main reasons why she came out of her writer's block and got back into the studio. "He suggested 'You Just Haven't Earned It Yet Baby'... saying 'Why aren't you doing anything? Get off your arse!'"

It was a sparkling album, comprising Kirsty's best, succinct song-writing, crisp production from Steve Lillywhite and extensive contributions from Johnny, who co-wrote two of the songs, 'The End Of A Perfect Day' and 'You And Me Baby'. The process brought out of Johnny what he describes as his "romantic melodic" thing, that of absolute love that engulfs the writing of certain songs. "When Kirsty asked me to write for her," he remembers, "she said 'I want one of those songs that make you feel happy and sad at the same time'... it can be almost upsetting when I make records [like that], that mixture of melancholia and vibrancy." Kirsty was asked by the press about her 'replacing' Morrissey as Johnny's wordsmith. "I don't think I have," she told *Melody Maker* in 1989. Citing Morrissey as her favourite lyricist since Ray Davies, she added "I think it would be terribly pretentious of me to think that." She did however, reference The Smiths' influence on a regular basis. "In my songs," she told *Cut* magazine in 1989, "I try to put things succinctly and make them not too depressing. Wit is very important... what seems like the end of the world today might not be so tomorrow." As an interviewee, Kirsty MacColl had few equals.

Inspired by her recent success with The Pogues over the Christmas of 1987 on the timeless 'Fairy Tale Of New York', the album also saw Pretenders/Average White Band guitarist Robbie McIntosh, Simple Mind's Mel Gaynor and The The drummer David Palmer on board alongside Johnny. They were, in Kirsty's own words, "people whose work I've always admired... The people I chose I'd either worked with before or knew the work they'd done for others." Fresh as a daisy, the album is led, of course, by Kirsty's impeccable vocal, but is essentially a guitar, bass and drums album, acoustic and discretely electric in its guitar sound. Sessions jumped between Townhouse and Ealing studios, and when the musical tracks were completed, Kirsty added finished vocals later. On 'Mother's Ruin', Johnny's triplets, trademark arpeggios and expanded chords lend an emotional weight to a touching song, the chorus of which could have come from Morrissey as much as MacColl. On the lovely cover of The Kinks' 'Days', which took Kirsty back into the UK Top Twenty singles chart, Johnny is equally in evidence, colouring the chord changes with articulate picking and strumming throughout. 'No Victims' and 'Tread Lightly' had more of a Smiths feel, particular the latter, and Johnny's guitar annotations keep the rockabilly pace of the song up-tempo beneath MacColl's multi-tracked vocals. 'What Do Pretty Girls Do?' sounded like a Morrissey song too, at least in its title, but melodically, harmonically and lyrically the song is pure Kirsty.

The lilting, Beatle-like swagger of 'The End Of A Perfect Day' has trademark Johnny Marr fingerprints all over it: driven almost exclusively by fat, repeated guitar lines that carry the verses through punching accents from the cymbals, the lack of a clear chorus but the inevitable swirl around to a repeated vocal motif makes it a fine piece. At the end of a perfect album, Johnny's second co-write is beautifully arranged around his understated, cyclical chord structure, the guitar chorused and the vocals perfectly intimate and open-voiced. For the song, 'You And Me Baby', Kirsty layered a choir of her own vocal behind a melody that sits exquisitely on the top line of Marr's picking, while Fiachra Trench's string arrangement sets the whole piece alight in its closing bars. The song had been written at Johnny's home, crouched on his knees in the hallway, trying at once to both nail the song and not wake his new baby. "I was feeling kind of sad," he remembers, "and [Kirsty] captured the spirit of that very closely." Of the same song, Kirsty spoke of wanting to grace the track with lots of space and gaps using real strings to beautiful effect. The piece was a divine ending to a beautiful and perennially popular album, loved nearly twenty years later by Kirsty MacColl fans old and new.

Lillywhite's production values echoed Johnny's in many ways, often multi-layering guitars across a track, and building up Kirsty's harmonised vocal to the same degree that the Smiths' guitarist had developed with his own sound. Johnny would work on Kirsty's follow-up album *Electric Landlady*, but *Kite* remains probably her most perfect work. Across her all-too short career she rarely recorded a bad track. She wrote beautifully, sang even more so, and did the whole thing – interviews included – with an intelligence, grace and humour that is increasingly rare in post-Kirsty pop singers. Of all the rock 'n' roll deaths over the years – some tragic, some preposterous, some pathetic – Kirsty's pointless death in the winter of 2000 robbed the world of a beautiful and creative woman. RIP Kirsty.

★

The Smiths returned in September when Rough Trade put out their last 'original' Smiths album, the live release *Rank*. The collection was another number two in the charts, confirming the affection still held for the band a year after its demise. *Rank* was a live album taped at the National Ballroom in Kilburn in the autumn of 1986, a concert which captured the dual-guitar version of the band with Craig Gannon on stage with Marr. Johnny approved the album's release, which included a live version of Johnny's instrumental 'The Draize Train'. A month later the Strange Fruit label issued *The Peel Sessions,* while before Christmas twelve-inch versions of 'Barbarism Begins At Home' and 'The Headmaster Ritual' completed another chapter in the release schedule of the band.

Johnny might have appeared to be getting free of his past, but The Smiths still haunted him. "I felt hollow at that time," recalls Johnny. "The ugly situation with The Smiths split meant that trying to produce work after that was really difficult, almost unbearable." "I had to grow up a little bit, and develop a really thick skin," said Marr. While the hollowness prevailed, not only did Johnny find that writing was difficult, but he began to lose interest in even listening to music – a much more serious symptom. "What was scary was that I didn't want to listen to records, and to be robbed of that is much, much worse than being robbed of the impulse to write," said Marr.

Rumours began to circulate that Johnny was putting together a new band. Heat – almost a precursor of Marr's future band The Healers – would involve former Julian Cope bass player James Eller and ABC drummer Dave Palmer. In fact, it turned out to be a 'nearly' band. It was a natural progression for Johnny however, that in the autumn he became part of another project, and stayed within its confines for as long as he had been associated with The Smiths.

The The, however, was a very different concept. For starters, there was no band as such. While teenage founder Matt Johnson had started The The off as a band concept, by the time of his debut album The The was in essence only Johnson plus guests. The format of The The that Johnny was involved with was, however, the most traditional band line-up that the band enjoyed, touring and recording as a working unit.

The relationship between Johnson and Marr went back to that drizzly October night in 1981 when the pair were introduced, and the two had remained close friends still. From day one they had harboured a desire to work together. As mentioned, in 1983 the pair had been together while Johnson was writing and preparing the album *Soul Mining* in his flat near Arsenal's football stadium in Highbury, London. By the time Johnny came to work with him properly he was aware of Matt's writing methods and recording processes, his use of guesting artists, and his working methods with studio staff and producers. This was not a traditional band experience, as Johnny had always known it – more of a research process based upon superb song-writing: Johnson would write everything, play much of the instrumentation, handle a lot of the relevant programming and engineering, and bring in collaborators where needed. There were parallels with The Smiths to some degree – the work to date had been a mixture of the melancholic and the exuberant, often with those two emotions mixed within one song. But The The's output to date had been a more varied affair, at times punching with soul, at other glacial and distracted. It was a refined concept, one of the most critically acclaimed 'bands' of the era.

Mind Bomb would be released the following year as the result of their first official collaboration, though collaboration only to a degree. By the time Johnny was involved – the pair were by now sharing management, and there was a professional as well as personal logic to their working together – much of the song-writing had been completed. The album developed as a blend of finished pieces and demos that Matt wanted to develop within a group context, and this was largely how the piece progressed. With issues in his personal life defining the trajectory that the album would take – the break-up and re-building of a close relationship coloured Johnson's spiritual search at the time – the album became a roaring indictment of organised religion. By his own confession, Johnson was "pretty whacked out" and "into some very interesting states of mind" at the time. He was fasting, or living on very proscribing diets, drinking copious quantities of magic mushroom tea and meditating extensively. Matt was ready for Marr's input. "I wouldn't eat for days," said Johnson. "And then I'd do loads of magic mushrooms. I tried all sorts of things which I don't need to detail... I was putting myself through so much I lost it and began to hear voices."

The initial impetus to move away from the material on the hugely successful and previous The The album *Infected* came from the ubiquitous Billy Bragg, whom Johnson had met in Australia. Billy encouraged Matt to join in the activities of the Red Wedge campaign, and Johnson enjoyed the resulting shows to such a degree that he decided that the next The The album would be made by a more traditionally-structured band.

Johnny and Matt met up in Johnson's recently acquired East London home and studio, part of a converted department store. "We sat up talking till the sun came up," Johnson said in conversation with Johnny in 2002, "[and] lost all sense of time." Without even being aware of the existing friendship between the three, once Matt had Johnny on board he called James Eller and Dave Palmer, and they joined the band for the album that was to follow. Johnny was still working with Chrissie Hynde, and so an insane routine was established where he would work with Chrissie until the early hours of the morning and then load all his gear into the car and drive across London to Matt's studio. "I'd get there," Johnny remembered, "and we'd take loads of mushrooms and ecstasy. It was the most intense psychological and philosophical experiment."

The first session was particularly memorable. Due to arrive at noon, Johnny had spent the previous night on ecstasy, and – after what he called "a real psychedelic night" – he turned up two hours late "looking like one of the Thunderbirds with his strings cut." Johnny picked up on Johnson's own tenseness as they started work on 'The Beat(en) Generation', but it just wasn't happening. "I turned to Matt," Marr recalls, "and said 'Look – I'll be honest with you: I took a load of E for the last three nights and I'm feeling a bit wobbly." Honesty has never been one of Johnny's problems… While such an admission might have finished a Smiths session there and then, Johnson's response was to encourage the potential of the situation rather than act against it. "Matt looked at me," says Johnny, "and with great production acumen said 'Well, we'd better get some more then hadn't we!'" So the pair wore out their engineers and produced their masterwork against the odds.

Mind Bomb's was a perfect line-up, completing the traditional four-piece and co-incidentally bringing together the band that might have become Heat. Johnny was to describe this incarnation of The The "as much of a band as any band I've ever been in", and the entire process of putting the album together was both relaxing and intense. The band itself was a perfectly formed group, under Johnson's directing eye. Nor were the foursome alone in the recording process; some seventeen performers appeared on the album in addition to a choir and the Astarti string section. Included in the cast were bass supremo Danny Thompson and Sinead O'Connor, who sang beautifully on 'Kingdom of Rain'.

'Good Morning Beautiful' was one of the band's favourite pieces, based upon field recordings of Islamic voices in Indonesia brought to the project by Johnson's girlfriend. With a glance towards David Bowie's *Station To Station* in its opening, the piece uses samples in quite a different way to Byrne and Eno's use of similar sounds on *My Life In The Bush Of Ghosts*. Where they used samples as the central tenet of the song, The The use them as colourings, illustrations to the musical tracks, and the effect is very pleasing. Directing the piece to the band, Johnson instructed Johnny to make his contribution sound "like Jesus meeting the Devil.""I was thinking... 'Right – that's a new one!'" said Johnny afterwards.

'Armageddon Days' had one of the strongest lyrics on the album, a brave piece augmented by a full choir, inspired by the current worsening issues between the Islamic world and the West. "People have forgotten how serious that whole situation was," Johnson was to comment later in reference to the Salman Rushdie affair that also went off over the coming months. "'Armageddon' started to pick up radio play, and at least one station got a phone call from someone... basically, 'don't play this, or else.'" Had it been released as a single, the opening few bars would have been familiar to anyone who remembered Sweet, the glam rock band whose 'Ballroom Blitz' was a huge hit in the early Seventies. It was clear however, that the wrath of Matt was levelled not at God but at organised religion *per se* – divinity is fine, but how we use it for our own means is the most divisive flaw in mankind's make-up. Track three, 'The Violence Of Truth', featured Mark Feltham on harmonica (though the harmonica on 'Beyond Love' *was* Johnny), a faux–glam riff from Johnny electrifying the track that demonstrated Marr's continuous search for a feel or vibe. "The only way I could get that sound," says Johnny, "was to pick the most horrible guitar I had, tape up the top four strings and just whack the bottom ones. It turned out almost like glam sax!"

'Kingdom Of Rain' contains the images of blood and rain that appear throughout the album, and Sinead's duet with Johnson as passionate as one would expect. Although O'Connor had had hits already, it was to be another nine months before she moved the whole world with own version of Prince's 'Nothing Compares 2 U'.

'The Beat(en) Generation' was named after a painting by Johnson's brother Andy, a warning shot fired across the bows of a generation of youngsters so hip that they had lost the connection with the real issues of their lives. Matt described it as a message for people who were living "all icing and no cake." The song has an engaging immediacy, reflecting the fact that Johnson wrote it from start to finish in two hours. The jaunty, country feel of Johnny's 12-string Stratocaster and Mark Feltham's irresistible harmonica drew a lot of listeners to the album, and was Johnson's first, deliberate attempt to do just that – to bring an audience into an album via a hit single. "I realised that I had been making life difficult for myself," Matt told *Alternative Press*. "Commercially, I'd always made the wrong moves for all the right reasons… In retrospect I couldn't have done it any other way." If the newly-found singles audience was expecting an album filled with rockabilly Marr, then they had not listened closely to the lyric – deeper waters awaited the listener to *Mind Bomb* in the politically-charged world order.

'August & September' was lifted wholesale from Johnson's personal diary, written on an island in the Mediterranean, a passionate love song of break-up and despair. 'Gravitate To Me', another single off the album, was the penultimate track, with more bluesy harmonica, this time set above Johnny's Chic-style guitar. "Beyond Love' was Johnson's personal favourite from the album. "It has some of the strongest lyrics I've written," Matt was to tell Martin Roach, also in *The Right To Imagination And Madness*, and the images of drops of blood and semen struck a haunting chord with many listeners too.

In The The, Johnny found a new soul-mate. While he was not necessarily looking for replacements for Morrissey, Rourke and Joyce, he clearly needed some grounded process to work on, and in Johnson he found not only a friend but a polished and articulate song-writer who was also a guitar player whose work suited his own playing, like jigsaw pieces fitting together. At the end of the sessions, Johnny – ever generous with his guitars – presented his sunburst 12-string Strat to Matt as a present.

Johnson was the only player who Johnny could consider working with at the time, noting cryptically that "I don't fit well with other guitarists." *Mind Bomb* was work that he felt he could "embellish and feel very comfortable with," and when the album was finally mixed at Air Studios off Oxford Street, there was a palpable feeling that The The had produced something unique and brave, a charged album that addressed some heavy and unpopular issues. Consequently the critical response was mixed. As it has been often for Billy Bragg, commentators who don't like his overtly political stance choose to ignore the searing and heart-wrenching love songs that he has produced, and so with *Mind Bomb* – reviewers took against its political and religious content and failed to record some of the warmer songs on an album that Johnny was very proud of. Both Marr and Johnson felt that there was a critical backlash because of who they were, not because of the content of the album. "A lot of people had it in for [Johnny]," Matt told Heather Bell, "and [for] me – for getting a bit cocky. So we just battened down the hatches."

In fact, *Mind Bomb* has aged particularly well, and remains a remarkably warm, melodic, passionate and eloquent piece of work. Musically it is varied, beautifully arranged and played with a precision and care only evident in works that are labours of love. Lyrically it is articulate and fervent, and delivered with evident passion. One reviewer likened it to TS Eliot's 'The Waste Land'. Johnson himself looked back on the album with mixed feelings. "I was obviously taking myself too seriously, and probably got what was coming to me," he says. "But in my defence I was trying to bring something new to the songs with the angle I took on religion." The album was, Matt admitted, ahead of its time. "If it had been Ice T doing that in 1991 everyone would have considered it a revelation," he said, concluding that – probably encapsulating the response to both him and Johnny – "Britain loves its people to be as humble as possible!"

CHAPTER SEVEN

Getting Away With It

19 89 saw The Stone Roses finally hit the big time, with their eponymous debut album. The Stone Roses was quickly established as an indie two-fingered classic, a new band sending post cards from Manchester with love. By the end of the year, the Roses were filling London's Alexandra Palace with 7,500 punters. After The Smiths and before Oasis, The Stone Roses were the guitar's saving grace and the precursors of the next ten years of real dance music in the UK. At the same time, New Order presented Technique. One of Morrissey's greatest solo singles, 'The Last Of The Famous International Playboys' continued his interest in cultural icons of the Sixties as his gaze turned to the Kray Twins and the London underworld. 'The Last Of The Famous International Playboys' so impressed Johnny (and the record-buying public, who took it to within one place of the top five) that, according to Johnny Rogan in The Severed Alliance, he sent Morrissey a congratulatory postcard.

Neil Young, a long-time hero for Johnny, released his hugely influential 'Rockin' In The Free World', beating the hell out of the guitar that had influenced Johnny so much in his early years. In March the first single from *Mind Bomb* was released. While 'The Beat(en) Generation' was a huge success, it was not the first choice of single, which initially was slated as 'Armageddon Days'. As mentioned, just days before the release however, the *Satanic Verses* affair kicked off, the political, religious, ideological and moral fracas inspired by the novel by Salman Rushdie, and the release was canned. While Rushdie was under sentence of fatwa, he was given a round-the-clock guard by security forces. Rumours abounded as to where Rushdie had sought refuge, and the story was a major feature in international news. Astonishingly, Johnny later claimed that Rushdie had been living in the apartment above him in London!

"I'd go and get the mail," Marr remembered in conversation with Matt Johnson later, "and I'd see all these letters for 'S Rushdie'... and I'd think 'Shit! – he's got to have a few words with his friends.'" While the pair apparently never met, when Oasis' Noel Gallagher was living in the same flat some time later, the post had still not been redirected. He was still receiving mail for a Mr S Rushdie.

It was a period of convoluted family ties for Johnny. In April, Chrissie Hynde's Pretenders released 'Windows On The World', at the same time as Morrissey released his own single 'Interesting Drug'. One of the singer's finest solo-single moments, this song featured Kirsty MacColl on backing vocals, and at the same time Kirsty was promoting her own album *Kite,* she had also covered the Smiths song 'You Just Haven't Earned It Yet Baby' as the B-side of her 12-inch version of the biting chart hit 'Free World', on which, of course, Johnny featured. Was there a conflict of interests for Kirsty, as she guested on one Smith's record, had another Smith appear on her own album, and covered a song written by the pair of them at the same time?

According to Kirsty there was no issue. She candidly explained to *Melody Maker* that both Morrissey and Johnny had contacted her independently and that both records were a 'natural progression' from her having worked previously with The Smiths on 'Ask'. On the subject of Morrissey and Marr possibly never working together again, Kirsty again pointed out that "I don't think it's really any of my business... but I think it would be a shame if they never wrote together again because the standard of their songs was so brilliant."

After *Mind Bomb* was released in May, Johnson decided to tour the album worldwide. In July 'Gravitate To Me' was released as a single. Johnny joined the tour, and the hundred shows around the globe were a resounding success, bringing in audiences beyond all expectations from twenty-two countries between the USA and Australia. For Johnson it was an affirmation that putting the band together had been the right decision for his own work at the time. For Johnny it was his favourite – and most extensive – touring experience to date. The tour concluded with three superb nights at London's Royal Albert Hall, which was filmed for video release as *The The Versus The World*. After the final date at Dublin's The Point in mid-July, Johnny returned to Manchester.

The The provided Johnny with a vehicle that carried him over a period of several years. In 1989 he tentatively began another such project, however, that would arguably become his most successful and would certainly rival The Smiths in terms of commercial, chart and – almost – critical success. Electronic was glibly labelled a 'supergroup' in some corners of the media: a former Smith, a member of New Order, and, though not a permanent member, a Pet Shop Boy, the threesome making a Cream for the Nineties. The blend was irresistible, though its genesis was low key. Initially Johnny and Bernard intended the project to, at best, produce "a white label twelve-inch and maybe an album," but – with typical understatement – Johnny admits that "things turned out okay."

The pair had met back when Sumner was producing Quando Quango, but they were also introduced by DJ Andrew Berry. "We knew each other," said Sumner, "but we didn't know each other that well." It was the former Hacienda hairdresser who suggested to Bernard that he get in touch with Johnny, and – tired of the stresses and strains of working in his own rehearsal studio alone – Sumner did contact him and ask Johnny if he fancied working together. "We started working weekends," remembered Johnny. "Really, really long writing sessions." As mentioned, these sessions ran concurrently with recording with The The, often on the same day.

For Bernard, Electronic was an opportunity to work outside of the strictures placed upon him by New Order. "I really needed a bit more freedom than I was getting," he recalls. "I felt that too many things I wanted to do were treading on people's feet. If I wanted to do a track, for instance, [that was] just me and a synthesizer, or me and an acoustic guitar, I couldn't do it in New Order because everybody's got to play their bit." While Bernard was looking for personal space, Johnny was looking also to find room to work for himself, away from collaborations. "It's an opportunity for me to work on other instruments," Marr was to say, "and pursue the ideas that I've only been able to explore in demos for other people really… and explore them more fully."

Electronic was a slow starter. "We were formed very much as an anti-group," said Johnny. Given their histories, there was a relief to simply be able to go away and make music for themselves. "[It] was almost like a refuge for the two of us to be still able to make music." It took the pair a long time to get to know one another's working methods and to gel personally. "Johnny had to get his head around the way I worked," said Bernard, "and I had to get my head around the way he worked, because Johnny is a very accomplished musician." Neither he nor New Order as a band had the level of sophistication that he found in Johnny's work. "[We] don't really know what we're doing – but we end up doing it!" said Bernard, but admitted that working with Johnny had made him a better musician himself.

If Electronic at times seemed overly serious, the humour within the band was evident from many of the interviews that Johnny or Bernard gave. In one of the funniest interviews on record, for a Canadian radio station, Johnny was asked who out of Chrissie Hynde, Matt Johnson, Beck or Morrissey, was the biggest diva. After a moment's pause he chose someone else instead. "Bernard Sumner," said Johnny with enthusiasm. "He's terrible. You're not allowed to make eye contact. The wrong kind of flowers in the dressing room send him into an all-day tizz. [He's always] talking about how he wrote 'Blue Monday' incessantly, when no-one really cares... or likes it!" Johnny's tongue was, of course, firmly in his cheek, but the immediate leap to cite Bernard as a diva was very entertaining. It also offered him the chance to dodge answering the original question with utmost professionalism! "I was a [young] guy," Johnny would say later, "living in a city that was just exploding with a new culture. I'd been waiting for my city to do that since punk, because I was too young for punk." The excitement around Manchester was tangible. "Suddenly the place was experiencing new music, new technology, new clubs, new drugs." As always for Johnny, the moment was the key thing – there was no career plan, it was simply this music at this moment in this town.

Electronic fused Bernard Sumner and Johnny's pop sensibilities and song-writing skills, Marr's structural proficiency with Sumner's programming ability, and – with Neil Tennant as part of the team – the gorgeous, rich voice of the Pet Shop Boys. Marr was keen to work with the Pet Shop Boys, and when Neil expressed interest in being involved with Electronic, Johnny jumped at the chance. As well as wanting to work with him, Johnny was also aware that to be involved with such an out-and-out pop act would shake up some of the Smiths community too. The Pet Shop Boy connection also brought a great sense of fun to the project too. The four guys got to know one another when Bernard and Johnny invited Tennant and Lowe to Manchester. "We got them down to The Hacienda within about five minutes of them getting there," remembered Bernard, "and they experienced the delights of the Manchester scene."

Johnny has analysed his work and working practices over the years and has come to the conclusion that each 'generation' of his career is a natural progression from the last. "The sort of person I was in The Smiths needed to write the songs that [he] did for *that* group," Marr observes... "I wanted to find my feet as a writer." The The expanded his musical vocabulary and consciousness further. By the time of Electronic, the work that Marr and Sumner produced was very much a representation of a particular scene and lifestyle that the pair shared. But it wasn't cosy. Working in Manchester, with The Hacienda still a priority for Sumner, put all kinds of things at risk. "That whole scene was a lot more complex than [just] a lot of people wearing flares," remembers Marr. "There was a lot of violence around, and guns. People were swallowing ecstasy and all that, but there were gangsters around, and violence." The scene came up against the media-heavy local Chief of Police, James Anderton, determined to stamp down on the increasing violence engulfing the southern suburbs of Manchester in particular. It was a heady, dangerous time – the press nicknamed the city 'Gunchester'.

The intensity of the circumstances made for a remarkable working relationship between Johnny and Bernard, the 'extremes' of the situation particularly good for the creative process. While The Smiths and Joy Division/New Order walked different paths throughout the Eighties, each had clearly always kept an eye on what was happening along the other track. In a sense, the duo were Manchester 'united', but there was one problem for the Sky Blue Marr however – working with Bernard also meant working with a Man U fan.

Near-neighbours, Johnny was deeply passionate about the work they began to do in 1989, as he has been with every project with which he has been involved. It was the first time Johnny had got involved with MIDI guitar playing, giving a synthetic feel to much of the music. Bernard was the perfect partner in this for Johnny, able – as Marr put it – to set up great sounds on a vast bank of keyboards whilst almost having the volume in the studio turned off.

As Johnny had with Morrissey and Matt Johnson, with Sumner and himself at the centre of the project they were able to bring a thousand different influences to bear while trawling through a shared love of similar kinds of music, from The Kinks to Kraftwerk. While The Smiths had given Johnny the experience of co-writing with a remarkable lyricist and The The had given him extra experience of working on material largely completed in the writing process by someone else, Electronic was a revelation. "For the first time," Johnny enthused, "I am totally writing with another musician." Sometimes Johnny would write all the music. Sometimes the roles were reversed and Sumner would do the same – it was a genuinely shared experience, as at other times they would literally write together. 'Getting Away With It', the timeless first fruit of the partnership, was a perfect example. "He wrote the verse," said Marr, "and I wrote the chorus... that is when the real sparks fly!" Johnny's initial intent with the song had been to write the song as if it were "Sister Sledge, with the Pet Shop Boys as a backing band," and he felt that the finished piece was a perfect pop song. To prove him right, the single went into the US top forty and sold over 350,000 copies, while in the UK it made it to number eleven in the chart.

Electronic reached a new audience for both partners. While The The and New Order were commercial and critical successes, Electronic proved that serial collaborators Sumner and Marr had found their own voices within the format of the duo. The new venture was a breath of fresh air, although the two often seemed to come to the task from different directions. "Bernard thinks the whole 'born with a guitar in your mouth' story very corny," says Johnny. While easy bucks had never been Johnny's priority in the past – it has always been *the work* rather than the income that motivates him – Marr has always loved commercial pop, whether it be glam stomps, cool grooves or out-and-out disco. And while income was not the driving force behind Electronic either, what was clear from day one was that both Sumner and Marr had developed a new kind of pop sensibility. Electronic – especially with their link to the Pet Shop Boys – just happened to be a very saleable concept. At the same time, lest the critics accuse them of trying to make a fast buck while their other bands were no longer clawing the top reaches of the singles charts, Johnny was keen to emphasise that his involvement with The The was still ongoing, and so was Bernard's with New Order.

This was by no means an idle hobby for a couple of rich musicians.

"We're intensely ambitious," Johnny told Stuart Maconie for *Select*, pointing out that while the project did not compete with their daytime jobs in other bands, it gave them both an outlet for other creative urges. Electronic had an air of the idealistic, a sense of refinement and of polish. Working with new machinery and escaping the 'Johnny Marr sound', Marr was also able to indulge his life-long passion for up-tempo dance music and electronica. "If it's a good song," Johnny told one interviewer. "I'll play alongside machines all day."

The relationship was immediately successful, the music vibrant and joyous. In December, within months of the duo coming together, Electronic – with Neil Tennant on vocals – released, 'Getting Away With It.' It was, of course, a huge success and one of the best-loved songs of the late Eighties, putting to bed the decade that Johnny's first band had so defined. While Morrissey's haunting and hysterical 'Ouija Board, Ouija Board' was also out over the closing weeks of the year, it was good to see both Johnny and Morrissey hitting the singles charts so successfully. The refined tone of Tennant's vocal, the killer melody and perfect production seemed to justify the careers of all three major performers on the record, as if to say, "See – we really *do* know what this is all about."

Some twenty-five miles west of Manchester, literally on the River Mersey itself and in the shadow of Runcorn bridge, Spike Island saw a festival in the summer of 1990 that was headlined by The Stone Roses. It was a mini-Woodstock for the generation, when many of the bands who went on to enliven Nineties pop were congregated in one place. Electronic made their live debut in Los Angeles in August, playing to a huge crowd at the Dodgers' Stadium. The concert came about after they were invited by Depeche Mode to play with them. Johnny explained, "I thought it was completely impossible," but it was an important date for the band in America. Neil Tennant – himself a pop junkie – told an amusing story about Johnny's obsessive love of pop music. "We're getting so used to this," Johnny said to Neil, "that we'll just be strolling across the stage soon chatting to each other about ancient pop music." Neil described Johnny 'strolling' across the stage towards him the following night. "During the drum beat in 'Getting Away With It', Johnny Marr comes over, playing away at his guitar, and says, 'What was Picketywitch's first hit?' It was dead funny." As Grant Showbiz confirms, "that sounds very, very Johnny! Good for him…" Meanwhile, Electronic's first UK gig was in January of the New Year when they appeared at The Hacienda, to celebrate the renewal of the club's licence.

With northern-born singer Lisa Stansfield cruising the charts in the late Eighties and early Nineties, there was a penchant among the record-buying public for soulful, breezy vocal acts with a bit of attitude. Another of Johnny's projects during 1990 was recording with Banderas, a duo who could have, but didn't, make it big. Their album *Ripe* was to be released in March of 1991, peopled by the likes of Jimmy Somerville and Bernard Sumner. Johnny appeared on the single, the distinctive album-opener 'This Is Your Life', which was released in February of 1991. It was an affirmative, Latin-style hustle, sung beautifully by one half of the Banderas duo, Caroline Buckley, with chugging 'Shaft' style funk guitar throughout. The project didn't quite sink without trace, but while the name of the band and the album's cover suggested a bunch of Spanish female skinheads, Banderas failed to hit the mark on either side of the Atlantic. It was a shame – 'This Is Your Life' had in spades the same kind of upbeat feel-good groove that had served Swing Out Sister and Stansfield so well in the previous few years.

By now though, Johnny had so many offers that he could afford to work with exactly who he chose and on what projects. One of the most productive was a more direct collboration with the Pet Shop Boys. Almost a decade into their career, Neil Tennant and Chris Lowe's *Behaviour* was the band's fifth studio album, and their perfect blend of distracted ironic pop lyrics and shimmering, faultless production values had rightly made them one of the world's biggest-selling acts. Marr, Tennant and Lowe obviously already had a working friendship via the Boys appearance with Electronic, and it was a continuation of that natural synergy that brought Johnny into the recording studio to work on two tracks with the duo.

Like Johnny, the Pet Shop Boys had a major-league work ethic, but their creativity was often glossed over by the interpretation of their techno-heavy production. "A lot of people have this idea that Neil and Chris just sit around the studio with machines making the music, while they read *Vogue*," Johnny was to say, reviewing the experience of working with PSB on jmarr.com, "which is very far from the truth." Attracted to the project for personal reasons – Johnny has always claimed that any working relationship he has, has to have a sound personal relationship going on for him to get involved – he was impressed with both the work rate of the band, and their musical abilities. "They both work constantly," he added, "and are never short of ideas." Marr was also quick to credit the proficiency of Lowe and Tennant, reminding fans that the guys proved themselves great musicians as well as great writers.

The album was produced by ex-Georgio Moroder keyboardist and future Grammy-winner Harold Faltermeyer, who found a rich and warm strain in the songs that Johnny was able to flesh out. In fact, the two tracks to which Johnny contributed were the most guitar-driven pieces in the Pet Shop Boys' catalogue to date. 'October Symphony' mirrored the more reflective tone that *Behaviour* signalled in the Pet Shop Boys' career. The track is a faultless, beautifully arranged piece, linking haunting strings and Johnny's Cry Baby wah-wah guitar with Tennant's beautifully delivered vocal, his tone less sardonic than on previous releases. As with Banderas, Johnny could not have been further away from The Smiths in terms of the work he was engaged in, but on the reflective 'This Must Be The Place I Waited Years To Leave' the tone is more Smith-like. Marr thoroughly enjoyed the experience of working with Tennant and Lowe, recalling "great memories" from the process. "I still really like those songs," he said later. "Especially 'This Must Be The Place'..."

Liverpool's The La's blended perfectly-produced guitar-based pop melody with a nostalgic slice of Sixties retro. 'There She Goes' drew a direct line in the sand back to The Smiths, and Johnny was a big fan, going on to work with that band's Lee Mavers on unreleased demos. Although the fruits of their labours have never seen the light of day, the pair spent several days playing together at Johnny's home studio, hanging out and jamming, each very much a fan of the other's music. What might have come out of a longer-term working relationship between the authors of 'There She Goes' and 'There Is A Light That Never Goes Out' is mouth-watering.

At the same time Morrissey delivered his own *Hatful Of Hollow*-style collection of hits and B-sides, *Bona Drag*, neatly encapsulating his post-Smiths work. 1991 was in many ways the year of Massive Attack [aside, of course, from the approaching grunge juggernaut, heralded by Nirvana's 'Teen Spirit'], when dance music got serious, and the burgeoning Bristol-based trip hop scene provided the soundtrack to the next couple of years-worth of pop. Massive Attack's *Blue Lines* became one of the UK's best-loved and most-played albums for decades, while Nellee Hooper, Neneh Cherry and Tricky coloured the first half of the decade with some superb and innovative singles. Some of the movement appealed to Marr, and he stayed closer to his traditional roots over the coming year – soul, folk and the continuing work-in-progress that was Electronic.

The first release of his continuing work was an appearance on the Stex single 'Still Feel The Rain', with Johnny included on various different format releases of the A-side. The Banderas album was released to a fairly indifferent world, while Morrissey continued his solo schedule with the critically acclaimed *Kill Uncle*. April saw the release of the new Electronic single 'Get The Message/Free Will', the A-side one of Marr's favourite Electronic tracks of all. Rather than Johnny's usual speed of light composition, 'Get The Message' was a 'crafted' song, over which he spent many, many hours of searching before he was happy with the result. Sumner's vocal take was perfect too, a stream of consciousness piece expanded in one take to complete the song. "I knew I had a really great verse, and a potentially great chorus," Johnny told Martin Roach of the ardour of the song's composition. "I had to really rack my brains to nail it… had to really concentrate to get [that] middle eight." Accordingly, the rhythm track alone occupied Johnny for five days solid.

In July 1991, Billy Bragg released another of his pristine, beautifully-judged collaborations with Johnny as a single. For Marr fans it was another glorious outing for the pair, and everything Johnny did on the track worked perfectly alongside Bragg's lyric. The song 'Sexuality' was in fact a joint composition. "Thank God it was a co-write," says Billy of the song that was born of the newly-renewed partnership. The former Smiths soundman Grant Showbiz, a long-time working partner with Bragg too, was producing Billy's album *Don't Try This At Home*, and the pair presented Johnny with a number of tracks to elicit his input. "I was in the studio labouring with 'Sexuality' which originally sounded a lot more like 'Louis Louis' than the track we know and love," says Billy. "Johnny came down and just kind of got hold of it and played those glittering chords over it, and changed it completely." Marr took the track back to his attic-based studio at home in Manchester. To what he described as "a three-chord change [that was] kind of reggae-ish," Johnny added his own backing tracks, backing vocals, and completely re-worked the song for Bragg, who was stunned by the piece that he heard. "[He] gave us back this beautiful shining pop song," remembers Billy.

152

"And me and Grant looked at one another and thought 'Christ – now what are we going to do? We're going to have to make an album that sounds like this.'"

Inspired, the pair made one of Bragg's best-loved albums. "That's how that album became a big pop album. We were trying to work up to the level of Johnny's production on 'Sexuality' – he did an incredible job. A really, really incredible job. He has a great melodic ear."

As well as the single – which enjoyed five weeks on the chart – Johnny also played on the lovely 'Cindy Of A Thousand Lives.' "'Cindy' was another one of the tracks he took when he took 'Sexuality'," recalls Billy. "He took that and 'Accident Waiting To Happen'. He did spooky, scary things with them." Bragg travelled up to Manchester to join Johnny in the process, and watched him at work. "I went up and stayed with him and watched him do it, but *how* he did it I have no idea" says Billy, mystified. Buried away in Johnny's attic, his song came to life once again. "'Cindy…' is a great feel," Bragg recalls fondly. "And it's got Kirsty all over it too, singing away."

While the melodic ear of Marr helped set fire to Bragg's writing, so too did his work with Kirsty MacColl continue to progress, and Johnny co-wrote one of her most moving and exciting songs to date. 'Walking Down Madison' was a groove-led departure for Kirsty and a perfect snapshot of Johnny's creative flavour at the time, all loops and heavy dance riffs set against a lightness of melody and touching modulation, a track completed by Johnny and presented to Kirsty intact, much as he had in the past with Morrissey.

June saw the long-awaited release of *Electronic*, and the debut album did not disappoint. For those not knowing quite what to expect, the overall flavour was more New Order than Smiths, but Johnny's fingerprints were all over the album and his guitar high in the mix. Marr had clearly shed his former band both emotionally and musically. Electronic declared a future with no past, an opportunity for Marr to graze new pastures and for Sumner to indulge his time outside of New Order. The band exercised Marr one hundred per cent. The first track, 'Idiot Country', featured a cool Mancunian rap from Bernard, Johnny's guitar as funky as it had ever appeared on record to date as the synthesized harmonies drifted over the complex rhythm track. The majority of the album was tight funk grooves, dance tracks with attitude, but often suffused with strong melody and a sense of claustrophobia too. 'Reality' was based on a synth riff, with Johnny's tight guitar filling the spaces in the drum track. While the rhythms are very 'up', Sumner's vocal is sparse and emotionally distracted. If this was dance music it would appeal lyrically to Smiths fans. Outside of the musical context, Bernard's lyric and delivery could easily have been that of a New Order or Joy Division song.

'Tighten Up' featured Johnny's strumming high in the mix, adding a warmth to the synth riff that started the song. 'Patience Of A Saint' was based upon Bernard's drum beat and a handful of chords dropped onto it by Chris Lowe. Johnny added the bass line, and the whole song – a pure Pet Shop Boys/Electronic collaboration – was completed very quickly. Tennant's vocal contrasted superbly well with Bernard's; although Electronic were always a duo, the contrast of the two voices over the course of an album was fascinating.

'Getting Away With It' featured the drums of David Palmer, the sticksman with whom Johnny had probably worked more than any other. Bernard's plaintive vocal again harmonized perfectly with Neil's – the song is another perfect happy/sad concoction, so typical of much of the work that Johnny has been involved with over the years. After 'Gangster' and 'Soviet' came the single 'Get The Message', featuring Primal Scream's Denise Johnson on vocals, one of the highlights of the album.

Electronic later went on to claim that their music was dance music for people who don't go to dance clubs. As more time passes and the band's first album becomes more of an archaeological relic of the early Nineties, the synth bass lines and metronomic beats that defined the dance grooves of the time give way to Sumner's vocals. There is a timeless-ness to Bernard's delivery, halfway between tender and dead-pan, that works on so many levels. This is particularly evident on 'Some Distant Memory', which has the plangent wistfulness of The Blue Nile, but on an E-fuelled night out in Manchester rather than wandering the wet streets of late night Glasgow. Johnny's glissando acoustic guitar is a real treat on the track too. The closer, 'Feel Every Beat' opens with some of Johnny's backwards guitar, swelling until the opening riff rocks more than anywhere else on the album. Palmer's drumming is supplemented by Donald Johnson. The album vamps into the distance with Johnny's harmonica pumping away...

Electronic made it to the number two slot in the UK album charts – like so many of Johnny's albums over the years, not *quite* getting to number one. It was, as Johnny might have said at the time, a fantastic piece of vinyl.

CHAPTER EIGHT

True Happiness
This Way Lies

Sessions and demos for the next The The album had begun as far
back as summer of the previous year, but through 1992 they
increased in intensity and gradually the album Dusk began to
take shape. The record was to prove at odds with what was happening
elsewhere in music. As the tide of influence wavers between the UK
and America, the attention turned to an American band called
Nirvana. 1992 was the year that Nirvana took off, their album
Nevermind released in the autumn. With the attendant so-called
grunge movement introducing bands such as Pearl Jam and Smashing
Pumpkins to UK audiences, the gap left by the under-employed
Stone Roses was filled. Nirvana – and indeed Pearl Jam and the
Pumpkins – were worthwhile bands, but much of the grunge
phenomenon was dire. There was clearly a gap in the market, and –
quietly – the phenomenon that came to be known as Britpop
gradually crept from the net-curtained bedrooms of London and
elsewhere to take over from Nirvana after the death of Kurt Cobain
in 1994.

In the meantime, *Dusk* was Johnny's second extended work-out
with The The and Matt Johnson. While elements of the writing
process had started during the *Mind Bomb* tour, the album was

recorded live in Johnson's own home studio in East London; the *Mind Bomb* four-piece band reconvened and recorded live, while the process was captured by film-maker Tim Pope. Writing on tour helped Johnson pare down the values that he engaged with the songs – cleaner, clearer. "I became more sensitive to the idea of dynamics," he told one interviewer at the time and the songs written for *Dusk* became more and more concise. Still reeling from the death of his brother, Johnson found the entire process difficult, sometimes losing the studio control that he had managed so clearly on previous albums. The influence of darker blues powers such as Robert Johnson and Howlin' Wolf were immediately to hand, and Matt described the entire process of making the album as "intensely personal." That isn't to say that the album itself lacked control: in fact *Dusk's* reigning-in of personal nightmares and visions has made it one of The The's most loved and affecting albums. The leap from the universal themes of *Mind Bomb* to the diary-like pages of *Dusk* was not a sales-orientated calculation, but the appeal to the audience was reflected in the fact that the collection of songs ultimately made it to number two in the album charts.

Much of the album was composed on acoustic guitar, with a drum machine fleshing out the basic demos. The massed ranks of contributors that enlightened *Mind Bomb* was reduced to a more stable central core of players – and the album has a much more rootsy, R&B feel to it – there was still room for a brass section on some tracks and guest artists such as Danny Thompson were brought in again where required. Musically the project was less of a 'band' than on *Mind Bomb*, the songs more finished as they came to the studio, but the sessions themselves were still intense, with blood red projections and incense burning around the basement studio. The band nicknamed it the 'psychic sauna,' the heat in the studio deliberately intense. Johnson arranged huge heaters, turned up full, to raise the studio temperature, and this was easily matched by the emotional heat. Johnny – established as the most contributing member of the band besides Johnson himself – remembered turning up at the sessions bright and breezy in his new open-topped Italian sports car, only to step down into the cellars and join the almost religious intensity of the recording studio.

The atmosphere appealed to Johnny immensely, the studio vibe creating a weird but very creative atmosphere. "He got these very intense, interesting dynamics, that captured your attention completely," says Johnny. "Too many bands are just record collectors, and four guys in a room with a big record collection each doesn't mean you can come up with the goods." But while the atmosphere was intense, it wasn't glum. "I can't work if I am down" says Johnny. "I get things done by being genuinely positive – and using that [kind of] energy."

Generous to a fault, Johnny also encouraged Johnson to play and develop more of his own guitar parts, and Johnson spoke of how one of Johnny's greatest contributions to the album was the encouragement he gave. "He understands what I am trying to do and he believes in it," Matt told Michael Leonard, adding neatly that his own role remained rather one of a "benevolent dictator."

Engaged in the success of these The The sessions, Johnny turned down the opportunity of producing one of the best-selling albums of the era. A Smiths-like frenzy had whipped up around Irish band The Cranberries following the release of their first EP in 1991, and by the following year they had signed to Island for a six-album deal. Sessions for the first album had foundered, and Johnny remembers being asked if he was interested. In fact, Stephen Street took the band to Windmill Studios in Dublin and produced the phenomenally successful *Everybody Else is Doing It, So Why Can't We?* It took a while for the album to take off, but there was a neat symmetry to the route that the record took before it hit the top of the album charts. Snubbed by the fickle UK market, the band took of on a six-week tour of the USA in support of another British band in the summer of 1993, and found a rabid audience on the US college circuit. The Cranberries picked up plaudits everywhere and the album began to sell and sell, finally reaching the number one slot in the UK more than a year after its release. The band who gave their Stateside support slot to The Cranberries in the summer of 1993 was The The... without Johnny Marr.

Although the target of Morrissey's latest single 'We Hate It When Our Friends Become Successful' was never identified, Johnny's former partner described the "vicious sense of competition in Manchester" when asked what the song was about. Described in *NME* as "by far and away the ex-Smith's worst single", Morrissey was happy to reference the "jealous, vile creatures" around the Manchester music scene in promoting it. In particular, Morrissey despised the response to success that his city's brethren heaped upon anyone who actually made it. "In Manchester," he said to *Q* magazine, "you are

159

accepted as long as you are scrambling and on your knees. But if you have any success, or are independent... they hate you." No longer on his knees, both Johnny and Morrissey were now happily successful *and* independent.

One of Morrissey's best solo albums, *Your Arsenal,* appeared in the mid-summer. Morrissey fused a big glam rock with a rockabilly roll on the album that was produced by Bowie sideman Mick Ronson, a wonderful blend of the old and the new, and – in the closing months of Ronson's life (he was to succumb to cancer in 1993) – a fitting piece by which to remember one of the most influential guitarists of the Seventies. Equally fittingly, there was no irony but maybe a quiet sense of achievement when Ronson's former employer David Bowie later covered one of the album's best tracks, 'I Know It's Going to Happen Someday.' The best Christmas presents for the festive season in 1992 were undoubtedly the two Smiths 'greatest hits' albums released in August and November respectively. While of course they were more than simply 'hits' albums, *Best I* and *Best II* did exactly what it said on the jacket, compiling some of the most memorable Smiths tracks together.

★

Throughout Johnny's career, personal relationships have come to define some of his most long-lasting professional relationships. It took years from their first getting to know one another for Marr and Matt Johnson to finally work together, and Electronic took a similarly long time to ferment. In Noel Gallagher, a fan became a friend. More than a decade earlier, the young Gallagher had lapped up the Smiths, alongside The Beatles, T. Rex and Slade. Gallagher hailed from the same streets down which the teenage Johnny had ridden his bicycle and yelled the songs of Marc Bolan. He was working for Oldham's Inspiral Carpets, one of the bands that had been 'most likely to,' alongside the Charlatans, Mondays, James and Roses. As a guitar tech for Clint Boon's band, Gallagher travelled extensively, learning the rock 'n' roll lifestyle and watching from within how a proper band operated. The potential of his younger brother Liam, singing in local band called Rain, soon became evident and, with Noel's guitar and songs on board, Oasis was ready to take on the world.

In May they played a now legendary gig in Glasgow and were spotted by the founder of Creation Records, Alan McGee. The five songs they played changed the pop world forever, as McGee fell hook, line and sinker for the Manchester miscreants, offering them a contract on the spot, from which they conquered the world. Although it was some time after the gig that the band actually signed with Creation, in the meantime a copy of their demo had fallen into Johnny's hands, and he was (excusing the pun) instrumental in helping them establish themselves. "I used to go to The Hacienda on a Saturday night," remembered Noel. He would regularly bump into the same guy there and chat to him. "I told him I was in a band and he said, 'Give us a tape, I'll give it to our kid.'" Every time Noel saw the guy, he would say the same thing – "give us a tape." "And then I saw him just after we had the offer from Creation… and he says 'How's the band going?'" Noel remembers having a copy of the new The The album in his hand, and the guy saying "Fucking hell – you'll definitely have to get a tape to our kid." The guy was Ian Marr. "And then it clicked," says Gallagher, "…Johnny Marr!"

"I gets him a tape," Noel remembered. "And two hours later I had Johnny Marr on the phone. I fucking freaked out." Johnny thought the tape was fantastic. "We went out for a drink that night," said Gallagher, "and he came along and brought his manager, Marcus Russell."

Noel Gallagher's story illustrates beautifully the way Johnny would happily oil any wheels that he thought ought to be turning more easily within the business. Russell, of course, went on to be Oasis's manager and to oversee their major successes. While there might have appeared much musical water between Oasis and The Smiths (swaggering loudmouths versus sauntering bibliophiles), in fact the bands had much in common, not least their Irish catholic upbringing in the southern suburbs of Manchester. Johnny immediately took to the duo. "When I first met Noel," Johnny was to say years later, "he took so long tuning up between songs that I had to lend him a guitar. He fell in love with it – and I didn't have the heart to ask for it back!" Over the forthcoming months, that guitar would be the one on which Gallagher wrote some of the biggest rock anthems of the decade, including 'Live Forever'. Quick to get to the point, when asked about that, Johnny jokes, "If that's the case, then I reckon he owes me a couple of million in royalties!"

Within the year, Oasis were headline news. In their famed spat with Blur, it became clear why it was that Oasis – while they sold fewer records than Blur at the time – went on to be a much bigger phenomenon in the long term. While the development of 'lad culture' – and magazines such as *Loaded* and *FHM* embraced unreconstructed maleness amongst the under-thirties – Britpop as a whole struggled to manage its sense of irony. Were Blur being ironic? Was Jarvis? Were Sleeper? While the message of Britpop was open to misinterpretation, Oasis suffered from no irony. Compared to the art school graduates of many of the London bands, Oasis brought the swagger and the fun back into rock 'n' roll.

One of the most obvious comparisons with The Smiths – apart from the Gallagher brothers' style bearing a passing visual resemblance to Marr's (down, perhaps, to them sharing a hairdresser in Manchester) – was that however much they attracted column inches for all the wrong (ie. non-musical) reasons, their reputation was backed up by some of the best rock 'n' roll of their era. Because their music was *so* good, their antics elsewhere could carry the day. However much the UK press tried to knock Morrissey off his pedestal, as long as The Smiths made the best music around they would always succeed. Ditto Oasis – their swaggering confidence recalled The Faces, their boogie was heavy with the pop influence of Slade, The Beatles and Dr Feelgood. And in Johnny Marr they had a champion who knew the ropes. Marr has remained close to both the brothers. The relentless glare of publicity that the Gallaghers have endured over the years has been more punishing even than that which shone on The Smiths; Johnny understands that it isn't easy being a Gallagher, just as it wasn't easy being a Smith.

★

Over the course of 1993, Johnny would work with K-Klass, make some demos with Ian McCulloch, record with Nelee Hooper and, of course, watch the release of that The The material, while much of the year belonged to Electronic. For starters though, 1993 saw The The release *Dusk,* a dark, city-night album, perhaps Matt Johnson's most personal piece of work. 'Love Is Stronger Than Death' was one particular favourite of Marr, a difficult song for Johnson, concerning as it does the death of Eugene Johnson, one which captured the writer's intention perfectly. Rather than indulging in melancholy, the song is remarkably positive and optimistic, Johnson's vocal at once tender and strong, the lyric intense but couched in images of blue skies, springtime, beating hearts and smiles. The acoustic guitar is Matt, but Johnny created his own harmonica part, and its wistful and

162

haunting tone perfectly sets off the swelling Hammond organ of DC Collard. After the swaggering anarchy of the opening track this is a soulful, moving piece.

The R&B harmonica that Johnny plays to introduce 'Dogs Of Lust' is as distinctive as any of his rootsy guitar on the album, the song bathed in a rawness that Jack White would seek out a decade later. DC Collard's honky tonk piano triplets establish 'This Is The Night' in a similar way, though the music is a very different proposition. As the drama of the track develops, Johnny's electric guitar soars over the rich melody, setting it in a warm but disturbing light.

'Slow Emotional Replay' typified the album's central issue, the disparity between the perceived and the perceiver, the internal and the external forces at work on the writer. Johnny featured on backing vocals on this, probably the most accessible track on the record, his introductory harp playing casting a glance back over his own shoulder to the days of 'Hand In Glove'. Johnny's harp playing is interesting in that he doesn't cradle the harp deep in his fists and try to pump out bluesy, Dr Feelgood-style notes, but plays the instrument melodically, picking out the lines as cleanly as he does on the guitar.

Tim Pope's video for the track took Johnny and Matt to New York to film among a bewildering cast of porn stars, psychic cab drivers and drunks. The basic premise of the film was "to go right up to all these weird street characters we had been told about, stick a microphone in their faces and ask them, 'What is wrong with the world?'" Quentin Crisp, the notably camp 'Englishman In New York' appeared in the film, as did a character known as Danny The Wonderpony who, naked, wore a saddle and gave rides around New York on his back. The whole surreal experience was emotionally draining for Johnny. Apart from anything else, he was aware that it was the end of a process of working with Johnson, at least for the time being. In New York, Marr didn't sleep for three days. The entire process brought Johnny to tears – "It was one of the most unbelievable experiences I have ever been through." Pope dragged them around snuff movie sets and introduced them to some extreme characters. "We went into this one innocuous-looking building," says Marr. "He told me I was going to need my guitar to mime. I walked in, and I was on live porn TV, being interviewed by this guy." The various characters that peopled the film were supposed to be down-and-outs and losers of every colour, but they came up with the most moving observations on life, or displayed emotional extremes that came out of the blue. Interviewing a 'very down' Irish guy, and asking him – as with the others – about what he thought was wrong with the world, Johnny remembers that "in front of our faces he just broke up, this massive guy. He completely broke down over the course of three minutes… it was like turning a key in him, and he cried." "Fucking horrible" was how Johnny summed up the moment.

While 'Slow Emotional Replay' brought some weird moments, the rest of the album was no less emotionally complex. 'Helpline Operator' was the result of hours of 'research' spent on the phone to The Samaritans ("I'm a method song-writer," Matt told *Guitar Magazine*). 'Sodium Light Baby' perfectly captured Johnson's visions of New York, a city where he had worked extensively to date and to which he moved permanently after the *Dusk* project was completed. The central riff, bouncing across the cool rhythm tracks, was Johnny's, a rare occasion of being given his head in the composition process in which it was usually Matt's lines that the musicians on the album played. Taped sounds, flugel horns, French horns and 'unknown' female voices added to Matt's piano on 'Lung Shadows', while he and Johnny shared guitar duties. One of the most haunting pieces that Marr had ever worked on, a beautifully painted sonic picture touched with delayed guitar notes and muted brass, the piece sounded like a cross between Miles Davies and *Music For Films*-era Brian Eno.

The same tone opened up 'Bluer than Midnight', a track on which Johnny did not appear. Starring Matt Johnson as John Lennon, 'Lonely Planet' closes the album, with discrete guitar lines from both Johnson and Marr throughout. *Dusk* is a fantastic album, born of the time in which it was produced, but years later nothing about the record has dated: it could have been released as easily in 2003 as 1993, and a decade after that it will probably sound as fresh again.

As he had with *Mind Bomb*, Matt toured the album extensively – with The Cranberries in support as noted, but this time Johnny stayed at home. The birth of his and Angela's first child, a little boy, gave him domestic responsibilities and a reason to stay put. His professional reasons were also more complex than that though – there were Johnny's other babies to look after too, as he preferred the confines of the studio to those of the tour bus.

His place in Johnson's The The touring band was taken by Keith Joyner, and The The entered a new period in its ever-changing story *sans* Marr. "It wasn't the right time for me to go away," Johnny told *Select* magazine, reflecting on how much he had enjoyed the first The

The tour, his first (The Pretenders aside) since the last Smiths tour. Although it resulted in only two full-length albums, Johnny's creativity with The The almost matched his high intensity Smiths period. It is clear that the experiences differed greatly. If The Smiths had been an incredibly close-knit unit of relatively new friends, with Matt Johnson, Johnny extended a long-lasting friendship into a working relationship of which he was never less than immensely proud. Johnson's writing is very different to Morrissey's but the two writers share an increasingly rare intensity and commitment to the veracity of their output. The significant difference for Johnny, of course, was that Johnson was not simply a lyricist, but a composer of immense skill, with a courage and indefatigability as rare as his ability with the pen. "Johnny and myself didn't really write as much as we should have done together," said Johnson in 1999, and it was clear that perhaps The The missed an opportunity for more collaboration.

One of the reasons why Johnny enjoyed The The so much was because Johnson brought finished compositions to the studio, often directing his fellow musicians in exactly what to play, thus Marr was spared some of the immense responsibility and pressure that being the musical mind of The Smiths incurred. In The The, he could simply be a band member, albeit the one with probably the most input after Matt himself. "People assume that my role in The The was to pop down to the studios and do the odd harmonica part and be in the videos, but I was in a group twenty-four hours a day for three years." This band was clearly a labour of love.

Johnny and Matt Johnson remain in close and constant touch today, emailing and phoning regularly, and Matt has described his friend as "one of my favourite people." Both believe that they will work together again; indeed Johnny has stated that – rather than the ever-requested Smiths reunion – he would be far more interested in working within The The again than he would with 'his other band.' After the release of *Dusk*, it seemed that more work would come from the pair, but it hasn't happened yet. While The Smiths was an incandescent experience that offered Johnny an education and the step into the limelight that he had dreamed of as a teenager, The The was far closer to the band that the seventeen-year-old Marr had imagined being a part of. And – if less high in profile than his work with Morrissey, Rourke and Joyce – the two albums that The The released with Marr on board remain amongst his most significant material to date.

While Oasis were racking up the column inches in the 'rough and ready' department, the 'fey and wasted' pages of the tabloids and music press belonged to another bunch of Smiths-influenced darlings. Mike Joyce apparently tried out for the drum position in Suede, and Morrissey was so taken with 'My Insatiable One' that it eventually made it into his live set. A decade later guitarist Bernard Butler would work with Johnny on the Bert Jansch album *Crimson Moon*. Suede and The Smiths had much in common. Their eponymous first album featured rocking guitar, homoerotic lyrics and a sexually uncertain image on the cover – familiar territory for Smiths fans. Singer Brett Anderson clearly bore profound influences of Morrissey and Bowie, and knew how to get the media's attention. What drew a huge number of fans to the band was the relationship between Anderson and Butler, who seemed to have re-invented the Morrissey/Marr axis for a new generation. Bernard's obvious debt to Johnny's glam-heavy guitar style was evident across the album and its follow-up *Dog Man Star*, but by the time the world woke up to Suede, Butler had left the band. At the time, and early in their career, Suede seemed a Smiths-lite stop gap for Morrissey and Marr fans who would soon bore of their retro posturing. In fact, they made some great records, their influences more glam than glum, and both Anderson and Butler have more than lasted the distance. In their own sweet way, they have also done something that Morrissey and Marr have never done. In 2004 the pair reconvened as The Tears – proving that there's always hope! Equally influential, the year also saw the release of Pulp's *Modern Life Is Rubbish*, and in Jarvis Cocker there was another distant echo of The Smiths as Cocker gently picked at the bones of post-Thatcher's Britain.

By the end of 1993, Electronic were gearing up for their next album. It wouldn't see the light of day until 1996, during which time Bernard's 'other band' would release both *Republic*, a number one album, and a *Best Of...* compilation, another top five hit. But the pairing of Sumner and Marr worked constantly on the Electronic project too.

If Johnny's work rate in The Smiths had been prodigious, there was no sign of him letting up now, as he ran from one project to another without pausing for breath. Admitting to spending up to sixteen hours a day in the studio, Marr was still refining his writing, still swimming with intent rather than simply going with the flow. Working closely with Bernard Sumner, Johnny was always trying to be a better guitarist, still looking for the chords and the melody of a better song. As the pair began to discuss the project in interviews, likely co-workers such as Karl Bartos, ex- of Kraftwerk, and Chic's Nile Rodgers were name-checked. Rodgers was one of Johnny's own long-time guitar heroes, and although the best years of Chic were long behind, he was in constant demand after his work on David Bowie's *Let's Dance* album had stormed the world a decade earlier. If you were into innovative pop with a creative bite and a commercial edge, then Johnny Marr was interested in what you were doing.

As Nirvana had been picked up in the wake of The Stone Roses' hiatus, so the Roses' natural successors Oasis filled the void left by the tragic demise of Nirvana. In August they released their most important album, *Definitely Maybe,* containing some of their best-loved tracks. Meanwhile, March 1994 saw the release of Morrissey's *Vauxhall And I.* Following the success of his collaboration with Mick Ronson, he reached the top of the UK album charts with a collection co-written with Boz Boorer and Alain Whyte, who had also appeared on *Your Arsenal.* Lyrically, the album was probably Morrissey's strongest since his days with The Smiths, prompting *Select* magazine to suggest that is he continued at this pace "you won't want The Smiths back." Praise indeed.

It was at this point that Britpop really took hold of the mainstream, with Blur's 'Boys And Girls' grabbing the attention of everyone between the ages of fifteen and thirty. *Parklife* was to follow, and a generation was affected/infected. A whole raft of new English bands became more visible. Shed Seven, Menswear, Sleeper, Supergrass – many of them focused around The Good Mixer, a pub in Camden Town, London, where Morrissey would also occasionally be seen. The Britpop scene had a distinct debt to The Smiths, though they were only one of any number of influences, from Ray Davis and The Small Faces onwards. Blur's Damon Albarn spoke extensively of how offensive he found the increasing influence of poor American design and culture in late Eighties and Nineties Britain. It was a time when – for better or worse –it began to be cool to think British again. Arch, angular, guitar-driven pop – Britpop as a phenomenon produced some great bands, some very dodgy ones, and some great headlines. Blur's first major tour of the UK, supported by Sleeper, was a revelation. As these kids grew up over the next couple of years, it proved to be so. In May, the leader of the Labour Party, John Smith, died suddenly. He was to be replaced in the role by Tony Blair. It was almost as though, after fifteen years of hurt, the youth of Britain was beginning to realise that there was life beyond the endless years of Conservative hegemony.

CHAPTER NINE

The Healing Process

By early 1995 Raise The Pressure, the new Electronic album, was well under way. It was a more ambitious work than Electronic – the tracks that emerged included more dance music than Johnny's trademark guitar, but 'Forbidden City', which Marr cited as one of his favourite Electronic tracks, and 'For You' featured his guitar more. The emotional 'Out Of My League' was another of Johnny's favourites. At the same time, Oasis released 'Some Might Say', their first number one single in the summer, and when NME set the band up head to head against Blur with its 'British Heavyweight Championship' front cover, they were guaranteed headlines in both the music and the general press – indeed the story of who would get the coveted number one single slot when the two bands released their singles on the same day, became an item on the prime BBC news show that evening.

Meanwhile, Morrissey's career took a turn for the worse on the release of *Southpaw Grammar*, of which one reviewer unkindly noted that there was no reason why anyone who already owned something by Morrissey "should ever want to hear this record." For Morrissey and Johnny, however, there was far worse ahead, as the former members of The Smiths prepared with their respective lawyers for a court case that would bring them all back into the headlines.

1996 proved a miserable year for the four members of 'the best British band since The Beatles' as Mike Joyce's claim over royalties came to court. The case consisted of the fact that – while song-writing royalties to Morrissey and Johnny were not in question – he had received an unfair percentage of the band's performance royalties. Going right back to the original contract with Rough Trade, on which only the names of Morrissey and Johnny had appeared, making them, legally, the only actual members of The Smiths, Mike argued that the 10% share of income that he and Andy Rourke had received was unfair in comparison with the remaining 40% each share enjoyed by Johnny and Morrissey.

Alongside equally famed cases such as George Michael's against Sony, Lol Tolhurst's against The Cure, or Prince's against Warner Bros, the case of The Smiths has gone down as one of the most dramatic and bitter in rock legal history. The press had a field day – it had been a long time since the British press had had a chance to take a pop against Morrissey in particular, and, regardless of the rights or wrongs of the case, it was largely the singer who unfairly took the brunt of the bad press. Andy Rourke had previously accepted a settlement with his former band-mates over the issue, but for Joyce it was clearly a matter to take further. While *The Manchester Evening News* noted that "the four band members barely acknowledged each others' presence throughout the court hearing", the esteemed local newspaper also observed a notable description of Johnny by his representative in court. Robert Englehart QC described Marr as "a very decent, honest person – scrupulously fair – who was not going to cheat his friends." The press estimated the outcome in favour of Joyce to be somewhere nearing £1 million pounds, a huge sum of money if that was accurate, and consequently the bitterness between band members was long-lasting.

Of the two song-writers, only Johnny was in court to hear the judge's decision, described by *The Times* as "looking shocked, pale and refusing to comment" as he left the courtroom. Described by the as an "engaging personality" and a "reasonable character", the affair clearly affected Johnny significantly. Despite his losing the case, Marr came out of the debacle with generally positive press. But not only were his former band-mates at odds with him, in Andy – who had given evidence during the case himself – he was in court with a near life-long friend. Morrissey was to appeal against the judge's decision made in favour of Joyce, though he was to lose that appeal, while Johnny accepted and settled the amounts proscribed by the judge. Years later the acrimony was still evident between Morrissey and Mike, though Johnny has kept a low profile on the subject. The British press gleefully attacked Morrissey, quoting and mis-quoting the judge's words *ad infinitum*. Ten years on, Johnny and Andy prepared to take the stage together again for the first time since the demise of the band, and Marr hinted at the agony that the case must have caused him: "Andy and I go way back before The Smiths," he told journalist Pete Paphides on the subject of their appearance in the high court. "Our friendship was bigger than that."

With the case behind him, Johnny – and indeed Morrissey – got back to work, though for Johnny it was a relatively quiet time. The release of *Raise The Pressure* kept Electronic's stock high, a collection of breezy-but-melancholic dance tracks and slower pop numbers featuring some of Johnny's loveliest guitar work for a long time.

'Forbidden City' had an air of the Pet Shop Boys in its graceful melody, but is pure Sumner in the lyric, while Johnny's acoustic strumming has a fantastic crispness and lightness to it. The discrete electric accents that he puts into the track, and the stretching, yearning solo make 'Forbidden City' one of Electronic's best tracks, and a beautiful album opener. 'For You' maintains the tone of guitar-driven pop, with Johnny again carrying Sumner's vocal perfectly. The orchestral clouds that open the next track give way to the metronomic keyboards of 'Dark Angel', the first song on the album not co-written with Kraftwerk's Karl Bartos, and a lovely blend of the optimistic and the melancholic.

'One Day' is powered by Marr's guitars again – pulsating acoustic, howls of feedback and rich, atmospheric chords that lead into one of Johnny's best, aggressive riffs on the album, though the verse is highly melodic. More glacial, orchestral keyboards introduced 'Until The End Of Time', another song with a Pet Shop Boy feel to it – refined, restrained dance music with an air of distraction. 'Second Nature' was a more reflective track, bringing the pace of the album down. 'If You've Got Love' pumped the energy up a level again. Johnny was particularly happy with 'Out Of My League', a song that combines the pace of 'There Is Light That Never Goes Out' with the kind of melodic transparency straight out of the kind of carefree early Seventies pop of which Johnny has always been a fan. 'Interlude' was a short piece combining the claustrophobia of David Bowie's *Diamond Dogs* with the textured, pastoral feel of Tomita. Brooding electronica defined 'Freefall', while 'Visit Me' was another gentle piece in which keyboard and Johnny's acoustic guitar complement Sumner's assured vocal perfectly. 'How Long' and 'Time Can Tell' closed the album, the latter gently strummed by Johnny around cool, jazzy chords.

Raising The Pressure was a mature piece, the sound of writers and musicians at ease with one another and the music they created. Despite the heightened energy of many of the tracks, it was a reflective album, removed from the frenetic force that defined Bernard and Johnny's previous outing.

Early in the New Year, 'Second Nature' was released as a single. Johnny then worked with another old friend from Manchester, Mike Pickering. Formerly A&R man at Factory Records, Pickering had been responsible for bringing both James and The Happy Mondays into the Factory stable, and latterly Guru Josh and Black Box to Deconstruction, to where he moved after Factory. Then, fronted by Heather Small, and including former Orange Juice keyboardist Paul Heard and Pickering, M-People had had a club-land hit with 'How Can I Love You More?' in 1991. It was the album *Elegant Slumming* in 1993 that launched the hits 'Moving On Up' and 'One Night in Heaven' on the world.

By the time *Fresco* was released in the autumn of 1997, the band were on something of a slide, with critical reaction to the previous two albums being luke warm. The new album was another rich collection of highly polished pop soul tracks, on two of which Johnny appeared. 'Believe It' was a funky dance number based around a repeated riff, and 'Rhythm And Blues" a mid-paced number featuring Johnny's echoing, wah-wah solo. Both tracks were, once again, a diversion from Johnny's more familiar work, and were also – like so many of his diversions – steps into soul and dance.

At the same time, Morrissey's critical standing was re-adjusted by the release of *Maladjusted,* after the under-whelming *Southpaw Grammar.* The album, according to *Uncut,* "confounded the obituary writers." Morrissey and Marr could still cut it, however far apart.

★

In November, one of Johnny's chance meetings while in the USA led to the genesis of his first truly solo work some years later. In an elevator in New York he "bumped into" a young guy. "We started talking, and we hit it off," explained Johnny much later. When he discovered that the guy was a musician, the pair arranged to meet up and play back at Johnny's house when they were back in the UK. At first, remembered Marr, "I wasn't even aware that he was a musician." Of course the young man was Zak Starkey, son of Ringo and drummer to the stars. Starkey's career went back to the early Eighties, although technically of course, being the son of a Beatle, it had in all likelihood started at birth. Sean and Julian Lennon, Danni Harrison, and Sir Paul's son James McCartney have all followed their dads into the business. By 1985, Zak was working with Roger Daltrey on his album *Under A Raging Moon*, with former Moody Blue and member of Wings Denny Laine on *Hometown Girls,* and was soon established not only as a touring member of The Who but also in his old man's All Starr band.

"He'd go off with The Who, and then I'd get back and be writing with Beth Orton," said Marr. "And he'd be doing some more Who stuff... We got to a point where we really liked the songs, and wanted to turn this into a band." The pair had a natural affinity, and by 1998 it was Starkey who was discussing in interviews the ongoing work with Johnny that eventually led to Johnny Marr's new band, The Healers. Johnny spoke of how he had been auditioning drummers who were so nervous that they couldn't hold their sticks properly, but that when he met Starkey the adulation was the other way round. Remembering what Marc Bolan and T. Rex had meant to the teenage Johnny, he laughed when he told the tale. "It was when he said he'd been on the set of *Born To Boogie* (the T. Rex movie directed by Ringo Starr)... I just thought, 'Oh my God!'"

1997 also saw eighteen years of Conservative drudgery come to an end. It was a heady few months: England beat Italy at football, the United Kingdom won the Eurovision song contest with – for a change – a proper band (Katrina And The Waves), and New Labour ousted the greying Tories under the banner of 'Cool Britannia'. Tony Blair's publicity machine recognised the new wave of optimism amongst the youth of the country, and – with the generation of acid housers and E-droppers who had gathered at Spike Island to witness The Stone Roses back in 1990 now all eligible to vote – Blair brought rock music on board to establish his own rock 'n' roll yoof credentials. In truth, the move was both a genuine inclusive gesture from Blair – he was after all the first British Prime Minister to play the electric guitar, having fronted his own band at University – but it was also a demeaning and cynical ploy to promote a political agenda. The sight of Noel Gallagher, suited and booted at 10 Downing Street, troubled some, but not Noel, who had happily supported New Labour and used the previous years' Brit Awards as an opportunity to tell the nation who to vote for. Since Liam Gallagher and Patsy Kensit had appeared on the front of posh style mag *Vanity Fair*, both the Gallagher brothers and Cool Britannia had become high profile across the British media. By the release of Oasis's 'difficult third album', the band were established as both the darlings and anti-heroes of a nation reeling from the death of Diana Spencer, the former wife of The Prince of Wales. *Be Here Now* sold more than three quarters of a million copies on its first day of release, but the album received a critical mauling.

Soon though there was turmoil within the Oasis camp itself. While Alan White had replaced original drummer Tony McCarroll in 1995, the year 1998 saw the departure of both Paul McGuigan and guitarist Paul Arthurs. The never-ending story of the Gallagher Brothers' band took another turn. 'Bonehead' Arthurs was a popular member of the band with fans, and his replacement would have to both fit in with the remaining members and appeal to the fan base. Who better?

Johnny denies that he was ever officially asked to join Oasis. That doesn't mean to say that behind locked doors and between friends the matter wasn't discussed. Of course, Johnny would play with them in the future, and tour with them with The Healers. For now Oasis was not for him, and the gig was taken on by Gem Archer of Heavy Stereo. Johnny is regularly linked with bands when their guitarist jumps ship – he was later to be associated with Blur, as a replacement for outgoing guitarist Graham Coxon, but of course this was even less likely to happen than his joining Oasis.

One of Johnny's production projects was released in September, when Marion's album *The Program* was released. The connection that brought Johnny in as producer on the second album by the Macclesfield-based Britpop band came via Joe Moss, who was managing Marion and invited Johnny down to the studio. The album was a follow-up to their first release *This World And Body,* for a band that had built up a strong live following around the country, including having played support roles for both Morrissey and Radiohead. "I wasn't particularly looking to produce a group," said Johnny.

"They invited me down to a rehearsal. Before we knew it, six hours had gone by and we'd worked on pretty much the whole album." As so often in Johnny's career, it is the personal connection that leads to the collaboration. "It soon became obvious," said Johnny, "that we were going to make a record."

While Marion's career was not long-lasting, the album they produced with him was well-received, and still sounds good nearly a decade on – unsurprisingly somewhere halfway between The Smiths and The Healers. Johnny's input was very similar to what he had injected into Billy Bragg's work: embellishment, re-writing, playing on the tracks and, in this case producing the band too. Marr also co-wrote 'Is That So?' and the single 'Miyako Hideaway'. As with Bragg, Sumner or Talking Heads, if Johnny heard elements in the songs that he felt could be developed further, the band themselves were open to his ideas. "They had a steaming chorus," Johnny said of the 'Miyako Hideaway'. "And I came up with a middle-eight and developed the verses a little."

Marion singer Jaime Harding watched Johnny at work on the tracks, and, like Billy Bragg, he too felt that there was a magical touch in what Marr brought to the party. Most of all, whatever Marr did, or added, or wiped, he never lost the feel of Marion themselves, never subjugated the band to his own ideas. "Johnny's input [on the album] was as big as anybody's, and he changed quite a lot of the music under the voice," explains Harding. "He made it richer and gave it a different feel, but… it's a Marion sound."

Unfortunately, although the album was a very powerful piece of work – the sound of an established band making big strides – *The Program* did not progress Marion into the big league. By the spring of the following year the band was in tatters, but several years on they still have a strong following. Guitarist Phil Cunningham went on to join New Order and – completing the circle as so many times has happened in Johnny's career – play with Electronic.

★

The death of Linda McCartney in 1998 had moved many people for whom Sir Paul and The Beatles had formed a backdrop to their life. While the turmoil that was The Beatles' closing years had entertained and dumbfounded most observers, Linda had forever been at Paul's side in the aftermath, and – as a member of Wings – become a pop star of sorts in her own right. Linda had also been dearly loved for her stand on behalf of vegetarianism and animal rights. Thus it was a congregation formed from many churches that mourned her death.

To mark the anniversary of her passing, an emotional concert was organised at London's Royal Albert Hall in April of 1999. Paul appeared, of course, alongside Marianne Faithful, Tom Jones, Neil Finn, Elvis Costello and others. For Smiths fans, the appearance of Johnny getting back with Chrissie Hynde and The Pretenders to sing 'Meat Is Murder' was a highlight of the show, and a natural synergy as Hynde had long ago joined Linda in the animal rights movement herself. It was moving to see Johnny put the past behind him to perform a Smiths song for a cause he felt truly noble. "There was a bigger principle at stake other than some silly sort of pop notions," said Johnny, happy that the larger share of the proceeds from the event would go to the charity Animaline. Johnny also performed on the night with Marianne Faithful and – in a surprising coda to the performance of George Michael – added his weight to a performance of Michael's 'Faith'. How The Smiths fans of the Eighties must have smiled.

"[It] was pretty incredible really," said Johnny. "I felt kind of honoured to play there... very grateful to be asked. And I felt quite flattered to have known [Linda] because she was a very beautiful person." The event was the first time that Johnny met up with Neil Finn, with whom he would work closely, though their conversation was short. For all concerned, the Linda McCartney tribute was a delight all round.

In April, Johnny appeared on *Top Of The Pops* again, with Electronic, to promote the current single 'Vivid'. Asked what the new album was going to be like, Marr and Sumner were in good form. "It's not very good," joked Barney. "It wasn't worth making." Marr denied having anything to do with it at all. "We're not really on it," he claimed on www.worldinmotion.net. "We got our friends to do it!" *Twisted Tenderness* was in fact a departure for Electronic, a rock album retaining their trademark sense of melody but this time heavy on guitar. In a sense, this was the first Electronic album proper, the first time that the band defined their own sound *as a band*. Bernard and Johnny were both keen to explain how much each had influenced the other's work over the long period that they had been working together. "People don't realise that we've lived in each other's pockets for eight or nine years," Johnny reflected. Despite being forever linked with Morrissey in people's minds, Marr was proud of the relationship he now had with Bernard Sumner, saying that "this is the longest-running partnership I've been involved with."

Whereas *Raise The Pressure* had been the product of years' of work, *Twisted Tenderness* was completed in only a few months. The difference was that the duo, reversing their usual writing/recording process of composing on keyboards and overdubbing, wrote the songs on guitar instead of keyboards. Marr found the process exhilarating – perhaps having reached the end of a natural cycle of experimentation and wishing to get back to the basics of what he did best. The resulting creativity brought a number of songs out of Johnny that he felt needed a different context – songs that required a bunch of guys in a room playing as a traditional rock band. So began the process – though a number of these tracks ended up as Electronic songs – of composing tracks for what eventually became The Healers.

The band for Electronic's album was fleshed out again by adding Black Grape's Ged Lynch on drums, Jimi Goodwin on bass and Astrid Williamson on backing vocals. It wasn't only Johnny who played guitar. With a lot of what Marr called "coaxing and bullying", he talked Bernard into including his own guitar lines on the final recordings too, just as he had encouraged Matt Johnson in the past.

Twisted Tenderness was another labour of love. When Johnny spoke of there being a unique sound quality to his material that he could only achieve when he worked with Sumner, it recalled his absolute devotion to the songs he had done with Matt Johnson. Sumner's lyrics – aided and abetted by Johnny, who "helped out" on the writing – had an increased weight to them, beyond much of what he had written elsewhere, and for the first time his lyrics were printed on the album's sleeve. These were not jobbing workaday fancies for wealthy freelance musicians, but projects of great worth and meaning to Johnny. He seemed to care as much about the music of *Twisted Tenderness* as he had about *The Smiths* more than fifteen years earlier. "I'm very proud of this record," he told the BBC, "and want to promote it as much as possible." Interestingly, the album was only released in the USA nearly a year after it's European and Japanese release, including a handful of extra tracks.

'Make It Happen' and 'Haze' featured Johnny on vocals; 'Vivid' was one of the songs that Johnny had written and demoed initially with Zak Starkey and that Bernard jumped on for Electronic; 'Can't Find My Way Home' was the first cover version that Bernard had ever recorded, an ironic selection in itself. At the birth of Electronic, Neil Tennant had glibly called the band 'the Blind Faith of the Nineties', referencing the Sixties supergroup that combined Ginger Baker, Eric Clapton and Steve Winwood. So many years on, it was apposite that the group's first cover should be one of Blind Faith's best-known songs. Johnny was particularly proud of 'Prodigal Son', another song originally demoed with Starkey. On the album's release, the band toured as a group proper, the first time that Johnny felt comfortable doing so with Electronic, which – in essence – was effectively a duo.

While Johnny openly admitted that Electronic's mandate included commercial success alongside artistic honesty, it was felt that the release was under-promoted. Yet despite Johnny's misgivings, the album made it to the top ten, eventually stalling at number nine. As it was, *Twisted Tenderness* proved to be – at least until now – the last album release from Electronic. A cycle of ten years had come to an end for Bernard and Johnny, during which time their work rate had been prodigious and the quality of their output – like everything else Marr has worked on – impeccable. As always – because partners such as Sumner, Bragg or Johnson were friends before they were working colleagues – Johnny would not write off the chances of Electronic convening again in the future.

For now though, *Twisted Tenderness* marked the end of an era. "I am really proud that we still [have] a friendship that is really strong," Johnny said of his ongoing relationship with Sumner. "As I do with Matt Johnson and Chrissie Hynde, and pretty much everyone I've worked with." The relationship with Bernard was perhaps closer than with any former collaborator. "When we took a break... we would get on a boat and go sailing together. I have never been closer to anyone."

There were always distractions however, and not always welcome ones for Johnny. The year of *Twisted Tenderness* was also the year of Manchester United's treble victory in the FA Cup, Premiership and in Europe – a momentous night for Manchester's 'other team', but not one savoured by supporters of the blue side of the city. Marr and Sumner joked that while Bernard was becoming increasingly smug at Utd's success, Johnny was becoming more and more 'twisted' in his perverse desire to see The Reds stuffed. With City's form getting worse, Bernard would tease Marr that Man City "would be playing Salford Grammar School next."

Electronic had run its course, but Johnny and Bernard remained close friends. "It's one of the rare examples of a band that split up with no acrimony whatsoever," said Johnny, and his friendship with Sumner – who he describes as "a *real* punk" – remains intact.

One of Johnny's least-expected moves in the late Nineties took him back twenty years and more. Looking back to their early encounters around the Manchester scene in the early Eighties, Mike Joyce remembers how his future band-mate always stood out from the crowd, because, he claimed, Marr was "always his own little fashion industry." In 1999 his life-long interest in matters fashionable led him to team up with one of Manchester's coolest designers, and set up their own fashion label.

Marr had started out in 'the fashion trade' – as mentioned, before The Smiths he had worked in X Clothes and hung out at Joe Moss's Crazy Face boutiques in central Manchester. Noted by everyone who remembers him back then for his sartorial elegance, Johnny had run back and forth to London fetching biker boots and berets back to put around town. An unlikely fashion leader for the new millennium perhaps, but the entire indie scene, Oasis and The Stone Roses all had a genetic link back to the look of Johnny Marr about them. Johnny had always been interested in cool.

'Elk' was a partnership with designer Nigel Lawson – no relation to the English Tory MP famed for his weight loss plan and notorious offspring. Lawson grew up in Hazel Grove, one of Stockport's more affluent suburbs only a few miles from Manchester city centre. In the late Eighties he had opened a store called Quad in Manchester's collective retail warehouse Affleck's Palace, *the* place in Manchester to buy your second-hand duds, joss sticks and groovy clothes from young, yet-to-be-established fashion designers. Quad supplied, amongst other things, Henri Lloyd jackets – snapped up by Manchester's fashion-conscious football fans, among them a young Mr L Gallagher. After Quad closed, Nigel took time travelling before a meeting with Johnny led them to found their own fashion label. The look was, according to Johnny, "a weird mix of native American, outdoor wear, Mod and other bits." Marr spoke of how the enterprise was as much ideological as business-orientated, though the gear was certainly visible in exclusive circles, and in the UK it could be found at Selfridge's, at Manchester's Geese and Dr Jives in Glasgow, while Johnny had established outlets in Boston, San Fransisco, and New York. Bernard Sumner and various members of Oasis could be

179

spotted in the self-styled 'desert and forest clothing' over the next year
or so, in particular in leather cagoules 'built in Manchester.' "It's like a
band," Marr said. "If you keep the ideas pure and the enthusiasm up,
then people can realise it's not a corporate thing." Elk hung up its
horns after a couple of years. But for a while Johnny was not just a
fashion leader, but a fashion entrepreneur.

In the summer of 1999 another new friend entered Johnny's life
via a casual meeting in the USA, and led to a beautiful track with
which Johnny was closely involved. Norfolk-born UK singer Beth
Orton's debut album *Trailer Park* was a splendid, folky debut from a
singer-songwriter who immediately turned heads and ears with her
mellow, trippy songs. The follow-up, *Central Reservation* showed
Orton very much on a journey both musical and spiritual. In 1999,
Orton was appearing in the Lillith Fair, the women-only travelling
festival founded by Sarah McLachlan. Backstage after one of her
shows, she came off stage to find a friend in deep conversation with
someone she didn't recognise.

"I was just chatting to the two of them," said Orton.
The conversation lasted half an hour before Beth eventually asked
the 'other guy' what his job was. "And he was like, 'Oh, I play guitar.'
And I said, 'Oh, is that right? Anyone I've heard of?'" Johnny
introduced himself modestly as the guitar player in The Smiths.
"I was like, 'Oh no, you're Johnny Marr!'" said Orton. While she
might have been showered in embarrassment, she needn't have
worried. Johnny was cool. "He's such a sweetheart," said Beth.
"We just carried on."

"She knew who I was," agreed Johnny, "but she didn't know
it was me." The pair hit it off immediately. Discovering that they
were staying in the same hotel, Johnny and Beth would sit into the
small hours on the balcony with the requisite guitars and promises
that they would work together again. Orton had songs unfinished,
and one caught Johnny's ear in particular. "He got very excited
about one song in particular," says Orton, "and started adding these
chords underneath. And then sort of... 'What about this idea for
the bridge?'"

"I wrestled the guitar out of her hands when I thought she'd got
to a bit that was wrong," laughed Johnny. "That's how it happens...
If I've got something in common with someone it is very likely that
I'm going to like what they're doing in the studio." Johnny kept
adding bits here and there, fixing up the chorus. "He got all these

chords out of the cupboard," said Beth. "And he was putting in all these little things... he just added this other dimension."

The result – 'Concrete Sky' – is a beautiful track on a beautiful album. By the time Beth Orton got around to recording *Daybreaker*, Johnny was on tour with Neil Finn, and not available for the sessions. Although he had sung the gorgeous harmony on the demo, Beth roped in Ryan Adams, and the resulting track is the peak of an album that was itself one of the highlights of 2002.

While Johnny was in the States, he was also introduced to current wunderkind Beck Hansen, who he visited in the studio during the making of the latter's album *Midnight Vultures*. The pair got on immediately, and Johnny added some guitar parts to a couple of tracks, most notably 'Milk And Honey'. Beck's articulate writing and lush, rich arrangements suited Johnny perfectly, and the lengthy, cinematic track was a highlight of a landmark album. Beck reminded Johnny of David Byrne, his wicked sense of humour and sense of the absurd combined with a truly unique creative gift. "He's not afraid to go down some necessary side roads rather than just take the main road," said Johnny. "He'll be discussed in the same way as Neil Young... and David Bowie."

Johnny's thoughts continued to turn to solo material, and he was keen to formulate a more coherent solo project. To a degree, Marr's success as a 'solo' performer to date had been his undoing. Given that almost every project he had worked on had been very successful, commercially as much as artistically, it was increasingly difficult to find the space to really identify what he considered his 'own' work, to distinguish exactly which creation was his and and which that of his partner. As a writer, that was one problem. As a producer, Johnny noted also that there was no distinction between what was his input and how much directly came from the artists themselves. Increasingly frustrated – collaboration with other artists having been the mainstay of Marr's career – Johnny was becoming more and more keen to put the shared responsibilities of Electronic and The The to bed and to work on his own material. "When I've worked with other artists," Johnny told an interviewer for www.worldinmotion.net early in 1999, "my first thought in the morning is fretting about the production... If I'm going to do that then I might as well do it for myself." While Electronic had been his priority, he would use the other priorities of his partner to excuse himself from the project as soon as possible. "When Bernard does his stuff with New Order, I'm going to kick that [solo stuff] off. I'll be singing and getting a band together."

★

Into the new millennium, Johnny continued to be involved in a number of projects with friends, new acquaintances, and – most notably – more formative work on his solo ambitions. Friends had been encouraging Johnny to develop his own material, and to get a solo album together for years. Matt Johnson was one of the 'encouragers', himself having been on the receiving end of Marr's own enthusiasm in the development of The The. "I think the world of Johnny," he told one interviewer in 1999. "I've been telling him to do a solo record ever since I've known him. I've been kicking him up the arse… and he's finally doing it." Chrissie Hynde was another advocate. While Johnny's material was developing, almost in a mirror of his teenage years, he realised that he needed a band to front the songs that he was writing.

Inspired by a slew of bands like Santana and Jefferson Airplane (instead of Leiber and Stoller!) he began to formulise a band structure that would have at its core a fundamental looseness, a 'tribal band' with many members. Early in 2000, Marr met bass player Alonza Bevan, late of retro-rockers Kula Shaker, and with Zak Starkey on board he already had the nucleus of the band. Appropriately, Kula Shaker had been a band that could recreate in a modern context the hazy, pot-fuelled years of the first wave of Britpop in the mid- and late-Sixties. Under the heavy influence of The Beatles, Small Faces and Traffic, the group achieved considerable success in the singles and the album charts, and with Crispian Mills on vocals had ready-made headlines as Mills was the son of actress Hayley and the grandson of actor Sir John Mills. From 1996, the band enjoyed a couple of years in the sun, but then the music press turned on them, and by the end of the decade – despite claiming that by then they would be the biggest band on the planet – Mills had left and the band was in tatters.

With two high-profile members of his band in place, Johnny might have been accused of cherry-picking celebrity members. But he had met Starkey and liked the guy before he had any idea of who he was; further, while Johnny had seen Kula Shaker live a couple of times and been impressed by their performances, it was another mutual friend who'd introduced the pair. "I was fully aware of his reputation as a musician," said Marr, "[but] the crucial thing was that a mutual friend said we'd get along as people. And that is really what counts for me. We need to have that friendship."

The comment once again illustrates Johnny's fundamental working ethic: friendship first, work to follow. Of all the people that Marr has worked with over the years, he cites only three examples where the idea of working with a third party came before knowing them well. Beck, Talking Heads and Bryan Ferry are the three instances where he was so intrigued that he went ahead with the work before really knowing his partners.

During the year, Johnny also worked with one of his childhood heroes, appearing – alongside Bernard Butler – on Bert Jansch's twenty-first album *Crimson Moon*. Jansch had inspired a generation and more of guitar pickers, his idiosyncratic but wonderfully compelling playing being an inspiration for anyone who sought out his work. For Johnny it was a dream come true – a dream he first had way back when he was learning to play as a young boy. *Dreamweaver*, the accompanying TV documentary on Jansch, also featured Johnny and Bernard, while the following year saw Johnny present Bert with a 'Lifetime Achievement Award' at the BBC Radio 2 Folk Awards.

Marr and Butler's playing on *Crimson Moon* is delightful, with Bernard's perhaps being the more erratic – appropriate for a player like Jansch, who has no concept of 'middle-eights' or bar lines. Particularly haunting was Johnny's plaintive harmonica on 'The River Bank', while his backing vocals on 'Looking For Love' were beautiful too. Johnny appeared on *Later With Jools Holland* in July, with Bernard and Bert alongside him, playing 'The River Bank' live. It was a briliant performance.

Bert Jansch was rightly feted in celebration of his sixtieth birthday in 2003. The BBC arranged and filmed the event in which characters as diverse as Bernard Butler and Ralph McTell teamed up to celebrate Jansch's life and music. Even if they didn't play together, for Bert it was remarkable that such a diversity of players should appear on the same bill. Marr, of course, was in his element.

For Jansch, Bernard Butler was a bit of an unknown quantity, but he knew that he had come to his work via Johnny's love for it. Johnny Marr he knew well. "Johnny is unstoppable," said Jansch. "He is guitar-mad! Endless – he just goes on and on!" On the subject of the famous rock guitarist, who has someone to tune his guitars for him,

Bert smiled wryly, "I didn't know what a 'guitar tech' was until I met those two!"

★

It was the members of the coalescing new band who talked Marr into standing up and fronting the ensemble. Whilst a decade before he had re-iterated his lack of ambition as a front man, now it seemed an inevitability, and he adopted the role with relish. Back in 1989, Johnny had told *NME* that he never wanted to stand in front of a group: "I know I will never be as popular, sell as many records or be as famous as Morrissey or any other singer I work with… and I don't want that." However, in The Healers he took centre stage for the first time. It was also a joint decision between Johnny, the band, management and label, that the band be called (in full) 'Johnny Marr And The Healers.' "'The Healers' on the posters – we may get 500 people," said Johnny, explaining that that is how he would have preferred it. "But if it has my name on it, we may get 504."

As Johnny came up with the basic concept of The Healers and recorded demos of the songs likely to be worked on, he also sang the vocals. All along he figured that he would ultimately add a singer to the band to take care of the final vocal job, and had listened to a number of demos from prospective vocalists around Manchester. One or two were even in mind for the job. What happened was that a democratic process proved to Johnny that he was actually the best man for the job himself. Presenting the demos to the band, the musicians themselves decided who they wanted for their singer, and elected Starkey to deliver their ultimatum: they wanted their lead vocalist to be their guitar player. By the time The Healers were his priority, Johnny was cool enough and confident enough in his abilities to accept the job.

Singing live toned up Johnny's vocal chords. The band played their first gigs in the spring of 2000, kicking off in the northern England town of Lancaster, where they played for nearly an hour and a half. While Lancaster was a 'secret' warm-up gig, their first advertised show was in Coventry, to an audience of about three hundred people, too many of whom clamoured for Smiths songs throughout. More importantly, the gig was a warm-up for dates to come, because The Healers were booked to support Oasis on their forthcoming tour. Johnny was asked whether it was 'humbling' to be

184

supporting a band that he had helped get off the ground in the first place. It wasn't as though Marr had had to beg for the gig. "I didn't ask to support them," he answered. "They invited me out."

In fact, by now it was pretty obvious to anyone concerned that what really motivated Johnny Marr was the studio, and that any gig, headlining or supporting, was more about fun and the transference and sharing of energy rather than ego. "I didn't really give a shit about supporting Oasis, and I didn't see it as being humbling," he said. "And I think humbling experiences are good for you, anyway." Johnny had also enjoyed recent tours more than he had ever done in the days of The Smiths, and for the first outings of The Healers everything went well. The bands played six shows in seven days, in Milan, Zurich, Vienna, Leipzig, Warsaw and Berlin before returning to the UK for two dates at Bolton's football ground, the Reebok Stadium, where they shared the support slot with the reformed Happy Mondays.

After Bolton, the band headed way out East, appearing at the Fuji Rock Fest in Japan, then in Barcelona. By September, the band was back in the UK, playing gigs in Portsmouth and London. As the writer, guitarist and singer, Marr invested more of himself in the experience than ever before, but thankfully the gigs routinely received a good reception. The first incarnation of The Healers tended to ramble through the songs live. "I wanted to really stretch them out and jam," said Johnny. People were curious, but went away impressed by The Healers, by Johnny, and – in many cases – particularly by Zak Starkey. Taking the full glare of the spotlight was clearly a risky strategy for Johnny, but he carried it off with aplomb. He would draw comparison with other notable Mancunian vocalists, of which there were of course many to choose from, but perhaps a rock audience in the twenty-first century could forgive and forget the past, and take Johnny Marr on his own terms. For Johnny, as always, his eyes were on the present and the future, not on the past, and if the comparisons irked him, he kept a dignified silence. If he was compared to Ian Brown or Liam Gallagher, so what? As Morrissey used to tell some of the early Smiths audiences – if you don't like it, leave.

In September Johnny joined an all-star bash to celebrate the sixtieth anniversary of the birth of John Lennon. The sessions were held at George Martin's Air Studios in Hampstead, and included the Gallagher brothers, Ron Wood, Donovan, Lonnie Donegan, as well as

Sharleen Spiteri and Jools Holland. Sounding fantastic, the evening was kicked off by Johnny, Noel and Gem Archer playing the Lennon classic 'Tomorrow Never Knows', accompanied by sitar and percussion. Towards the end of the year, Johnny followed up the dates that he had played with Oasis by sitting down with Liam Gallagher and laying down some songs. Within a week, Liam was reported to have written, and Johnny played on ten songs that would be considered for the next Oasis album. Liam apparently said the songs were better than anything by either Radiohead or John Lennon. The tracks remain unreleased as recorded with Johnny, but the next Oasis album – which Marr would ultimately play on – featured three of Liam's songs.

Outside of The Healers, Johnny was also busy on tracks with two of his former collaborators, Chris Lowe and Neil Tennant of the Pet Shop Boys. Nearly twenty years into their own career, the sessions for *Release*, to be heard publicly in 2002, saw the band eschewing again the synth pop of their early years and developing a more rounded, organic sound, with Johnny's guitars prominent in the mix. With Johnny approaching the tender age of forty, there was no sign of any kind of mid-life crisis as the team worked on tracks at Tennant's home in north-eastern England.

"We were very much on our own," Chris Lowe told Sylvie Simmons, "in a very organic situation, and it all just sort of evolved." While Tennant and Lowe had written many of the songs on guitar, Johnny's final input was paramount, and the tracks that worked the best were the ones that were more guitar-oriented. A few years previously, Johnny had joked with an interviewer that Neil Tennant was 'a closet Ritchie Blackmore', but – he noted – was very melodic in his playing. One of Johnny's roles on *Release* was to 're-do' Tennant's own guitar parts, digging into the tracks that Tennant and Lowe had put together, picking out elements on the guitar that brought them even further to life, just as he had done with Billy Bragg over a decade before. If the album was a departure for the Pet Shop Boys, nothing could encapsulate this more than the fact that the piece was critically compared to Oasis, surely as far away from what the Pet Shop Boys were perceived to be by their public as possible. "If we had wanted to," admitted Tennant, asked about the songs on the album, "we could have turned them all into dance tracks... [but] we just felt there's so much dance music around nowadays what was the point?"

186

Much of the middle of the 2001 was occupied with a tour that Johnny undertook alongside Neil Finn. After that brief meeeting at the Linda McCartney tribute concert, Finn simply called Johnny out of the blue and asked him if he wanted to go out on the road again.

Finn had been playing a few low key gigs around New Zealand with bands made up of local amateur musicians, who would cover his hits and those of Crowded House and Split Enz, the two bands with whom Neil is most closely associated. To end the tour, Finn decided to form a little band of his own and contacted Johnny, Pearl Jam's Eddie Vedder, Phil Sedway and Ed O'Brien from Radiohead amongst others about sharing a bill.

"It was a whimsical notion I had around Christmas," said Neil Finn. For the gig in Auckland, Neil decided his new little band could be something special for the town. "I was going out to do a tour with a band of strangers every night," Neil continued, "and I thought it would be good in Auckland... to do something in Auckland that Auckland would never normally get." As Finn explained, "it took a few phone calls."

Johnny was intrigued – Finn's new material, the album *One Nil*, had impressed him, and the more he thought about it the more he really wanted to get out and do the gigs. On arrival, the band rehearsed for three or four days, and when the band hit the stage they were supported by Betchadupa, Neil's eldest son's band. Dates in the Antipodes were followed by a European tour ("which I had no idea I was going to do," said Johnny, "until I got back from New Zealand!"), and according to Marr it was one of the best experiences of his career. "In the past," said Johnny, "I always had to be dragged by the collar by the lead singer," whereas this tour was a joy. "I didn't realise how great Neil was until I started playing with him," Marr admitted, "[but] when you get inside those songs you realise what a talent he's got." During the tour, Johnny 'allowed' Neil to cover much protected/little played Smiths songs. They included 'There Is A Light That Never Goes Out' and 'How Soon Is Now?' – perhaps two of the most sacred songs in Johnny's back-catalogue. The pair shared the vocal duty. "We got better as we went on," said Finn.

Meanwhile, Johnny was working hard on his own new material too. The new Healers song 'Down On The Corner' was played at virtually every gig, and often Neil would ask Johnny to run through the song for the purposes of sound-checking too.

By the time the tour reached the UK, and Manchester, they were really flying. Of the gig in his local home theatre, Johnny observed that "I haven't seen the Manchester Apollo rock that much since Thin Lizzy." In the spring of the following year, Johnny re-joined Finn for a series of concerts on the west coast of America. The response from the Californian audiences was as enthusiastic as it had been elsewhere. The ensuing live release, *Seven Worlds Collide*, was testament to the fantastic experience that the band enjoyed. As well as becoming friends with Neil Finn – who Johnny clearly respects extremely highly, Johnny got to know Eddie Vedder from Pearl Jam and Lisa Germano too. Johnny was to work on two of Germano's own solo albums in the next few years.

Although The Healers had been out alone and had toured with Oasis, there was still no published evidence of Johnny's 'solo' project. Nonetheless, work continued on his return from the Finn tour, and the first fruits of it were released in early October. The EP 'The Last Ride' was completely unlike anything Johnny had released before, and he was happy for it to be considered a new beginning. "It's really nice for people to know where I am at," he told one interviewer, "and not have to talk about the past all the time." 'The Last Ride' was a postcard from where Johnny was at in the early years of the new century, and that was certainly a mighty long way away from The Smiths which was, after all, nearly two decades previous.

Heathen Chemistry, the dull new Oasis album, was released in the summer of 2002 to a better critical response than some recent Oasis records. To some degree the media love affair with Burnage's finest had run its course, and the Oasis congregation was now a more settled church, a firm fan base rather than a Pavlovian response to anything the Gallagher brothers did. The album featured a number of contributions from Johnny. With a laid-back feel from Oasis, the record showcased several of Liam's songs as well as one each by 'new boys' Gem Archer and Andy Bell. While Johnny was never likely to have replaced Paul Arthurs, his relationship with the Gallaghers was still good. '(Probably) All In The Mind' was very reminiscent of The Beatles' 'Tomorrow Never Knows', and Johnny added an uncomplicated but raw and effective solo. 'Born On A Different Cloud' – one of Liam's songs – featured Johnny on slide guitar. He played a really effective session that recalled the slide of George Harrison as much as Liam's fantastic vocal revisited John Lennon's. 'Better Man', a rocking track much in the tradition of The Stone Roses' 'Love Spreads' was Johnny's final cut on the album, another one of Liam's songs on which – as well as guitar – Johnny also contributed backing vocals.

On the subject of Johnny Marr, Noel Gallagher is hysterically funny. "There's nothing he can't do on a guitar," says Gallagher. "You can't be influenced by Johnny Marr, because he's unique. You can't play what he plays." Noel rises to his subject with enthusiasm. "Even *he* can't play what he plays. He told me a story of trying to recreate 'How Soon Is Now?', and it was like an Abbot and Costello sketch... even *he's* not as good as he is!"

Another production credit came Johnny's way in 2002 when he worked on the first album by Joe Moss's recent signing Haven. *Between The Senses* was a strong album, compared in parts to Travis and Coldplay. In a series of events closely resembling the birth of The Smiths, Joe Moss, on holiday in Cornwall, was invited to see the band play live. Although Moss was still managing Marion, and they were gradually dissolving under his gaze, he liked the band that he saw, and invited them up to Manchester, getting them some support slots with Badly Drawn Boy in the process. Haven and Joe Moss got on really well, but the band and Johnny hit it off straight away. Johnny and Haven were to work on the follow-up album in a year or so's time.

*

In the spring of 2003, the BBC marked the twentieth anniversary of the release of 'Hand In Glove' by broadcasting live from Salford Lads Club, by now firmly ensconced as The Smiths' 'own Abbey Road'. Andy Rourke had been playing with Badly Drawn Boy, the Mancunian sensation whose work had rightly become feted nationwide. Mike Joyce was drumming with new band The Dogs, including former Oasis guitarist Bonehead. Johnny was of course playing with The Healers. Lisa Germano, who had met Johnny through the Neil Finn tour, released her critically acclaimed album *Lullaby For Liquid Pig,* on which Johnny played a part. Germano's solo career – she first appeared in the mid-Eighties playing violin for John Mellencamp – was well-established, and her *Geek The Girl* was one of the highlight albums of the previous few years.

Despite so much activity, The Healers took off on tour, and their dates through 2003 made it one of the most extensive jaunts of Johnny's career to date, encompassing a dozen countries and varying from small clubs to major stadia. The band kicked off in the USA in mid-January in Hoboken, New Jersey. Although Johnny had played many times in the USA, and loves the country dearly, he was as nervous as hell when he took the stage at Maxwell's. His first words to an American audience as a Healer summed his pre-gig nerves up perfectly. "I can't speak for everyone else," Johnny told the crowd, "but I've been shitting myself!" The band played three dates at Maxwell's before heading to Philadelphia, Washington and New York. By February, via Toronto, the tour arrived on the West Coast, where The Healers played at venues such as LA's Troubadour and appeared live on *The Late Show* with David Letterman. Apart from playing songs from the album, Johnny also regularly performed the Bob Dylan classic 'Don't Think Twice, It's Alright' to the delight of audiences.

Still avoiding Smiths covers in the set, and sticking to largely tracks from *Boomslang*, the band played two gigs at the beginning of March to finish off the world tour. The first was back in the home town of Manchester, while the second was a triumph at the ULU, where so long ago The Smiths had been introduced to John Walters, had been invited to their first session for John Peel, and had set off on the mighty journey that Johnny was very much still a part of.

Long-awaited, The Healers' first album *Boomslang* was finally released to a modest but generally enthusiastic reception in February 2003. Inevitably the album was compared to The Smiths and to all the other bands who had come out of Manchester shouting, from Oasis to The Stone Roses and The Happy Mondays. The comparisons were not always entirely fair, nor were they by any means all positive, but many reviewers and fans fell in love with the record. The fact was that the idea of a Johnny Marr album on which Johnny sings all the songs was hard to get our heads around, but as always with his work, the album works perfectly if it is viewed as a snapshot of where he stood at a given time and in a given place. The album isn't the culmination of Johnny's career, and critics looking for the 'final solution' to twenty years of shunning publicity while crafting immaculate pop year after year were searching in vain. Johnny wasn't trying to sound 'like' anyone, not least any of his former bands. With his ears constantly on contemporary bands, he was aware of how much his output would be likely to be compared to others too. "It would be undignified for me to try and sound like The Strokes, or Coldplay," he explained. "God Forbid! I just wanted to make sure the [album] was wide awake, and natural and honest."

The fact that Marr took the microphone and the centre stage for the first time in his adult career signalled that this was a different Johnny Marr altogether from the one we were used to. Not least the confidence he exuded in discussing the project. For one riotous Canadian interview, Johnny was asked whether, looking back at the Linda McCartney tribute concert, Sir Paul had been familiar with Johnny's own work. "Linda was a fan," said Johnny. "And Chrissie Hynde probably played him some stuff. He just said I should have started singing a long time earlier. He said I was amazing, and he'd wished The Beatles had had five people in it!"

The title came to Johnny in a dream, in which a snake (a 'boomslang' is a breed of snake, and the word is a Dutch translation of the name 'tree snake') approached Johnny and revealed its name. The album was the result of a long period of waiting for Marr; since the last Electronic album he had been talking the project up. It started as a solo process and turned into a band, which then turned into an album. Johnny had a clear concept of what the album would be from the beginning, but as time went on he refined the concept when needed. "I wanted to make a record that was less layered," Johnny explained. "But when I came to finish the record, I decided to do what came naturally, and what excites me." The agenda was out of the window, and Johnny decided to add as many 'colours' as he could, if they were the right colours. It was irresistible for Johnny to "put a capo on a Gretsch and see what happens."

Grant Showbiz heard demos of much of the album before its release, and knew that the project was high quality stuff. "There were versions of that Healers' album that I just thought were stunning – I heard versions… that I just thought were killer." The opening track, 'The Last Ride', clearly sets the tone for the whole collection. Johnny's vocal has a Mancunian drawl that is, of course, immediately comparable to Liam Gallagher – perhaps the slight distortion applied hinted that he was not entirely confident in his voice. There's a feel of John Squire in some of the linking riffs, but that points more to a combination of shared influences than to Marr's referencing the Roses: there's far more George Harrison, Cream and Rory Gallagher in the track than there is John Squire. Underpinning the entire track – fluent and melodic and fired by fine percussion – is heavy strumming on Johnny's favoured acoustic. While the opening two tracks have a very Beatles-feel, Marr is in Neil Young territory on 'Down On The Corner': acoustic and breezy, it builds over acoustic guitar and piano to a lilting pace, the electric picking of which does recall a few Smiths moments. The rising crescendo, treated guitar sounds, Bo Diddley riff and harmonica that introduce 'Need It' suggest more Smiths reference, but again this is far more Rory Gallagher than Marr, Joyce and Rourke. Johnny's solos are more extended chorus riffs than showboating, his vocals tight within a narrow range that suits the chugging boogie of the track.

'You Are The Magic' strums off in Oasis fashion, but is soon coloured with sonic details that mark it out as something else. Johnny's wah-wah, discrete percussion and rootsy bass recall some of the Madchester dance scene of ten years before, it's funky, dissonant and groovy, ending on gently looped guitar sounds, and Johnny was pleased that it was also compared to 'Crazy Horse'. 'InBetweens' is another rocker reminiscent of album-track Oasis, but the song was very much about himself and people of his generation who were 'between labels'. "They're interested in esoteric things, like what's going on in the ether," said Johnny, "but at the same time they know that it's important to [match] the right shirt with the right shoes!" For Johnny, the people caught up in the in-between corners of life are the ones with their eyes pointing in the right direction. As he expanded, "they're not sitting on the couch getting sucked into so-called reality TV and the shopping channel."

Six tracks in, Johnny's vocal style is well-established – he sounds confident and assured at the microphone. Of course this was not what many Marr fans had expected, but if they had been looking for rockabilly Johnny with esoteric Morrissey-lite lyrics then they hadn't watched Marr closely enough over the last few years. 'Another Day' has a simplicity of approach tempered by tambourine and a John Lennon vocal, major seventh chords and gentle harmonies that belie someone steeped in country rock as well as in grinding rock 'n' roll, a major key psychedelic optimism that is very pleasing. 'Headland', at a little over a minute and a half, is the shortest track on the album, an acoustic instrumental loaded with atonal guitar clips, threatening feedback growls and bubbling undercurrents in a lighter tone. It introduces 'Long Gone', another heavily riffed, loose drummed song. Johnny described the song as being inspired by the rock 'n' roll carousel. "It's about hanging out with five pretty crazy fans after a The The concert in Los Angeles in 1992... ending up in the ocean at Venice Beach at around six in the morning, and getting my clothes wet...what happens to everybody really!"

'Something To Shout About' slows the pace again, acoustic strumming and lovely finger-picking on electric guitar. Johnny's vocal is one of the most affecting on the album, high in register and sincere amongst a wash of backing vocals. 'Sympathy for The Devil'-style percussion introduces the last track of the album, 'Bangin' On', with Johnny's chords hard and fast, Starkey's percussion heavy and tough.

★

While Johnny could probably have signed with any number of labels, he was keen that – in an echo of The Smiths first contract with Rough Trade –he did so on his own terms and not be 'managed' by people who didn't understand him. "Some of the people I would meet with had this look in their eye, like 'Shit – this guy's an anarchist,'" he said. The last thing Marr wanted was to have to make a video in which he had to "walk around Barcelona in a white suit with a model." Instead, he signed with the indie co-op label iMusic, led by old friend Marc Geiger, retaining control over the music rather than surrender to the whim of a major traditional label. Old habits die hard, and the parallels with the original deal Rough Trade are obvious. "I was pretty much in the same situation with The Smiths," recounted Johnny. "We were invited down to record companies, sitting under posters of people I couldn't relate to."

While setting up a deal that reflected his priorities in the early days of The Smiths, Johnny also cleaned up another element of his past when he reunited with early Smiths manager Joe Moss who became his manager once again. The pair go back a long way, before The Smiths, and it was Joe who first encouraged Johnny to realise that there was more than local bands and gigging around south Manchester ahead of him. The synergy of Johnny, band, label and management was complete.

Should Johnny Marr have waited so long before releasing what is effectively his debut solo album? Some have noted that if Johnny had released *something* under his own name early in his post-Smiths career, and perhaps put out half a dozen albums over the years, then his solo career might have followed a trajectory similar to Morrissey's and the critical surprise that greeted *Boomslang* have been avoided. The problem for *Boomslang* was that Johnny had no solo credentials for fans to compare it to: while Morrissey's next album might be a masterpiece, or it may disappoint, at least people had an *idea* of where he would be coming from. With *Boomslang*, nobody quite knew what to expect from Johnny Marr, and so it either met with the listeners expectations or disappointed them – there was little middle ground.

But such expectations missed the point of Johnny's career in its entirety. From working with Morrissey, through The The, Electronic and occasional one-offs with the likes of Kirsty MacColl, Billy Bragg or Beth Orton, all of Johnny's work has been about co-operation and collaboration. Whether forming a band with Andy Rourke or shacking up with Modest Mouse, whether lighting up a spliff at the desk in The Hacienda or joining The Pretenders on tour, music for Johnny has been constantly evolving 'community,' a social activity based around music. One of the key elements to Johnny's music over the years has been that it has always been the child of creative comradeship. If Morrissey's lyrics spoke to a body of people lonely within themselves and looking for a voice that mirrored their own relationships and agendas, Johnny's music did exactly the same, because it was born out of the very emotional correspondence that Morrissey's lyrics were. A Johnny Marr solo album was never going to be Johnny alone with a finely-picked acoustic, nor was it going to be simply a step on from The Smiths, as though the intervening years had never happened. It was always going to be a collaborative effort of some kind, again a snapshot of where he was on the journey at the time.

So, of course, while the world waited for Johnny to present an album all about The Smiths and his relationship with Morrissey, he couldn't win. We were post-Mondays, post-Oasis, post-Roses. If the album had been filled with Smiths-like grooves then Marr would have inevitably been accused of sitting back and resting on former glories. If he had made an experimental album of tape loops and guitar clicks he would have been guilty of excessive self-regard. If he sounded anything like the bands who owed him so much debt themselves then again he would be chastised. Whichever way he turned there would be an enormous raft of fans ready to be disappointed, and just as many (more enlightened ones) ready to simply go and find out where Johnny was at.

In fact, the album rocks. Sonically varied, confident, laid back but punching its weight, it is an assured piece of work from some heavyweight talents. Given that this was generally perceived as his first solo outing, could listeners expect any revelations? *Were* any of the songs about Morrissey, The Smiths, or the time in Johnny's life that still meant so much to his fans? Johnny put the record straight on this one with aplomb. "None of my songs are about Morrissey," he said. "I think that would be a bit showbiz, a bit cheesy. A bit corny. Singing about someone I used to work with sixteen years ago in a cryptic fashion so that people could decode it? That would be a bit cheesy!"

Billy Bragg was a big fan of *Boomslang*. "I thought it was great," he said, when interviewed for this book. "I thought it was great of him to finally do what he wanted to do – his own project. If you are constantly working a lot with side-men it can be hard." Grant Showbiz also feels that to some degree *Boomslang* was Johnny coming home. To have lived through the exhilarating career of The Smiths at such a ridiculously young age and still to be contributing so many years later was a remarkable achievement. "I sort of looked at Johnny's life and thought, 'it's been fantastic, and he's been so lucky,'" says Grant. "But I don't know how I would have taken to being king of the world at twenty one, then had the rest of your life to go on [to]." Simply getting to *Boomslang* intact, and with such a creditable body of work behind him *apart* from The Smiths was remarkable. What was pleasing was that Johnny simply decided to follow his own nose on the project. With friends like Bernard Sumner telling him that he should have the confidence to just sound like himself ("What the fuck is wrong with sounding like you?" Sumner had asked him), Johnny had come to the same conclusion. "I had to tell myself, 'Come on Johnny, make the assumption that your audience wants you to sound like you,'" he told one interviewer.

According to Bragg, it was evident that the album was a personal labour of love. "He put a lot of himself in that record I think," he said, and – in response to the critics who unfavourably compared the album to Oasis – noted that such a comparison was "bitterly unfair", given the support that Johnny had given to the Gallaghers himself. Johnny pointed out that if listeners thought he was influenced by Oasis, they should go check out the rock family tree. "I'm *not* influenced by Oasis," he said. "The Smiths were very, very influenced by the *White Album*, so – years later – [Noel's] obviously heard the *White Album* a few times!" The message is clear – if we sound similar it's because we are coming from the same places, not because one of us copies the other. Billy has suffered a similar backlash at times himself. "The point is that the public get a fixed idea of you in their heads… it's like me with my politics: if I don't make those kind of records people aren't interested." Bragg sees a classic opportunity to knock someone down being taken by the press, who had – in the main – supported Marr since the demise of The Smiths. "There is an element of... they've lauded you all that time, they want to give you a going over now," he says. "A lot of us have had to put up with that sort of mentality."

In the wake of *Boomslang's* release, Johnny ceaselessly fielded the endless questions about The Smiths and why – after so many years – he suddenly want to be a singer. With the tour over, there was more production work to finish off, as Johnny handled the second Haven album, *All For A Reason*. The record was released in March 2004. Marr once again brought the best out of the four-piece, playing the role of producer again but adding harmonica and backing vocals too. Since *Between The Senses*, although it was tiring for the band to be constantly asked about The Smiths, they had found a supplementary audience that came to them because of Johnny's history. "In America," said vocalist Gary Briggs, "a quarter of our audiences were curious Smiths fans. You've got to respect that, so we'll answer as many Smiths questions as [are] put to us!" In some respects that probably made it easier for Johnny Marr.

CHAPTER TEN

Back To the Old House

In October 2004, the world was rocked by the sudden death of John Peel. To say 'the world was rocked' is no exaggeration – Peel's death touched everyone who had ever heard of him, from megastar bands who had received a leg up from him, to bedsit radio junkies who had listened to him under the duvet for decades. The BBC and the record industry in general went into justifiable overdrive in trying to pay tribute to a remarkable man, whose input into the pop music of the last thirty and more years was perhaps the greatest single contribution to the genre.

Johnny was understandably distraught at the news, Peel having been *the* early champion of The Smiths. He summarised his feelings at the loss thus: "John Peel was very important to The Smiths, particularly in the early days. He was the first person to play our single, and we would often try out new songs when we did sessions for his show. He knew what was going on, and went out of his way to promote good music, and the underdog." Johnny added one more modest observation. "He was a nice guy too!"

While the world mourned John Peel, Johnny, who was appearing with the brothers Neil and Tim Finn, honoured the late DJ with an impromptu version of his favourite song at a couple of gigs, notably in Liverpool. Having already kicked the audience's backside with 'There Is A Light That Never Goes Out', Johnny introduced the classic Gerry and The Pacemakers' 'Ferry Across The Mersey' in tribute to Peel. "A few people in the audience started shouting 'Teenage Kicks' (famously Peel's favourite song)" remembered Marr. "I just went into it. Never played it before in my life! It was a good moment."

By 2005, Zak Starkey had joined Oasis for their tour, an arrangement that Johnny appeared totally cool with. David Tolan had joined on drums, and Iwan Gronow of Haven was playing the bass. Johnny was back in his home studio, making demos for new Healers material alone. Some of the songs would appear in forthcoming gigs over the next couple of years, but at the point that this book went to press, no follow-up to *Boomslang* has appeared or been publicly scheduled. Early in the summer, Johnny played with a number of his teenage heroes at the Meltdown festival in London, this year (each season has a different curator who chooses themes and performers to appear) curated by Patti Smith and Lenny Kaye. Johnny was on the bill with Beth Orton, Bert Jansch and others, including fellow-Mancunian Roy Harper. The year 2005 was one of the most memorable of recent seasons, when American and British folk artists stole the show but where perhaps the guitar was the major star.

Bert Jansch played a beautiful solo set, and was joined on stage by Beth Orton, whose gorgeous, modest voice blended perfectly with Bert's faultless playing. Johnny came on after Beth and, locked together as though there was only one guitar on stage, the seated pair played acoustic versions of 'Pretty Saro' and 'Pretty Polly' like old guys who had played together for years. The Healers replaced Jansch when he left the stage, and the band leapt into 'Please Please Please Let Me Get What I Want'. After Neil Finn had sung *a cappella*, Johnny returned with Tony Shanahan to join him on 'Throw Your Arms Around Me' and sang a verse of 'Lay Me Down' with the all-star line-up for a finale.

While Johnny was busy working, The Smiths continued to be a part of the present as much as the past. While Smiths conventions have become *de rigeur* on both sides of the Atlantic, in April of 2005, Manchester Metropolitan University and the city's Institute of Popular culture ran an academic conference with The Smiths as the subject of the two day brain-fest. The supposed purpose of the event was to redress the lack of 'serious examinations' of the band over the years. 'Why Pamper Life's Complexities?: A Symposium On The Smiths' was opened by author Dave Haslam, and included seminars with titles like 'Architecture Through Music: Experiencing Manchester and Expressing Manchester' and 'When In Hulme Do As The Humans Do: Remapping Manchester and The Smiths Using Psychogeographics', the latter chaired by the redoubtable CP Lee. The event was rounded off with a gig by The Smyths tribute band and an exhibition of Stephen Wright's photos at Salford Lads Club. It was nice to know that a band dedicated to the memory of Morrissey, Marr, Rourke and Joyce could still, nearly twenty years on, turn the toe of a psychogeographicisist.

In December, Johnny appeared on another collaboration, this time providing guitar and harmonica to *Fictions,* the new album from Anglo-French chanteuse Jane Birkin. His contributions were amongst others on a variety of songs both original and covers, provided by Rufus Wainwright, Beth Gibbons, Neil Hannon, Kate Bush and others. Rumours started to appear towards the end of the year that, while the band were booked onto the bill for a charity concert in Manchester, The Smiths would be reforming for the event. While these were pretty quickly scotched, the line that at least Andy and Johnny would play together was not.

By 2006, even the most ardent of rock 'n' roll rumour mongers had realised that the 'Beatles To Reform' stories were unlikely to have any credence. Despite the deaths of both Keith Moon and John Entwistle, however, Roger Daltrey and Pete Townsend would still appear billed as The Who. It was no surprise then, that the Eighties band least likely to reform was still under pressure to do just that. While any remaining wounds between Johnny and Andy Rourke seemed healed, the various relationships between the four members were simply not active enough for a reunion to take place. Johnny wouldn't confirm the amounts on the table, but it was rumoured that they were offered $5 million to play the Coachella festival in the USA. "I was offered twice as much for us to play in New York," he confirmed. "And Hyde Park. And God knows where else." It was nice to know that money at least would not be the deciding factor in whether The Smiths ever did reform.

Just as the Linda McCartney tribute concert had involved agendas bigger than simple issues of pop music, it was for similar reasons that Johnny played a gig in Manchester in January of 2006 that warmed the hearts of Smiths fans everywhere and did give them a little taste of what a reunion might have offered. Manchester's MEN Arena was the venue for the Manchester Versus Cancer Concert. The bands that appeared were booked by Andy Rourke. He drew on the great and the good of the Manchester music scene and beyond over twenty and more years, bringing in New Order, Badly Drawn Boy, Shaun Ryder and Bez from The Happy Mondays, Doves, Elbow, 808 State and more. One of the acts booked to appear was, of course, Johnny Marr And The Healers. Johnny was introduced by Damon Gough, aka Badly Drawn Boy. The first song that the band launched into was 'There Is A Light That Never Goes Out', and the audience joined Johnny and the band in singing every word of the classic Smiths song. The Healers premiered two new songs, slated to appear on the next album, and reprised 'Down On The Corner' from *Boomslang*. When Johnny spoke to the crowd, he confirmed his support for the cause for which they were all there, before introducing "someone I first played in school with in 1978," and followed that up with "tonight seems like a good time to play together again." Andy came on stage to join the band, who hit into the opening bars of 'How Soon Is Now?', and the crowd went beserk.

"It was beautiful really," said Johnny after the show. Before packing his gear and moving on to the after-show party, Johnny and Bernard Sumner joined Doves on stage and played through the Lou Reed classic 'Vicious', from *Tranformer*, and the Motown standard, 'There's a Ghost In My House.' In three songs he had covered his love of Seventies glam, Sixties soul and reprised The Smiths – from a fan's point of view, not a bad night's work. While New Order limited their set to a Joy Division–only collection of songs, there was a Live Aid–style crowd on stage for the closing number, as Johnny rejoined Hook, Sumner, Rourke, Ryder and Bez, with the Doves, for a rousing finale of 'Wrote For Luck'.

Over the course of 2006, Johnny was immersed in a project that took him to the southern states of America, working with the critically acclaimed Modest Mouse. Both the Modest Mouse boys and Johnny himself are said to be very excited by the project, that – at the time of going to press – is still unrevealed. Still contributing wherever he can, Johnny also appeared on Lisa Germano's first album since *Lullaby For Liquid Pig*, his appearances on *In The Maybe World* receiving critical acclaim once again.

Throughout 2006 Morrissey was in evidence everywhere. His latest album, *Ringleader Of The Tormentors* was rightly praised by reviewers worldwide as perhaps his strongest collection of songs since The Smiths. One thing was for sure, while Johnny continued to experiment and develop his work, Morrissey showed no signs of slowing down either. It was a fantastic, trenchant, savage album. Morrissey continued to develop as a writer and as a vocalist, and finally seemed to receive the independently earned plaudits he deserved. Over the course of 2006, Morrissey presented himself with decorum and grace. One would guess he would hate to be described as an 'elder statesman of rock,' but he appeared with great dignity, a stylish, mature man with a more–than–stylish and vastly mature talent. Brushing off questions about Smiths reformations and court cases with ease, it seemed that we had got the original Morrissey back amongst us – witty, urbane, articulate and entertaining, but serious about his substantial work.

Summer 2006 saw the twentieth anniversary of the release of *The Queen Is Dead*, widely seen as the most important Smiths' release. The music press had a field day. One of the most entertaining spectacles was the visit to the UK of Sweet And Tender Hooligans, the California-based Smiths tribute band. The Hooligans career was, by 2006, far more long-lived than that of the band they recreate on stage: formed in 1992, the original line-up performed their own material and threw Smiths songs into the set as crowd pleasers. They were soon exclusively playing Smiths songs, appearing at conventions, and attracting the attention of members of the band themselves. Their act is convincing and – oddly – moving. Jose Maldonado almost seems inhabited by Morrissey, as he throws the singer's shapes and tugs at his ever-loosening shirt in a perfect recreation of the master. Visually, it is sometimes easy to forget that it is not Morrissey behind the mic at all, though off stage only the haircut would perhaps betray Jose's chosen profession. David Collett, on guitar, doesn't look like Johnny Marr, and neither does Karey DeLeon on second guitar, but between them they emulate Johnny's sound with precision.

The band played a short UK tour, culminating with a gig in Manchester on the anniversary of the very day of *The Queen Is Dead*'s original release. The Hooligans' set consisted of the entire album, track by track, followed by a selection of Smiths and Morrissey solo numbers. The audience reception was ecstatic – 'Cemetry Gates', 'There Is A Light That Never Goes Out' and 'Panic' were the biggest audience pleasers. Dancing started shyly towards the back of the hall, and by the end of the gig Smiths fans ranging in age from twenty to fifty were at the front of the stage, waving wildly and singing along to every song. Suitably, there was an affectionate stage invasion, and Jose tugged back at the outstretched hands, visibly moved by the reception in the home town of *The Queen Is Dead* on its anniversary. It is clear that, while The Smiths are no longer with us as a performing entity, they are treasured with a remarkable affection by a broad population of fans old and new. "For me," says Maldonado, "it's like when I was seven-years-old and put on my Superman cloak. I could fly. Today I put on my Morrissey cloak…"

★

Johnny Marr continues to live in the wealthy suburbs of southern Manchester, on the edge of the Cheshire countryside. It's an area of trendy wine bars and footballers' wives, a two-minute drive from long country walks and lakeside picnics, but Marr lives surrounded by guitars, constantly called upon by friends and colleagues for matters musical. Spirituality ("I don't really have 'spare time'" he admits, "but I do like to lie on my back and go into a trance"), the books of Carlos Castaneda or Carl Jung, the history of Native Americans and Tibet, the fate of Manchester City football club… many things continue to exercise Marr's mind when he is not playing the guitar. But one gets the impression that Johnny Marr is always playing the guitar, for himself, for Angie, for his kids and for friends.

Or he's listening to music. Grant Showbiz looks back on his years working with Johnny with great affection. He remembers a time when the pair would simply sit and listen to records, in exactly the same way that Marr did with his teenage friends in the years before The Smiths. And Showbiz remembers the warmth and companionship of the man. A pleasure simply to *be* with, "Johnny is probably one of the nicest people to sit and just play records with," he says. "He has that wonderful ability to compress time." The former Smiths' sound engineer sees parallels between Johnny and another *wunderkind* guitar player from another era. "I've been vaguely seeing comparisons between him and Jeff Beck recently," says Showbiz. While Beck's career has been eclipsed by 'flashier' guitarists of his own generation, while Johnny's reputation as a guitarist has gone from strength to strength over the years, Grant feels that the pair have followed similar paths. Especially in the way Beck went from being the hottest gun in town to a point where he could pursue his own projects and itinerary at his own speed. "He has kind of avoided all that 'fashionable' stuff really, and has become a Sixties icon and just... *carried on*." In coming out of The Smiths and simply working, working and working, Marr has done the same. Showbiz compares the two in terms of character too, and finds more similarities. "[Beck] is an interesting, quiet man – a nice guy to hang out with too." Grant imagines that the Jeff Beck of today is slightly less obsessed with music than he supposes Johnny is. When interviewed for this book, Grant summed up Johnny's passion: "I assume that Johnny [will be] listening to music as we speak!"

If he's not working with an up-and-coming band, or playing around with friends on material never to be released, if he's not working on a co-write with someone or planning a gig or two, Johnny will probably be strumming away on his own. One thing crops up over and over again in the Johnny Marr story: *the guitar, the point of it all*.

It's hard to find anyone with a bad word to say about him. Johnny appears to be universally popular with everyone he has worked with. Even at the depths of the break-up of The Smiths, or during the court case of 1996, nobody dissed Johnny on a personal level. Even the High Court judge summed up all his charity and described him as 'engaging.' For Noel Gallagher, Johnny Marr is "euphoric – an 'up' kind of guy." He can walk into any recording studio in the world and enhance the work in progress, either with his guitar or harmonica, or with some element of production, advice or encouragement. He's modest – he knows how good he is, because he has studied what he does for more than thirty years, but he retains a self-effacing air. He's generous – he'll listen to demo tapes from unknowns still, and will give his guitars away if he feels someone will benefit. Is he some kind of saint? He's certainly a Healer.

If Johnny Marr *is* some kind of saint, it is probably for the patience with which he deals with the question which everyone asks him. Every interviewer seems to trot out the same old line: "Will he work with Morrissey again?" And his answer is always the same. He won't. Or – maybe, one day in the future – he will. Who cares? It would be lovely to see them on stage together, but then again, it might be dreadful. It would be just as interesting to know if Johnny is going to work with Billy Bragg again, or Matt Johnson or Neil Finn or Bernard Sumner... For his part, Morrissey appears happy to let sleeping Smiths lie too, and for the fans who would so like to see them reunited, they can comfort themselves that both the former band-mates are happy to include Smiths songs into their own live sets again.

With wife and life-partner Angie, Johnny shares his home with their two kids, both in their early teenage years. His relationship with Angie pre-dates even his career with The Smiths, and the kids have grown up surrounded by music and musicians, and are familiar with the globe-trotting celebrity world that their father inhabits. There's an element of pride in Johnny's tone when he admits that their tastes aren't just the latest teen fodder. "My kids love music," he confided on a webcast. In a house where musical instruments are literally part of the furniture, their tastes are broad. "[They like] all kinds of things," says Johnny. "But not Britney Spears." Shame.

The Marr family have also continued to 'do the right thing' wherever possible. Johnny remains a vegetarian, and over the years has given much support to *The Big Issue* magazine. Via the auspices of UNICEF, he has also sponsored a child in India, and of course, was seen supporting the Manchester Versus Cancer gig with Andy Rourke.

In terms of what motivates him most, Johnny Marr admits that, "I'd rather have silence than bad music," reflecting at the same time that what he loves best hasn't changed too much over the years either. "I have to be drugged and kidnapped to get me out of the studio" he says. One of the most endearing and re-assuring things about Marr is that he has, over the years, so often been close friends with the people he works with. His friendships are long and lasting as well as productive. In 2006, when he was appearing on stage with Andy Rourke, that was a friendship more than thirty years old. With the likes of Matt Johnson, Bernard Sumner, or Billy Bragg, he has never publicly closed the door on the idea of working with any of them again. There is always a hope or a declared intention that "we will work together again one day." Even with Morrissey, with whom Marr went through so much and with whom he shared earth-shattering experiences at an age when neither of them ought to have been expected to cope, there seems no lasting animosity, although neither side will ever admit any likelihood of their actually working together again. He considers himself a lucky man, rejoicing in the fact that he can "just live his life and get paid for it." And if it had all happened differently, what would Johnny Marr be today? Had there been no Morrissey, no Andy, no Mike? No Kirsty, no Bernard, no Healers? No Matt, no Billy, no Beth Orton?

With his usual down-to-earth modesty and understatement, this deeply inspiring musician, whose entire professional life has been devoted to the instrument that put him in the spotlight as a teenager, is under no illusion. "If I hadn't made it," says Johnny, "I'd have been the biggest hasn't-been in south Manchester."

Thankfully Johnny made it. And in doing so, he made it better for all of us along the way. Without him the last twenty years of music would have been a lot less graceful and a lot less delightful. Here's to twenty more...

"I just regard what I'm doing as a journey, you know?" says Marr today. "I feel very blessed."

Discography

This is a discography of the fundamental recordings on which Johnny Marr was predominant. There are, of course, boundless numbers of Smiths bootlegs available, but these are beyond the scope of this listing. The usual internet resources are available to the intrepid bootleg collector!

THE SMITHS
These are the original, fundamental Smiths releases. Post-Smiths re-issues are noted where it is thought that this is appropriate, but of necessity there may be some omissions amongst the re-releases.

Singles

Hand In Glove / Handsome Devil
Rough Trade, May 1983

This Charming Man / Jeane
Rough Trade, November 1983
(12-inch included 'Accept Yourself' and 'Wonderful Woman')

What Difference Does It Make? / Back To The Old House
Rough Trade, January 1984
(12-inch included 'These Things Take Time')

Heaven Knows I'm Miserable Now / Suffer Little Children
Rough Trade, May 1984
(12-inch included 'Girl Afraid')

William It Was Really Nothing / Please Please Please Let Me
Get What I Want
Rough Trade, August 1984
(12-inch included 'How Soon Is Now?')

How Soon Is Now? / Well I Wonder
Rough Trade, January 1985
(12-inch included 'Oscillate Wildly')

How Soon Is Now? / The Headmaster Ritual
Rough Trade, February 1985

Shakespeare's Sister / What She Said
Rough Trade, February 1985
(12-inch included 'Stretch Out And Wait')

That Joke Isn't Funny Anymore / Meat Is Murder (live)
Rough Trade, July 1985
(12-inch included 'Nowhere Fast', 'Shakespeare's Sister', 'Stretch
Out & Wait', live versions)

The Boy With The Thorn In His Side / Asleep
Rough Trade, September 1985
(12-inch included 'Rubber Ring')

Bigmouth Strikes Again / Money Changes Everything
Rough Trade, May 1986
(12-inch included 'Unloveable')

Panic / Vicar In A Tutu
Rough Trade, July 1986
(12-inch included 'The Draize Train')

Ask / Cemetry Gates
Rough Trade, October 1986
(12-inch included 'Golden Lights')

Shoplifters Of The World Unite / Half A Person
Rough Trade, February 1987
(12-inch included 'London')

Sheila Take A Bow / Is It Really So Strange?
Rough Trade, April 1987
(12-inch included 'Sweet And Tender Hooligan')

Girlfriend In A Coma / Work Is A Four-Letter Word
Rough Trade, August 1987
(12-inch included 'I Keep Mine Hidden')

Stop Me If You Think You've Heard This One Before /
I Keep Mine Hidden
Rough Trade, October 1987

I Started Something I Couldn't Finish / Pretty Girls Make Graves
Rough Trade, November 1987
(12-inch included 'Some Girls Are Bigger Than Others')

Last Night I Dreamt That Somebody Loved Me / Nowhere Fast
(BBC recording)
Rough Trade, December 1987
(12-inch included 'Rusholme Ruffians' (BBC recording))

Albums

The Smiths
Reel Around The Fountain / You've Got Everything Now /
Miserable Lie / Pretty Girls Make Graves / The Hand That Rocks
The Cradle / Still Ill / Hand In Glove / What Difference Does It
Make? / I Don't Owe You Anything / Suffer Little Children
Rough Trade February 1984
1993 WEA re-issue included 'This Charming Man'

Hatful Of Hollow
William, It Was Really Nothing / What Difference Does It Make? /
These Things Take Time / This Charming Man / How Soon Is
Now? / Handsome Devil / Hand In Glove / Still Ill / Heaven
Knows I'm Miserable Now / This Night Has Opened My Eyes /
You've Got Everything Now / Accept Yourself / Girl Afraid / Back
To The Old House / Reel Around The Fountain / Please Please
Please Let Me Get What I Want
Rough Trade November 1984

Meat Is Murder
The Headmaster Ritual / Rusholme Ruffians / I Want The One
I Can't Have / What She Said / That Joke Isn't Funny Anymore /
Nowhere Fast / Well I Wonder / Barbarism Begins At Home /
Meat Is Murder
Rough Trade February 1985
1993 WEA re-issue included 'How Soon Is Now?'

The Queen Is Dead
The Queen Is Dead / Frankly Mr Shankly / I Know It's Over /
Never Had No One Ever / Cemetery Gates / Bigmouth Strikes
Again / The Boy With The Thorn In His Side / Vicar In A Tutu /
There Is A Light That Never Foes Out / Some Girls Are Bigger
Than Others
Rough Trade June 1986

The World Won't Listen
Panic / Ask / London / Bigmoug Strikes Again / Shakespeare's Sister / There Is A Light That Never Goes Out / Shoplifters Of The World Unite / The Boy With The Thorn In His Side / Asleep / Unloveable / Half A Person / Stretch Out And Wait / That Joke Isn't Funny Anymore / Oscillate Wildly / You Just Haven't Earned It Yet, Baby / Rubber Ring
Rough Trade March 1987
1993 WEA re-issue included 'Money Changes Everything' and 'Golden Lights"

Louder Than Bombs
Is It Really So Strange? / Sheila Take A Bow / Shoplifters Of The World Unite / Sweet And Tender Hooligan / Half A Person / London / Panic / Girl Afraid / Shakespeare's Sister / William, It Was Really Nothing / You Just Haven't Earned It Yet Baby / Heaven Knows I'm Miserable Now / Ask / Golden Lights / Oscillate Wildly / These Things Take Time / Rubber Ring / Back To The Old House / Hand In Glove / Stretch Out And Wait / Please Please Please Let Me Get What I Want / This Night Has Opened My Eyes / Unloveable
Sire June 1987, later released on Rough Trade

Strangeways Here We Come
A Rush And A Push And The Land Is Ours / I Started Something I Couldn't Finish / Death Of A Disco Dancer / Girlfriend In A Coma / Stop Me If You Think You've Heard This One Before / Last Night I Dreamt That Somebody Loved Me / Unhappy Birthday / Paint A Vulgar Picture / Death At One's Elbow / I Won't Share You
Rough Trade September 1987

'Rank' (live)
The Queen Is Dead / Panic / Vicar In A Tutu / Ask / (Marie's The Name) His Latest Flame & Rusholme Ruffians / The Boy With The Thorn In His Side / What She Said / Is It Really So Strange? / Cemetry Gates / London / I Know It's Over / The Draize Train / Still Ill / Bigmouth Strikes Again
Rough Trade September 1988

211

The Peel Session
What Difference Does It Make? / Miserable Lie / Reel Around
The Fountain / Handsome Devil
12-inch EP, Strange Fruit October 1991

'Best 1'
This Charming Man / William It Was Really Nothing / What
Difference Does It Make / Stop Me If You Think You've Heard
This One Before / Girlfriend In A Coma / Half A Person /
Rubber Ring / How Soon Is Now? / Hand In Glove / Shoplifters
Of The World Unite / Sheila Take A Bow / Some Girls Are Bigger
Than Others / Panic / Please Please Please Let Me Get What I
Want
WEA August 1992

'Best 2'
The Boy With The Thorn In His Side / The Headmaster Ritual /
Heaven Knows I'm Miserable Now / Ask / Oscillate Wildly /
Nowhere Fast / Still Ill / Bigmouth Strikes Again / That Joke Isn't
Funny Anymore / Shakespeare's Sister / Girl Afraid / Reel Around
The Fountain / Last Night I Dreamt That Somebody Loved Me /
There Is Alight That Never Goes Out
WEA November 1992

'The Very Best Of The Smiths'
Panic / The Boy With The Thorn In His Side / Heaven Knows I'm
Miserable Now / Ask / Bigmouth Strikes Again / How Soon Is
Now? / This Charming Man / What Difference Does It Make? /
William, It was really nothing / some girls are bigger than others /
girlfriend in a coma / Hand in Glove / There is a Light That Never
Goes Out / Please Please Please Let Me Get what I Want / That
Joke isn't Funny any More / I Know It's Over / Sheila Take a Bow
/ I Started Something I Couldn't Finish / Still Ill / Shakespeare's
Sister / Shoplifters of the World Unite / Last Night I Dreamt that
Somebody Loved me / Stop Me if you Think you've Heard This
one before
WEA June 2001

Video

The Complete Picture
This Charming Man / What Difference Does It Make? / Panic /
Heaven Knows I'm Miserable Now / Ask / The Boy With The
Thorn In His Side / How Soon Is Now? / Shoplifters Of The
World Unite / Girlfriend In A Coma / Sheila Take A Bow /
Stop Me If You Think You've Heard This One Before / The Queen
Is Dead (Including 'The Queen Is Dead', 'There Is A Light That
Never Goes Out' And 'Panic', a film by Derek Jarman)
WEA December 1992. Released on DVD later.

WITH THE THE

Singles

The Beaten Generation / Angel
Epic March 1989

Gravitate To Me / The Violence Of Truth
Epic July 1989

Armageddon Days Are Here (Again) + remixes and versions
Epic November 1989
Various 7, 10 and 12-inch versions with additional tracks.

Shades of Blue (EP)
Jealous Of Youth / Another Boy Drowning (live) / Solitude /
Dolphins
Epic February 1991

The Dogs Of Lust / The Violence Of Truth
Epic January 1993

Slow Emotion Replay / Dogs of Lust
Epic April 1993
Various formats and additional tracks available

Albums

Mind Bomb
Good Morning Beautiful / Armageddon Days Are Here (Again) /
The Violence Of Truth / Kingdom Of Rain / The Beat(en)
Generation / August & September / Gravitate To Me / Beyond
Love
May 1989

Dusk
True Happiness This Way Lies / Love Is Stronger Than Death /
Dogs Of Lust / This Is The Night / Slow Emotion Replay /
Helpline Operator / Sodium Light Baby / Lung Shadows / Bluer
Than Midnight / Lonely Planet
Jan 1993

WITH ELECTRONIC
Most Electronic releases involved a number of different mixes,
edits and formats. Only the main release is listed here.

Singles

Getting Away With It / Lucky Bag
Factory December 1989

Get The Message / Free Will
Factory April 1991

Feel Every Beat / Lean To The Inside
Factory September 1991

Disappointed / Idiot Country Two
Parlophone June 1992

Forbidden City / Imitation Of Life
Parlophone June 1996

For You / All That I Need
Parlophone September 1996

Second Nature / Turning Point
Parlophone February 1997

Vivid / Prodigal Son
Parlophone April 1999

Late At Night / Make It Happen / Make It Happen (remix)
July 1999

Albums

Electronic
Idiot Country / Reality / Tighten Up / The Patience Of A Saint /
Gangster / Soviet / Get The Message / Try All You Want / Some
Distant Memory / Feel Every Beat
Factory May 1991

Raise The Pressure
Forbidden City / For You / Dark Angel / One Day / Until The
End Of Time / Second Nature / If You've Got Love / Out Of My
League / Interlude / Freefall / Visit me / How Long / Time Can
Tell
Parlophone July 1996

Twisted Tenderness
Make It Happen / haze/ Vivid / Breakdown / Can't Find My Way
Home / Twisted Tenderness / Like No Other / Late At Night /
Prodigal Son / When She's Gone / Flicker
Parlophone April 1999

WITH BILLY BRAGG

Singles

Levi Stubbs' Tears / Walk Away Renee (as Duane Tremelo)
Go! Discs June 1986

Greetings To The New Brunette / Deportees / The Tatler
12-inch included 'Jeane' and 'There Is A Power In The Union'
Go! Discs December 1986

Sexuality / One Good Thing / Sexuality
Go! Discs July 1991

Albums

Talking With The Taxman About Poetry
– appears on 'Greetings'' and 'The Passion'
Go! Discs September 1986

Don't Try This At Home
– appears on 'Cindy'' and 'Sexuality'
Go! Discs September 1991

Bloke On Bloke
– appears on 'The Boy Done Good'
Cooking Vinyl June 1997

All Bragg's compilations are worth owning. According to budget
you'll search out Victim Of Geography, Reaching To The Converted
or Must I Paint You A Picture. The re-recorded version of
'Greetings', entitled 'Shirley' is on Reaching To The Converted.

THE SMITHS & THE ART OF GUN-SLINGING

WITH BRYAN FERRY

Singles

The Right Stuff / The Right Stuff (remix)
Virgin November 1987

Kiss and Tell / Zamba (Marr on A-side)
Virgin February 1988

Limbo / Limbo Remix)
Virgin June 1988

Album

Bete Noire
Virgin November 1987
Johnny appears on 'Limbo', 'The Right Stuff', 'Kiss And Tell' and
'Seven Deadly Sins'

WITH TALKING HEADS

Single

(Nothing But) Flowers / Ruby Dear
EMI April 1988

Album

Naked
EMI March 1988

Johnny appears on '(Nothing But) Flowers,' 'Ruby Dear', 'Cool Water' and 'Mommy, Daddy, You and I.' A UK 10-inch version of the single appeared with all of these except for 'Cool Water.'

WITH KIRSTY MacCOLL

Singles

Free World / Closer to God / You Just Haven't Earned It Yet Baby
Virgin February 1989

Days / Happy
Virgin June 1989

Walking Down Madison / One Good Thing
Virgin June 1991

Albums

Kite
Johnny plays on the majority of tracks, and co-wrote 'End Of A Perfect Day' and 'You And Me Baby.'
Virgin April 1989

Electric Landlady
Johnny plays on 'Walking Down Madison,' which he co-wrote, and 'Children of The Revolution.'
Virgin June 1991

WITH THE PRETENDERS

Single

Windows Of The World / 1969
Polydor April 1989

WITH QUANDO QUANGO

2 From Quando: Atom Rock / Triangle
Factory June 1984

WITH EVERYTHING BUT THE GIRL

Single

Native Land / River Bed Dry
Blanco Y Negro September 1984
(Johnny appears on the A-side)

WITH K-KLASS

Album

Universal
Parlophone December 1993
Johnny appears on 'Las Cassa'

WITH A CERTAIN RATIO

Single

Shack Up / Life's A Scream
Creation May 1994

WITH BLACK GRAPE
Single

Fat Neck / Yeah Yeah Brother / Pretty Vacant
Radioactive May 1996

WITH M PEOPLE

Album

Fresco
Deconstruction October 1997

WITH MARION

Album

The Program
London September 1998

WITH ANDREW BERRY

Single

Kiss Me I'm Cold / That's My Business
Fontana July 1990

WITH STEX

Single

Still Feel The Rain / Still Feel The Rain
Some Bizarre January 1991

WITH BANDERAS

Single

This Is Your Life / It's Written All Over My Face
London February 1991

Album

Ripe
London March 1991
Johnny appears on 'This Is Your Life'

WITH THE PET SHOP BOYS

Singles

Can You Forgive Her / Hey Headmaster
Parlophone, June 1993
Various formats included an extra track, Johnny's guitar/
remix version of 'I Want To Wake Up'

Liberation / Decadence
Parlophone April 1994
Johnny appeared on the B-side.

Albums

Behaviour
Parlophone October 1990
Johnny appeared on 'My October Symphony' and 'This Must
Be The Place.'

Release
Album – Parlophone April 2002
Johnny Appears on eight of the ten tracks

WITH BERT JANSCH

Album

Crimson Moon
Castle/When June 2000
Johnny appears on 'Fool's Mate', 'My Donald, 'Looking For Love',
'The River Bank.'

WITH BETH ORTON

Album

Daybreaker
Heavenly July 02
Johnny co-wrote 'Concrete Sky', also released as an EP in July 02
with various other tracks.

WITH BECK

Album

Midnight Vultures
Geffen November 1999

WITH NEIL FINN

Album

Seven Worlds Collide
Parlophone February 2002
Johnny plays guitar and vocals throughout this live collection, taking lead vocal on 'Down On The Corner.' He also plays ukulele and harmonica elsewhere. Includes Finn's version of 'There Is A Light That Never Goes Out.'

WITH HAVEN

Album
(as producer)

Between The Senses
Radiate February 2002

All For A Reason
Radiate March 2004

WITH OASIS

Album

Heathen Chemistry
July 2002
Johnny appeared on '(Probably) All In The Mind' and 'Born On A Different Cloud.'

WITH DENISE JOHNSON

Single

Rays Of The Rising Sun / (versions)
Magnet, June 1995

WITH JANE BIRKIN

Album

Fictions
Album – EMI March 2006
Johnny arranged and plays harmonica and guitar on several tracks, including Neil Hannon's 'Home' and 'Image Fantome,' a reading of Debussy's 'Pavane Pour Une Infente Defunte.'

WITH MODEST MOUSE

Album

We Were Dead Before The Ship Even Sank
Album unreleased at time of going to press. Johnny involved in
songwriting and playing.

JOHNNY MARR & THE HEALERS

Single

The Last Ride / Need It / Long Gone
Pacific October 2001

Album

Boomslang
The Last Ride / Caught Up / Down On The Corner / Need It /
You Are The Magic / In Betweens / Another Day / Headland /
Long Gone / Something To Shout About / Bangin' On
iMusic Feb 2003

WITH THE CHARLATANS

Album

Live It Like You Love It: The Best Of The Charlatans live
Album – MCA October 2002
Johnny appeared on stage with The Charlatans and appears on
'Weirdo' and 'Sproston Green'

WITH LISA GERMANO

Albums

Lullaby For Liquid Pig
Album – Reincarnate May 2003

In The Maybe World
Young God July 2006

Bibliography

There have been many books written about The Smiths. Some of them are rotten, some are excellent. The two most important references are:

Songs That Saved Your Life by Simon Goddard
Reynolds & Hearn, London (London 2002)

The Smiths: A Visual Documentary by Johnny Rogan
Omnibus Press, London (1993)

Goddard's book approaches the story of The Smiths through their recording sessions, and follows each song or track from its inception to its release and beyond, thereby telling the story of The Smiths themselves – one of the best rock music books in print. Rogan's *Visual Documentary* is a day–by–day, year–by–year account of the band. *Morrissey & Marr: The Severed Alliance* (Omnibus Press 1992), also by Rogan, was the first serious look at the history of The Smiths.

Also referred to in the text are:

Manchester England by Dave Haslam
Fourth Estate, London (2000)

Haslam's is a superbly readable history of the music business – largely its musical history – in Manchester, from the Victorian era to the present day. Not just a great book about Manchester, but a fine read in itself.

In Session Tonight by Ken Garner
BBC Books, London (1993)
Even more since his death, John Peel's legacy is immeasurable. For anyone who listened to Peel over the years, this is a wonderfully readable account of the various sessions recorded not just for Peel but for other Radio One shows such as Kid Jensen and Janice Long.

The Right To Imagination And Madness by Martin Roach
Independent Music Press, London (1994)
A superb collection of interviews with some of indie and left-field rock's most inspiring voices... not least the largest single interview in book form with Johnny Marr.

Morrissey: The Scandal And The Passion by David Brett
Robson, London (2002)
Not loved by many, the book took too great an interest in Morrissey's sexuality for most readers, but there are some interesting interviews included, whether one agrees with the authors' premises or not.

David Nolan's Granada TV documentary *These Things Take Time* (2002) was an interesting take on The Smiths, using specially commissioned cartoon versions of the band instead of the real McCoy to illustrate Vic Reeves' commentary. It also included a number of valuable interviews with members of the Smiths' entourage.

Web Sites

If ever a band was born to have its bones bared on the web, it was The Smiths. There are too many Smiths-orientated websites to even begin listing them all, good or bad, but a trawl through any search engine will throw up the best. The four members of the band, of course, all have their own official sites, and these ought to be the starting point for a week or so of wandering at leisure.

Primarily of course, Johnny's own website is *www.johnnymarr.com*, while *www.jmarr.com* contains a wealth of material, especially on The Healers. Morrissey resides at *www.morrisseymusic.com*; Andy Rourke at *www.andyrourke.info*; Mike Joyce at *www.mikejoyce.com*.

www.thethe.com is a fantastic resource on Matt Johnson, containing some fabulous published interviews with Johnson and Marr, while The Pet Shop Boys official site is *www.petshopboys.co.uk*. Billy Bragg's work is best represented at his own site, *www.billybragg.co.uk*, and likewise Kirsty MacColl at *www.kirstymaccoll.com*. Electronic benefit and suffer from being grouped in among many Joy Division and New Order sites, but *www.neworderonline.com* is a point of departure for all three bands, and packed with good content. I also like *www.talking-*

heads.net and David Byrne's own pages at *www.davidbyrne.com*. Paul Carrack can be found at his site, *www.carrack-uk.com*.

Jonathan Schofield runs independent tours of Manchester and the North West of England, and also writes regularly for *www.manchesteronline.co.uk*, a valuable resource on all things Mancunian.

Appendix

An Interview between Johnny Marr and Martin Roach for the latter's book, *The Right To Imagination And Madness*, published by Independent Music Press in 1994.

"I was writing this book about my favourite twenty songwriters and contacted Johnny's managment office. At the time, I had only two books to my name and was publishing this work on my own label. I didn't worked for any magazines and, in many ways, offered Marr little or no benefit in return for the interview. Further, he hadn't spoken to the press for several years. I was amazed and delighted when I got a phonecall to get myself to Manchester on a certain day and turn up at a central hotel. I waited anxiously and, bang on time, a blacked out BMW rolled up and Johnny Marr stepped out.

He walked straight up to me and introduced himself, not as 'Johnny' but as 'Johnny Marr'. We sat in the bar area and drank tea, while he spoke for four hours about his songs and the music that had affected him. He wouldn't let me pay for anything and offered to check any information he'd given me if I had any queries. He was a gentleman and a scholar of music. Oh, and he looked compeltely rock and roll, exactly as you would want Johnny Marr to look: shades, cool clothes and a rock star's barnet. I have never had the chance to thank him directly for his leap of faith in me – a totally unknown writer asking him about his songwriting – so, hearty respect and cheers, Johnny.

MR: How has your upbringing shaped your musical development?
JM: I think it shaped it massively, as I think it does with everybody really. I came from a particularly musical family. I grew up on the outskirts of the city, near the Ardnick Apollo, not the Harlem Apollo [laughs] and loads of my relatives lived on the same street. Four families lived next door to each other, all Irish immigrants, all very young families and so there were parties every night. Being an Irish situation there were always accordions and harmonicas and other instruments around. My first memory of guitar playing was this uncle who had big sideburns and Chelsea boots, he was well cool, he had a guitar and did a little bit of playing, I thought he was really hip. Because it was a big family there were always christenings and weddings and there was always what seemed like this same band playing at these functions. In between their sets I would go and have a look at the guitars. I remember this red Stratocaster, I can recall the smell of the case and everything. My parents had Beatles records but they were more into the Irish stuff, kind of country music, which spilled over into The Everly Brothers who were really popular in my household. No matter how much you believe otherwise, I think your upbringing indelibly affects your development, it gives you your musical personality and in some cases your entire musical vocabulary. Even when I started to rebel against that, when I was ten or eleven and I got into glam rock, it was still there. Even now, I hate country music, so the influence remains. Unwittingly or not, my family did shape my musical ideas and were very encouraging to my aspirations to play.

Was that domestic musical environment better than being at musical school?
From what I have seen definitely, yes. It seems there are two ways you can go and neither include musical school. You can either come from the genetic thing like I did, or you can come from a completely non-musical situation. Take Bernard Sumner for example, he got into music from a completely different, almost political need, when he left

school. He had no musical family at all. I don't know anyone who's had success from music school, that way always smacks for me of It Bites, too cerebral, too calculated, not very much soul. If you want it bad enough and connect with music on a spiritual level, tuition is completely irrelevant. Music is a purely spiritual connection.

So when did you first make that spiritual connection rather than listen to other bands?
From about ten.
That seems quite early.
Yes, very early. I had always had guitars for as long as I could remember. I thought once that maybe my parents were pushing me into it, but I soon realised that I was obsessed. I loved the feel and shape of them, so I always had toy guitars around. Then when I got to ten or eleven I heard Marc Bolan for the first time, like a lot of people, through Top of the Pops. The first record I ever bought was 'Jeepster' but it wasn't until 'Metal Guru' got to No.1 that I really made that connection for the first time. It was a feeling that I'll never forget, a new sensation. I got on my bike and rode and rode, singing this song, it was a spiritual elevation, one of the best moments of my life. The next day me and my mate went out and stole loads of glitter, put it all over our faces and started emulating our favourite bands. From then on my formative years were totally and utterly dedicated to music. I was into football like everyone else, but while most kids my age were into conkers and bikes, I was at home miming to 'Metal Guru' and 'Telegram Sam'.

So do you think you missed out at all in your childhood?
No, not at all, because I still think what I was doing was more interesting than what other kids were doing.

So was it always going to be music that you used as your expression?
Yes, it was. Undoubtedly. I'm very one-dimensional in that respect, music is everything. When I left school I had jobs and all that, but they were only a means to playing loads of records and tapes and getting paid for it. That was a natural apprenticeship for being in a band because Billy Duffy from The Cult worked around there.

He was my closest ally and a few years older than me, so he was kind of like my role model. Eventually he gave up everything to be involved in music and I kind of followed that.

How much did you follow him musically?
Very little, very little. I moved from the city to the south of Manchester, which was vaguely middle class, and looked like Beverly Hills compared to the staunch, working class, tough city. My new place was only a little housing estate, and now it is really dilapidated, but at the time it felt like nirvana. I met guys who were only 13 or 14 but took themselves so seriously as musicians, they were already legends in their own minds. Billy Duffy was one of those people. In those circles, it was okay to regard yourself a a serious musician, even though they were so young. Without that I would still have been a musician but I don't know whether I would have had the confidence to have done what I did. I used to walk around all the time with a guitar case, and there was actually a guitar in it, but there's not much I could do with it outside the shops! But it was just to let everybody know that my whole identity was as a guitar player. I was very cocky. But in terms of writing I realised certain limitations, after being in a few of my mates' bands. I knew that as a guitar player there are only so many times you can play someone else's songs. Someone had to start writing.

So when did you start writing your own material then?
As soon as as I could string a few chords together, I started putting them down on a cassette recorder. I was never really into being the typical guitar hero, I was always naturally into songs rather than all that. About 13, maybe earlier, I suppose, perhaps 11 or 12. I picked it up very quickly, it was only the physical discomfort of hurting my fingers that I struggled with.

So you landed your ideal vocation very early on in life?
Incredibly early. Coming from a punk mentality, Bernard thinks the whole 'born with a guitar in your mouth' story is really corny.

You DJ-ed with Andrew Berry at the Exit club - did that have an affect on your development as a writer when you saw how people reacted to certain tracks?
Not really in that respect. The most important thing about that whole period is that since then I have been able to look back and say to myself 'Yes, my musical intuition was always correct for me'. I was playing James Brown in 1980, stuff that later went on to influence the baggy scene, Fatback, Sly Stone.

That must have been unfashionable at that time?
It was very unfashionable! [laughs[There was nobody dancing to it either so I couldn't learn much from that!! [laughs] But it has held me in good stead since The Smiths split because if I had believed all the stuff about me being a musical megalomaniac I would have crumbled.

So how did that background help then at that difficult later time?
With the dance music I became involved in after I left The Smiths, it felt completely natural, because I was into all that well before The Smiths came along. I was listening to Chic in 1977, I have always had that schizophrenic attitude to music. But I think most people my age do, they are very open. If you'd talked to Shaun Ryder a few years ago he'd have been listening to Funkadelic and Rubber Soul as well. I think it is only the post–punk generation that understands that, because we have been left with a 30 year legacy of stuff that you can just take ideas from. You don't have to be in any mind set or cult to appreciate it. My sister was always into dance music and she introduced me to 12" singles, so the whole DJ phase was just a natural part of what I do.

Were you listening to these dance bands because you got nothing from punk?
I didn't get much from punk because of my age – I was too young to get into most clubs, although I did get to see Iggy Pop. I liked the American punk acts because they seemed to be more directly influenced by the British invasion of America, Patti Smith, The Stooges, New York Dolls, particularly The Dolls who were themselves interested in the girl groups whom I had already discovered. You see,

what happened was that after glam rock I furiously back tracked because there was nothing around for me. I didn't really get off on the records in the charts, I didn't like Manfred Mann's Band. The only records I liked were dance tracks at The Fair, all black music really. I used to go to The Fair to look at girls and clothes and listen to this stuff. In terms of material I could relate to as a writer, I had to go back even further which is when I got into Motown, and that led me onto Lieber & Stoller and Phil Spector and the Brill Building. Phil Spector was the second major influence on me behind Marc Bolan. That is why I got into American punk rather than British, because Patti Smith used to do Ronnettes numbers and the Dolls would do the girl group stuff.

So how did Phil Spector influence your development?
The overall musician. Not purely sonically, but you could hear in his records that he was completely obsessed. There were no spaces in his music, any harmonic suggestion was realised. It's kind of a production thing. If you've got four or five musicians playing then you will get loads of natural harmonics and spaces in there between the instruments. Well, Phil Spector was someone who would hear all these tiny suggestions and then fill every one in. This big, big, dense apocalyptic sound which I definitely connected with.

How does that relate to your role as a guitarist?
Well, as I say, I have never related to the Jeff Beck's of this world, so it was completely natural - I have never seen the guitar as a solo instrument. When I started to write songs I wanted my one guitar to sound like a whole record, so I consequently developed almost a one-man-band style. I don't fit very well with another guitarist, other than Matt Johnson, whose work I can embellish and feel very comfortable with. In terms of my own songs I like to be able to hear the whole thing - I'll play a new song and hear piano and strings and then I try and play all that on my one guitar.

So who would you say is the closest to your own style?
Um. [Thinks long]. Neil Young I suppose. His stuff is very fashionable again now, but his electric guitar playing is similar. I hear echoes of that

in The Smiths. Or possibly Keith Richards and Brian Jones combined, 'Nineteenth Nervous Breakdown' and all that.

What aspects of those players do you see as similar?
The rhythm and melody really. Even if I play what can technically be called a solo, I regard it as a break. I believe music should be approached as composition, not as a free-form jam, everything has to be structured for a reason. I could always relate to Phil Spector far more than anyone else as a guitar player. For me you've got Jimi Hendrix and the rest is crap. As a musician, if you are going to be some kind of virtuoso, unless you can do it with the same spirit and depth of soul as Hendrix, you should forget it. I am a white English musician, born in the sixties in the Provinces, and that is the way it sounds. Too many people fall into the trap of the whole ethos and mythic identity of the guitar hero, which is largely a complete anachronism, the fastest gun and all that crap.

I am interested in where you draw the line with that – for example you are renowned for your use of pseudo-jazz chord progressions yet in its worst form jazz can be the ultimate in musical self-indulgence?
I'm not into jazz that much but what you said undoubtedly applies to bad jazz - however, the greats like Coltrane, and Miles Davies are the furthest I have been down that road. I don't dislike jazz because of indulgence, I just dislike indulgence of any kind. For example, there's a lot of indulgence in post-punk stuff, in fact some indie music has the worst kinds of indulgence. When that stuff is bad, it's the worst.

Okay, moving on to the actual mechanics of song writing, what are they for you and are there any patterns?
Yes. There's a pattern whereby I start to get a feeling, an uneasy feeling for a day or two and I try to harness that. I try not to party, I keep myself really straight and sober, which I guess is the opposite of what people might expect. I get up early and stay up late, sleep as little as possible and harness that disconcerting uneasiness. I feel a little bit uncensored and feel almost like a storm is coming and I know that something is going to happen.

Has that always been the case?
Well, no, The Smiths was a completely and utterly different situation. We spent so much time together and we were incredibly pragmatic in approach. We were really into singles and we'd do batches of three songs at a time. We would sit down and say 'Let's write a song'. For my part it was the discipline of Lieber & Stoller which was at the core of The Smiths. It was like 'this is what we do, we write songs and we can write thousands'. We recorded seventy songs in four and a half years. Morrissey would come round to my house and we'd do three songs just like that, then he would go away and do the lyrics and three days later he'd be in the studio recording it. When you have a partner who is so prolific and has that physical and emotional necessity to write, it makes things very easy for you, and in that way we propelled each other towards this endless supply of songs. I don't want that to sound too clinical and demystify the process though, because as well as being pragmatic it was incredibly romantic. The songwriting process and the songs we produced were sacred, and still are to me now. One of the things about making records is that for it to work you have to be totally and utterly in love with it for those three minutes and you have to be able to hear that love in the tracks. That might be a particular idiosyncrasy of mine, because I guess some of my more distinctive songs have that romantic melodic content. When Kirsty MacColl asked me to write for her she said ' I want one of those songs that make you feel happy and sad at the same time'. That is very much where I am at, I feel like that, it can almost be upsetting when I make records, that mixture of melancholia and vibrancy. I don't like to hear bone-head records, I look for poignancy. Those are the feelings that I harbour for a couple of days when I get that uneasy feeling.

If you can't release that feeling does that make you feel ill?
Absolutely, really ill. To avoid that heartache I sort a lot of stuff out in my mind first. Generally the best ideas are those that completely click in my head straight away and it's like 'Let's go let's go!!' I will pick up a guitar and play it and it's written really quickly. The songs that are crafted, I like less, although it can work well that way. An example of that is 'Get The Message' by Electronic, one of my favourite songs that I have written. It has this fragile element and could be from any time, and that was fairly well crafted. I knew I had a really great verse and

a potentially great chorus, but I really had to rack me brains to nail it. I had to really concentrate to get the middle eight.

Have you got an example of a song that by contrast came really quickly?
'Please, Please, Please, Let Me Get What I Want' by The Smiths, a simple song that just came out. That song perhaps more than any other has a great deal of my musical background in it - I think it sounds like a Del Shannon song.

When that happens, when a song suddenly arrives, how much do you feel that you are primarily a receiver for all these songs that are already out there?
I would go along with that school of the muse. When I write and I stay up late, my creative faculties are down and I think you are more open to receiving all that. That's when drugs can help. They can also hinder enormously, you can get on completely on the wrong track. But in whatever way, if you let your creative faculties down you can get more stuff written.

But surely if you over-do that and you're tired, won't you be less motivated and energetic to pursue those ideas?
No, because I prefer playing the guitar to sleeping. I hate getting up and that's why The Aphex Twin has it made. I wish I could do that! [laughs]. There is no way that I am going to get out of bed, no matter how good the idea is, not even to write a hit!! [Laughs loudly]

How often does that uneasy feeling come?
Well, it depends. Take this week. I am working on the next Electronic album and I want to get into more technical stuff, maybe guitar sounds, and I don't feel like writing anything. The feeling hasn't been there.

What if that feeling suddenly arrives when you are in the middle of some production?
I would just go into another room and get it down. One of the other

techniques you can work with is when you write a few songs, and think 'Great, they're pretty good' and because you are relaxed you carry on noodling and that way write another good track immediately afterwards. The songs after the initial batch can be just as good. For example, 'Idiot Country' by Electronic was written like that, when I had completed three songs and I carried on playing for the fun of it. Loads of Smiths' songs were written like that aswell, such as 'How Soon Is Now'. I had written 'William It Was Really Nothing', 'Please, Please, Please, Let Me Get What I Want' and 'Nowhere Fast' all very quickly, and I was left to my own devices in my flat and that way I wrote 'How Soon Is Now'. Another example was after a Radio 1 session. I was on the train home and I got loads of ideas that turned into 'Reel Around The Fountain', 'Still Ill' and then 'Pretty Girls Make Graves', which I recorded as soon as I got home in twenty minutes on a two track recorder. Fortunately I've got a good music memory for ideas I have when I am away from a recording environment. A lot of ideas come when I am about to go to sleep though, which I know is common and maybe a psychic or biological phenomena because of which I have since started to keep a notebook by my bed.

Have you got an example of a song which was written with the help of drugs?
[Laughs loudly] Have you got three hours to spare? Well, for a start you can pretty much include the entire Smiths back-catalogue. 'Disappointed' by Electronic was a total ecstasy song after a long night doing E. Funnily enough, I find that booze is not very good for creativity and I think you can hear the effect of drink in the tracks, too morbid, too dark. I have to say the best stuff I have written though, has been when I have been sober and on a natural high, through pure exuberance. The Smiths was a very exuberant time. I pretty much lived my life for twenty years like that. And then I just plummeted!!! Still, that's cool, you learn a lot about yourself with things like that. Joining The The was like going from Charlie Bubbles to Apocalypse Now.

Matt Johnson said about 'Mind Bomb' that he deliberately exposed himself to drugs for that project?
Yes. I don't want this to turn into some kind of Aerosmith drugs

interview, but there are some really interesting stories behind that. I was working with Chrissie Hynde at the time, which was a fantastic period of great learning and being with a good friend. Working with her didn't quite work out but just being around somebody so insightful and perceptive was brilliant. We came into the studio to write an album, although she wasn't really ready for that. Then Matt phones me up and asks if I want to work with The The. So what I would do was work with Chrissie until 2 in the morning and then load all my gear into the car and drive across town to the other studio and start work with Matt. I'd get there and we'd take loads of mushrooms and ecstasy. It was the most intense psychological and philosophical experiment. That is one of the bonds between Matt and I, that psychological intrigue. When I first heard that he wanted me to work with him I was well pleased, and the night before the first session I took loads of ecstasy and had a real psychedelic night. I was supposed to be at that first session for noon but uncharacteristically I didn't get there until 2pm. I walked in and I looked like one of the Thunderbirds with his strings cut. I glanced around and Matt was sitting there, looking incredibly intense, and the producer was the same, the atmosphere was unbelievably tense and dark, a really horrible vibe. The producer was staring at his hands and that was the day it transpired he had a nervous breakdown – Matt will do that to you. So we started 'The Beat(en) Generation' and I tried the harmonica and it just wasn't happening. The feeling just wasn't locked. The line I had to play was great and it should have been okay, but I just couldn't work with all this bad atmosphere around. It was going nowhere so I turned to Matt and said 'Look I'll be honest with you, I took a load of E for the last three nights and I'm feeling a bit wobbly'. Matt looked at me and with great production acumen said 'Well we'd better get some more then hadn't we.' So off goes the drummer and comes back with all this stuff and we just cocooned ourselves in the studio for five days and the results were amazing. Matt is intense. He'd be tripping and saying 'I want it to be like Jesus meets the devil' and I'd be like [Shrugs shoulders and smiles] 'Sure, okay, I get you' and it worked!!!

Are you disciplined?
There are many privileges that you inherit as a musician, so if I am not writing I will work in the studio on something else, even if it's

just refining a guitar sound or learning a new piece of technology. The point is that if you are sitting in the pub you are not going to write a song. I like to work in the studio because at least then I am in an environment where a song could come out.

Do you write to an imaginary listener?
Well, it's different for me because I write for a specific partner. For example, at the moment I am in the mode of writing for Bernard although I don't want that to sound too clinical, because there are many sounds I could produce that would suit him. He has such good musical tastes so I am very open to what I can write. When I am working with somebody we become very, very close and naturally from there I write stuff that works for them.

How do the projects you have been involved in compare from a songwriting point of view?
I regard them all as very natural stages of my life. It is almost like a chicken and egg situation. The sort of person I was in The Smiths needed to write the songs that I did for that group, very disciplined, yet exuberant and still feeling new to have a partner. With The The it was home for me, I wanted to find my feet as a writer and still make records. That is why I did so many sessions early on because I wanted to make records but not form a band – if I had started a band soon after The Smiths split I would have been expected to play with three young guys with quiffs and glasses and the spotlight on those three would have been unbearable. So when Matt called and said he wanted me to expand the sonic picture of his band and get into sound effects it was exactly what I wanted to do at that time. You see, the problem with The Smiths was that towards the end it was very restrictive. I was the only melodic factor in the band. We didn't use keyboards, sequencers or even backing vocals, so I was playing constantly and that became a bit tiresome for me really. So The The was very much expanding my musical consciousness and vocabulary. Electronic was very much a representation of a particular scene and lifestyle that Bernard and I both shared and found ourselves at the forefront of really, particularly Bernard because it was right on his doorstep at the Hacienda, the Manchester scene. That whole scene was a lot more complex than a lot of people wearing flares, it was very complex,

there was a lot of violence around, and guns – yes, people were swallowing ecstasy and all that but there were also gangsters around and violence. Extremes.

Did that affect the way you wrote with Bernard?

Yes, extremes are very conducive to being in a group. It shakes things up. That first Electronic album is very much of its time. For example, 'Feel Every Beat' may sound a little obscure but lyrically it makes total sense. It is vaguely political – there were serious head-on conflicts for Bernard with the Chief of Police James Anderton that threatened his very livelihood. Where we are at at the moment is a different thing and we'll have to see how that works.

What percentage of your work starts as music with the lyrics being put to that later?

The Smiths was entirely music first. I gave Morrissey the music and he'd fit stuff around that. I suspect he had lyrical fragments lying around and he would fit them in place to each song I gave him. There were one or two exceptions such as 'Rusholme Ruffians'. I knew he had written a song about The Fair, so I decided to use 'Marie's The Name' by Elvis Presley. Also, with 'Meat is Murder' I knew there would have to be that kind of heavy material content. Perhaps the main example of his lyrics prompting my music is 'Panic'. I had been over his house and I knew he had a new idea with a hook that was 'Hang the DJ' so I basically wrote 'Metal Guru'!! We even asked Toni Visconti to record it but he wasn't interested. The line 'It says nothing to me about my life' ironically reminded me of the role 'Metal Guru' had in my life as I explained earlier, so I used that Bolan track. With Electronic it is a perfect step for me at this stage because for the first time I am totally writing with another musician. Sometimes I'll write all the music, other times he will and I'll just put a guitar break down. Sometimes we'll both contribute to the music – for example, 'Getting Away With It': he wrote the verse and I wrote the chorus. That is when the real sparks fly when we write together, head to head. That is very new and fresh for me. Normally when people ask me to write a song they expect a whole backing track, such as Kirsty MacColl on 'Walking Down Madison'.

What is your approach to technology and its role in the songwriting process?
I treat technology really in much the same way as I would a drummer and a bass player in certain situations. I can be completely musically fascistic and technology allows you to do that. I use it to make that connection with Phil Spector, who would get musicians to play and play and play until every single drop of individual nuance had gone and he got it to exactly how he wanted. 'Get The Message' sounded like a really odd band and I spent a long time just getting that sound, five days on just the rhythm track.

Well, if you are that demanding of the correct feel for the music, isn't that very intimidating for the lyricist, in that he has to come up with a very specific lyric to match that feeling?
Well, touch wood, it works quite well. Something I do appears to inspire them to pick up on the mood I was after.

But when you write, do you have any specific situation in mind - for example, a lyricist may have a very particular event or occurrence in mind when he writes. What do you think of that inspires your sound?
A feeling. There were two songs for The Smiths that are good examples, the first two songs we ever did - 'Hand That Rocks The Cradle' and Suffer Little Children'. That demanded not too much doom or all minor chords, that would have been too obvious. At the end of the day I have learnt from all the people I have written with that they want it to sound like is me. But the problem is they usually means 'The Boy With The Thorn In His Side' when they say that. I wrote that track in about four minutes and just did it. I guess there is something in the guitar part that appeals. I heard it on the radio recently and I can see what people are looking for - that mix again between happy and sad. That is my nature.

Well, have you got any examples where the lyricist absolutely hit the nail on the head with their articulation as far as representing your own emotions and feelings that you created the song with?
Oh yeah, loads. 'I Know It's Over' by The Smiths. It isn't my favourite Smiths track but when I heard him sing that for the first time in the studio it was amazing. 'There Is A Light That Never Goes Out'

captures the atmosphere perfectly aswell. 'How Soon Is Now' is another example. Also, 'Disappointed' – Neil Tennant sang this great falsetto tone at the end which was spot on. Again 'Get The Message' as well. That song undoubtedly stamps Bernard's genius as a singer, his is an incredible performance on that track. That vocal performance is as good as anything that Lou Reed ever did. 'You And Me Babe' for Kirsty MacColl was also very appropriate – I wrote that track on my knees with a tape recorder in the hall-way 'cos the kids were asleep and I was feeling kind of sad, and she captured the spirit of that very closely.

Do you ever evoke a visual or actual scene to inspire songs?
Sometimes, yes. For example, much of The Smiths' work was an evocation of being on the bus to or from school, in the rain, going under all these Victorian bridges. That was something that I heard in Joy Division's music and it was something that Morrissey and I discussed and were both very aware of. It is a feeling that you can't avoid if you are a sensitive person in Manchester.

Is that why you clicked with Bernard so well?
Undoubtedly, and it is something that we are trying to address more now, especially with our slower, more atmospheric songs. A song called 'In A Lonely Place' which I believe was originally a Joy Division song but was released by New Order, is very Smiths-like, not in terms of sonic content but in terms of atmospherics. It has a certain melancholy that is almost beautiful and that is what those times were like. This is always in contrast to the other side of inspiration which is just pure driving exuberance, and I find I share that very much more with Matt. He is the only person that I have met that is able to draw on that peculiar environmental feeling I just mentioned, even though he lives in London. He seems to be able to focus on it, with songs like 'Heartland', 'Helpline Operator and 'Love Is Stronger Than Death', he evokes a young white sensitive boy living in a Victorian environment. It's not as obvious as Ray Davies because he did it lyrically, these little scenarios. We evoke it as a musical atmosphere, a feeling. It is not something that I particularly want to go back to, but I do recognise it, that unique melancholia.

You are renowned for mixing pseudo-jazz progressions with rock backdrops. Where was your inspiration for doing that?
Bert Jansch, the guitarist from Pentangle. Incredibly unfashionable group to mention but an amazing guitar player. When I moved to Wythenshawe, Billy Duffy and some of his mates introduced me to all that. There was Richard Thompson as well, but I could never really get it on with his singing, I couldn't get with all that finger in the ear stuff!! The way Jansch and Renbourn worked together was very jazz and that introduced me to tunings.

So is that contrast between the jazz and the rock elements the musical manifestation of your personal mix of melancholia and happiness?
Yes, I think it is, that captures that feeling. 'Unhappy Birthday' by The Smiths has really strange chords, but what happens on the left hand is quite jazzy. Also, 'Headmaster Ritual' is similarly written with different tunings, which I think doesn't sound like anyone except me. That was the song that took me the longest time to write, about three years. Each album had a new bit. First the chords, then the riff and suddenly three years had gone by. With that song if you analyse what I am doing on the left hand it is like Joni Mitchell, and what I am doing with the right hand is like Dave Davis.

Do you still experiment with tunings?
I am doing so again, yes. I get bored with the way a guitar is set up. The great thing about tunings is that you'll play two chords and think 'I've done it, I've come up with a chord sequence that no-one else has ever used. Then I put it back into concert tuning and it's C to F!! But again, using different tunings breaks down those critical and creative faculties that we were talking about earlier, you follow things that you might otherwise not go with because it sounds like a piece already out there. You don't second guess yourself, you find different harmonics and get more into it.

So would you advise young bands to use tunings and capos more often?
Definitely. Funnily enough, there was a piece in a guitar magazine a few years ago about my use of capos and I thought 'Shit am I the only

person who does it?' They cost about three quid and you get a new song out of it, you know, it's well worth it.

Have you got any examples of songs that wouldn't have been written without the use of a capo or tuning?
Loads. 'Big Mouth Strikes Again' because the chords are really quite simple but if it had been in regular concert tuning it would have been boring. 'Cemetry Gates' as well. 'Feel Every Beat' by Electronic. Those are kind of 'Headmaster Ritual'-Joni Mitchell chords that are really weird.

You said of 'The Boy With The Thorn In His Side' that you used a Strat because you were looking for that single coil purity. How much does the make of guitar affect the end track?
Very much sometimes.

But doesn't that mean that a young band with only one guitar is limited by their finances as to what they can create?
Yes, a little, but it does give you that first identifiable sound. A band's first album is quite often just a sound that people latch onto and that is great. Then on the second album they can afford more gear and so they can bring in more textures. I think that is a good thing. I always had a Les Paul and I thought I was getting too bluesy, so I got a Rickenbacker which is much less suited to solo-ing. The only solo I think that has ever worked on a Rickenbacker was 'Eight Miles High'. But yes, the make of guitar you write with can really dictate the songs.

Name a song written with a specific person in mind. Who is that person and why did you write it?
After about a minute and a half of writing 'Please, Please, Please, Let Me Get What I Want' it had a Del Shannon feel, so I continued to write that with my mother in mind, because she listened to so much of that. 'Back To The Old House' I wrote with my wife in mind.

When the lyrics have been put over those songs and they don't match the exact situations or person you were thinking of, what happens?
What you need to look for is one partner to give 100% and the other to give 100% and those two halves to make 300%, a chemical reaction that creates a song which is far greater than the sum of its parts. Again, 'Get The Message' is a very elementary song but the atmosphere of the vocal is superb. The vocal was actually a stream of consciousness. Bernard sang these two lines, recorded it then stopped the tape. Then he went [picks imaginary tunes out of the air with arms]... and put those two lines down and the whole track was done first take. It's not just about the content of the lyric, it's also about the delivery, the atmosphere. That fragility he captured mixed with my music in a way that was so simple, but it was so much bigger than the sum of the parts. The Smiths had it, and I had it with Matt but I have seen it the most with Bernard and Electronic.

When Bryan Ferry did the 'Right Stuff', putting lyrics to The Smiths' 'Money Changes Everything' did his lyrical and musical presentation match your original ideas?
Yes. I didn't really analyse the lyrics that much, because Bryan is more into phonetics anyway, and for me that song is very much phonetical and rhythmic. The fact that Bryan didn't write anything radical didn't worry me because phonetically he got it right and with those really high backing vocals it sounded perfect. And the band that Bryan used was much more true to the spirit of the track. He used Andy Newmark on drums from Sly Stone and Guy Pratt on bass which was exactly the nature of the track really. Perfect.

You have dropped knives onto open guitars to create certain effects and other tricks. Have you got any other examples?
Well, the knife thing was used on 'Stop Me If You Think You've Heard This One Before'. I do all kinds of stuff like that. I'll tape up the strings for example. Take 'Violence Of Truth' by The The, there is an almost glam rock riff that comes in where the lyric goes 'These are the rules of religion, these are the rules of the land' and the only way I could get that sound was to pick the most horrible guitar I had and then find the key, tune up the bottom string so the bass string was in sympathy with it, then tape the top four strings up and just

whack the bottom ones. It turned out almost like glam sax. Another one is for when you want really accurate warble and pitch bend like you normally would with a wammy bar, you sample it into a keyboard, use the pitch bender on the keyboard and then quantise it in the actual sequencing. Whatever it takes I will do to a guitar, tape strings whatever. The Nashville tuning method is quite good as well – put the high strings from a 12 string onto a six string – that can have good results.

Really, but isn't that the antithesis of The Smiths' purist approach?
Well, we weren't really that purist behind the scenes. Morrissey liked the ideas of sixties techniques, so we'd use sound effects from BBC sound effects records, whereas now we'd have used a CD Rom but told people it was from the BBC records! Take a look at the 'Strangeways Here We Come' sleeve and there is a picture of me with my head in my hands, and in the background there is an Akai sampler, clearly!! Having said that, we were a guitar group and if I wanted a certain sound I would use a guitar. So if I was looking for strings, I would get that through the guitar, using sustain and turning the tape upside down. That approach has its difficulties but it can also get great results and it's more interesting than doing it with synths. That is where I am at now, taking that experimentalist approach and using it for guitars rather than synths.

What is the balance between wearing your producer's hat and your songwriter's hat?
Absolutely none. No difference. Unless you're producing someone else. With Billy Bragg I showed his guitarist some tricks and that was great fun. Take S'Express – the distinction between the writer and the producer had completely gone and I think that gelling of the roles is completely healthy.

You still need to be creative within those parameters though...
Sure. Matt Johnson did it in reverse for example. He started in the early 80's with all this technology and yet now he has come round to real purist material. Years ahead of his time, always has been. But yes, I take your point, technological abuse has to be avoided, it's back to

that indulgence idea again. I think my sense of the song always stops me from doing that fortunately.

How much does structure dominate the writing process? Is unorthodoxy in structure appealing to you?
Yes, as I get older it appeals more. Paradoxically, I like changing things around, changing structures and playing around but still using some form.

Does the process of recording and the studio interest you?
As a kid I liked to hear records that you didn't know how they were achieved, where you get this environment that is almost from another planet, I love that. It is far more interesting than just four musicians playing in a room. If you are going to do that you have to do it like Matt did on 'Dusk' I think. He got these very intense, interesting dynamics that captured your attention completely. That degree of presence is pretty rare though. You see, too many bands are just record collectors and four guys in a room with a big record collection each doesn't mean you can come up with the goods. That is a mistake that has come through more and more in the eighties.

But you make no secret of your references to the past, so how do you balance that with plagiarist nostalgia?
It's the question of relativity. The thing I liked about the Beatles for example was that they made use of the technology that was available at the time. Bands who want to sound like the Beatles and only use the same gear they did are completely missing the point. If The Beatles had adopted that attitude they would have sounded like a swing band. Jimi Hendrix was all about capturing his own spirit and being obsessed with the power of music and taking his many references and building on it and making it his own. All the greats are about living in their era and saying something about their times. That was something that frustrated me about my detractors when I left The Smiths because they equated me with this fickle music careerist persona that was now into dance. There were two answers to that. One, what I was expressing in The Smiths was the spirit of the sixties but in its own time, in its own way. The pragmatic approach of those

sixties songwriters was what inspired us. It didn't sound like Gerry & The Pacemakers to me, it sounded very much like an eighties group. Also, I feel that we made it cool again to be on Top of the Pops. The second thing about that criticism was that I am a faddy person, unashamedly, I have always liked fashion. I think it is fascinating, fashion in music and fashion in clothes. There is a philosophy of some rock musicians that says a song has to be timeless to be great. If you pull that off then great, but one of the things that attracted me towards Marc Bolan was that he was of his time. That is why I have got the utmost respect for the Pet Shop Boys because they are not trying to write 'Blowin' in the Wind', they want it to sound like the year it was written.

How much does the mood you are in when you walk into a studio affect the outcome?
Totally. I can't work if I am down. I get things done by being genuinely positive and using that energy. There have been times in my life when I have tried to control it and drown my intensity and I did that for a couple of years but I got nowhere. I try not to succumb to cynicism. I have to be positive otherwise it goes nowhere.

Are you your biggest critic?
Yes.

Are you able to leave tracks when they are good enough rather than perfect?
Not really, but I have partners who do that for me.

Were you nervous when you first put your songs forward to people?
No. I sort of did things the other way around. When we first went down to London as The Smiths I wasn't nervous at all, because I was very cocky and I knew inside me that no-one had ever heard music like this before. I felt up against it and that confrontational element fired me up. I would be on stage thinking 'Don't go to the bar 'cos you've never heard anything like this before, check us out'. Then later when we were more successful I would be throwing up all day which is why I was always so thin!!!

How do you feel when people openly emulate you?
I do hear echoes of what I have done in one or two groups and it is very flattering and then I will watch those guys to see what they do next. One of the best things was when my friends and family started recognising my style. My sister phoned me up once and said 'I've just heard your new record, I knew it was our Johnny', and although that was The The's 'Slow Emotional Replay', it was a real triumph for me, because the harmonica was like nobody else but me.

Your harmonica playing is always viewed as secondary to your guitar?
Well, yes. I wouldn't have played that instrument with The Smiths unless I had met Matt Johnson. After I went for a record deal in London I stayed with him and slept on his floor. He had nearly finished 'Soul Mining' and he played me 'Perfect'. I thought 'I can do that' so I took it back to The Smiths. Originally though it was 'Love, Love Me Do' that started my whole interest in the harmonica.

What is at the core, the heart of your songwriting?
To me writing a song is about having a feeling and trying to catch it. It is much less cerebral than many people make out, much more spiritual, more about a feeling than anything else in my life. Once I have identified that feeling it might take a month or just five minutes, but I will capture that feeling in a song.

The insinuation of that is that you are pretty efficient?
Once I have the idea I am, yes. I have had enough experience to be efficient. In the early days it was a necessity because Morrissey was very, very demanding of me, he was always looking for songs, and without him I wouldn't have written as many songs in that fashion, with such speed. Bad songs don't tend to get beyond the second guitar overdub, I can hear by then that it isn't working. There is a lot of truth in the school of thought that if a song is any good you can play it on an acoustic guitar. Billy Duffy said that of the first Electronic album, that although it was a dance record you could play all the songs on an acoustic. I said 'Well, you'll have to teach me 'cos all I do is stand to the side at the ironing board playing keyboards!!!!'
[Laughs]

Has there ever been a phase when you lost the knack and felt hollow, that you had lost that passion?
Yes, when I got caught up in all the machinations of the fame game. It would have been incredibly hollow had I had nothing else to think about. Around 1989 me and Matt were ready to go on tour. The ugly situation with The Smiths split meant that trying to produce work after was really difficult, almost unbearable. I had to grow up a little bit and develop a really thick skin. I had to, otherwise I would have gone under. I felt hollow at that time, yes.

Was that a scary feeling?
No, what was scary was that I didn't want to listen to records and to be robbed of that is much, much worse than being robbed of the impulse to write. I have as much joy from having a son as I do from writing a song, but to lose the enjoyment of listening to records would really, really sadden me. I would be devastated if the music business gave me such a cynical ear that it would rob me of the love of my life.

What is the most important record in your life?
'Gimme Shelter' by The Rolling Stones. That was the soundtrack to my life from 14 to 22. The intro is amazing. I have tried to capture the spirit of that on the whole of 'The Queen Is Dead' but I would never try to lift it. It is a spiritual reaction between those people that could never be recreated.

What is the greatest accomplishment of your life, musically or otherwise?
Musically it is that I still make records with the same passion and exuberance that I had when I was a kid and that has taken some doing. On a personal level it is my kids and family.

What has been the biggest failure in your life?
The way The Smiths ended. We should have split when we did simply because we had lost the touch with basic emotional values which we all possessed, but were subverted by our egos which by then had turned us into caricatures. We were good people, but we did the split all wrong.

When and why did you last cry in front of someone?
New York in 1993. It was the last time I was going to work with Matt and I hadn't slept for three days. I had been exposed to the most incredible mind states, dragged through all these mind trips which were recorded as the video for 'Slow Emotional Replay' by Tim Pope. We went right into the heart of the New York porn world. The basic premise was to go right up to all these weird street characters we had been told about and stick a microphone in front of their faces and ask them 'What is wrong with the world?' Their reactions were just incredible. It was one of the most unbelievable experiences I have ever been through. Tim didn't tell us where we were going at all. We went into this one innocuous looking building and he told me I was going to need my guitar to mime. I walked in and I was on live porn TV being interviewed by this guy. Then we went to this meat district as they call it, and I saw this guy, tattoos, beard, a real trucker and he gets out of his truck and he was wearing a tutu. Then we met these transexuals who were so beautiful. These people, who were supposed to be down and outs and losers came out with the most humane answers and ideas about the world's problems. One guy was this Irish chap who seemed really down, not down and out but just very down, and we asked him the same question, and in front of our very faces he just broke up, this massive guy, he completely broke down over the course of three minutes. He completely went, it was like turning a key in him, and he cried. Fucking horrible. There was another club where we'd been told that snuff movies had been made in, the atmosphere was horrendous, dire. I was sitting on these plastic sheets and there was very little light, only a trickle coming through from the streets. It was so Twin Peaks. We were miming when this guy comes in called Danny The Wonder Pony, who makes his living going round these sex clubs with a saddle, giving people rides on his back. He had neon lights flashing from his mouth and when we asked him, this freak, he gave this real compassionate answer. After a while I became very numb, but at night-time I had the most graphic images, so I know that it all goes in to your head somewhere. It was a very surreal, weird experience. That reduced me to tears.

What are the musical constants in your entire catalogue?
Melodic guitar counter-point. You can hear it in all of The Smiths stuff. 'Sexuality' by Billy Bragg, 'Still Feel The Rain' by Stex, you hear

it in 'Disappointed' by Electronic, 'Beyond Love' by The The, 'Jealousy Of Youth' by The The. It is there throughout my work and absolutely essential to it.

If you were to be run over when you leave this interview what shall I say were your last words?
I wrote some good songs... didn't I?

Suggested tracks:

1. 'Last Night I Dreamt Somebody Loved Me' (The Smiths) has that sense of yearning which I feel mirrors certain aspects of my spirit.

2. 'Get The Message' (Electronic) displays the spirit of two partners, both putting in 100% of themselves and resulting in a creation that is more than than 200%.

3. 'How Soon is Now?' (The Smiths) shows that I'm a cool guitar player and that I can get it right when I really want to.

Visit our website at **www.impbooks.com**
for more information on our full list of titles including books on
System of a Down, Dave Grohl, Muse,
My Chemical Romance, Mick Ronson, Ian Hunter,
The Killers, The Streets,
Green Day, The Prodigy and many more.